Limiting Arbitrary Power

Marc Ribeiro
With a foreword by the Right Honourable Antonio Lamer,
P.C., C.C., Chief Justice of Canada (Ret.)

Limiting Arbitrary Power:
The Vagueness Doctrine in Canadian
Constitutional Law

UBCPress · Vancouver · Toronto

© UBC Press 2004

15   14   13   12   11   10   09   08   07   06   05   04   5   4   3   2   1

Printed in Canada on acid-free paper

National Library of Canada Cataloguing in Publication

Ribeiro, Marc, 1974-
    Limiting arbitrary power: the vagueness doctrine in Canadian constitutional law / Marc Ribeiro; with a foreword by Antonio Lamer.

    Includes bibliographical references and index.
    ISBN 0-7748-1050-5

    1. Constitutional law – Canada. 2. Vagueness (Philosophy) 3. Rule of law – Canada. 4. Law – Canada – Interpretation and construction. 5. Ex post facto laws – Canada. 6. Canada. Canadian Charter of Rights and Freedoms. I. Title.

KE4238.R52 2004   342.71   C2004-900292-9
KF4483.R75R52 2004

Canadä

UBC Press gratefully acknowledges the financial support for our publishing program of the Government of Canada through the Book Publishing Industry Development Program (BPIDP), and of the Canada Council for the Arts, and the British Columbia Arts Council.

This book has been published with the help of a grant from the Canadian Federation for the Humanities and Social Sciences, through the Aid to Scholarly Publications Programme, using funds provided by the Social Sciences and Humanities Research Council of Canada.

Printed and bound in Canada by Friesens
Set in Stone by Brenda and Neil West, BN Typographics West
Copy editor: Frank Chow
Proofreader: Susan Safyan

UBC Press
The University of British Columbia
2029 West Mall
Vancouver, BC V6T 1Z2
604-822-5959 / Fax: 604-822-6083
www.ubcpress.ca

Contents

Foreword

It is trite but true that words take on different meanings depending upon the context in which they are used. Not only can the meaning of words vary greatly in their written form, but tone or the body language employed can also affect the meaning of words when spoken.

Enunciating in legal form the parameters within which conduct will be unlawful is therefore one of the greatest challenges facing legislators who must enact laws or judges who must then develop or apply these laws.

Given these challenges, Marc Ribeiro's study of the void-for-vagueness doctrine and its place and effect in our Constitution is not only daring and courageous but also a major contribution to the legal community's understanding of the doctrine.

Dr. Ribeiro's past achievements were to be a guarantee of the excellence and thoroughness of his study. While a student at the University of Montreal Law School, he clerked for the Honourable Michèle Rivet, President of the Human Rights Tribunal of Quebec, and was the recipient of many scholarships and awards. After graduation, Dr. Ribeiro spent close to four years under the supervision of Professor Patrick J. Monahan of Osgoode Hall Law School in Toronto, successfully completing his doctoral thesis on the doctrine of "void for vagueness." In Toronto, he also worked as a research assistant for Professor Anne F. Bayefsky and did some supervised teaching.

The vagueness doctrine's ramifications are innumerable. Two of the most important are fair notice to the citizenry and limitations upon the discretion of law enforcement authorities, the latter being used in the widest sense so as to encompass judges, police officers, and all other persons empowered by law to curtail the freedom of a citizen's activity. In that context, the author examines the concepts of retroactive laws and *ex post facto* rule making by judges, as well as the principle of the rule of law, in order to assess their relationship to the basic rationales of the doctrine.

Dr. Ribeiro's text gives us insight into the American approach to "void for vagueness." Then, turning to its Canadian counterpart, his analysis of the majority rulings (there are few) of our Supreme Court makes, in my humble view, a strong case for revisiting the "legal debate" test set out in the *Nova Scotia Pharmaceutical*[1] case, which holds that a law is not vague if its interpretation is open to legal debate. He argues ably for the injection into the doctrine as it now stands of a more flexible and, depending on the context of a given law, a higher threshold than that found in the legal debate test.

On this point he is in good company. Many eminent jurists, such as Dean Peter W. Hogg,[2] Professors Don Stuart[3] and André Jodouin,[4] and Luc Huppé,[5] to name but a few, have expressed the view that the legal debate test's threshold is set too low.

Dr. Ribeiro notes some subsequent refinements of the legal debate test in the *Morales*[6] case and in the *Farinacci*[7] case regarding the relevance of the "legal context" for judges assessing legislative precision. He also refers us to other factors that should be considered in order to ensure, as he concludes, "a more adequate equilibrium between certainty and flexibility in the legal system by taking a more balanced approach towards the vagueness doctrine." Finally, recognizing that the legal debate approach is, though too generous, a clearer one than his suggested set of standards, he argues that it is "the nature of constitutional standards to be flexible," and that a fixed constitutional standard of statutory definiteness cannot promote adequately its purpose of protecting legality and the rule of law.

Dr. Ribeiro's contribution to the possible and eventual development of the vagueness doctrine is enormous. The legal community should be grateful to him for having unselfishly spent so many years making an important contribution to the quality of the debate on the doctrine and to the evolution of Canadian law.

The Right Honourable Antonio Lamer, P.C., C.C.
Chief Justice of Canada (Ret.)

Acknowledgments

I wish to express my gratitude to those people who have provided me with invaluable assistance, insight, and encouragement towards the completion of this book. First, I would like to thank Professor Patrick J. Monahan, of Osgoode Hall Law School (York University), who, from 1997 to 2001, supervised my doctoral work. He has always provided me with extremely helpful comments and thoughtful advice. I would also like to thank the other members of my doctoral examining committee: Professors Jamie Cameron and Bruce Ryder (both of whom also served on my supervisory committee), as well as Professors Janine Benedet, Ian Greene, and Richard Haigh, for the time they took to provide me with valuable feedback.

I wish to acknowledge with appreciation the Canadian Federation for the Humanities and Social Sciences, the Social Sciences and Humanities Research Council of Canada, as well as York University, for the funding they provided. I also wish to thank Professor Anne F. Bayefsky for having given me the pleasant opportunity to work with her as a graduate assistant at York University's Centre for Refugee Studies. I am very grateful to the librarians and staff of the Osgoode Hall Law School and University of Montreal Law School libraries for countless hours of extremely valuable assistance. I thank the editors of *La Revue Juridique Thémis* for having graciously permitted me to use in this book some parts of an article I published on vagueness in 1998 ("Le problème constitutionnel de l'imprécision des lois" [1998] 32 R.J.T. 663). This earlier paper was prepared under the supervision of Professor François Chevrette, from the University of Montreal Law School. I am greatly indebted to Professor Chevrette, not only for his insightful supervision of this paper but also for his devotion to the teaching of law and for the way he has contributed to framing my approach to legal thinking.

I am greatly indebted to the Honourable Mr. Justice Louis LeBel for the invaluable and extremely pleasant learning experience I enjoyed while working for him as a law clerk. I am grateful to him for his wise counsel and for the latitude he generously gave me to finish this book in 2001. I am also indebted to the Right Honourable Antonio Lamer, PC, CC, Chief Justice of Canada (Ret.), who had selected me to be his law clerk before his retirement. His support of and interest in this project have been greatly motivating, helpful, and rewarding. I would also like to express my thanks to my colleagues, the law clerks at the Supreme Court of Canada for the 2000-2001 term, for their friendly encouragement through the last stages of the completion of this book. I am especially grateful to Malcolm Thorburn for the helpful feedback he has provided, as well as to Christopher Rickerd for his very constructive advice and assistance.

I wish to convey my profound gratitude to my aunt, Luci Ribeiro-Morgan, for her extremely helpful cooperation in proofreading numerous earlier drafts. I also would like to thank her for the sensible advice she has been giving me for several years, ever since I started expressing an interest in law, on the orientation of my career. I wish to thank my friend and former co-worker at the Centre for Refugee Studies, Purushothman Panchalingam, for his invaluable technical help in preparing this study, as well as for his encouragement and his unique sense of humour, which greatly enlivened my stay in Toronto. I would not want to forget to thank the Anastacio and Morgan families, whose warmth and generosity gave me a home away from home when I was in Toronto.

Over the years, many other people have been supportive and have provided me with assistance and guidance, which I wish to acknowledge. They include the Honourable Madame Justice Michèle Rivet, President of the Human Rights Tribunal of Quebec, Professor Diane Labrèche (University of Montreal), Dr. Ogenga Ottunu, Antoinette Oudot, An-Lap Vo-Dignard, Peng Chao, Danny Boeuwens, Jean-Pierre Girouard, Jorge Fernandez, Louise Cyr, Martin Camilli, and the Sharp family.

But above all I must express my sincerest gratitude to my parents, Mireille and Herminio, as well as to my brother and best friend Olivier, for their unconditional support, the numerous sacrifices they have made, and the strength and inspiration they give me. I am forever indebted to them, especially for these last few years when I was away in Toronto and in Ottawa, and during which they have been incredibly understanding. I wish to dedicate this book to them with deepest affection. *Merci beaucoup.*

Limiting Arbitrary Power

Introduction

Under the *Canadian Charter of Rights and Freedoms*,[1] a theory has emerged pursuant to which a law lacking in precision may be declared invalid. Two essential rationales lie at the core of the vagueness doctrine. First, vague laws are constitutionally suspect because they do not provide "fair warning" to citizens as to what the law prescribes. Thus, individuals can be the victims of "unfair surprise" if a rule is applied to them when they could not have foreseen that such a rule would apply to their particular situation. Second, vague laws have the inevitable effect of increasing the discretionary power of law-enforcing authorities. This is problematic since as a result of these laws the rights and obligations of citizens may be subject to the arbitrary will of such authorities.

In the abstract, the essence of the vagueness doctrine – that laws must meet a certain level of precision – appears rather simple. This impression is misleading, however. In fact, this requirement of definiteness has an inevitable fluid nature that makes it difficult to assess. As Justice Frankfurter once noted in the American context: "'Indefiniteness' is not a quantitative concept. It is not even a technical concept of definite components. It is itself an indefinite concept. There is no such thing as 'indefiniteness' in the abstract, by which the sufficiency of the requirement expressed by the term may be ascertained."[2]

Consequently, attempts must be made to explore the boundaries of statutory vagueness under the Constitution. As Lon Fuller writes: "No matter how desirable a direction of human effort may appear to be, if we assert there is a duty to pursue it, we shall confront the responsibility of defining at what point that duty has been violated. It is easy to assert that the legislator has a moral duty to make his laws clear and understandable. But this remains at best an exhortation unless we are prepared to define the degree of clarity he must attain in order to discharge his duty."[3]

Although a multitude of elements (which will be discussed in this text) come into play in the assessment of legislative precision in a constitutional setting, the core of the debate inevitably reaches the basic opposition between legal certainty and flexibility. While the aspiration for certainty in the application of legislation lies behind the requirements of precision, it must always be balanced against the need for flexibility. It would be unrealistic to aim for a legal system governed exclusively by rules settled in advance and mechanically applied by judges. Because of the unforeseeable nature of circumstances that may be involved in the matters being regulated, as well as the inherent limitations of language, the flexibility afforded by vague statutory formulas is often needed to promote justice and efficiency in any legal system. In other words, discretion can often be a useful tool. The object of the vagueness doctrine is the appropriate balance between the two competing imperatives of certainty and flexibility.

The development of the vagueness doctrine in Canadian constitutional law is a relatively recent phenomenon. The issue was addressed for the first time briefly by the Supreme Court of Canada in the 1988 case of *R. v. Morgentaler*.[4] Then, in 1990, its roots were traced back to the principle of legality (*nullum crimen nulla poena sine lege* – no crime nor punishment without law) by Lamer J. (as he was then) in his concurring opinion in the *Reference re ss. 193 and 195.1(1)(c) of the Criminal Code (Man.)*.[5] In 1991, also in a concurring opinion, L'Heureux-Dubé J. linked the vagueness doctrine to the fundamental principle of the rule of law in the case of *Committee for the Commonwealth of Canada v. Canada*.[6]

It was not until 1992, however, that the Supreme Court purported to explain the content of the doctrine at length in the landmark decision of *R. v. Nova Scotia Pharmaceutical Society*.[7] In that case, a challenge was brought under s. 7 of the *Charter* against s. 32(1)(c) of the *Combines Investigation Act*,[8] which makes it a criminal offence "to prevent, or lessen, unduly competition." The Court upheld the validity of the provision and purported to define the vagueness doctrine in a comprehensive manner.

First, Gonthier J. examined the appropriate place of the vagueness doctrine in the *Charter*. As there is no particular provision in the Constitution that expressly requires precision in legislation, he noted that the vagueness doctrine can be derived implicitly from certain provisions of the *Charter*. Thus, provisions that contain an "internal limitation," such as s. 7 can render the doctrine relevant.[9] The doctrine can also be made applicable under s. 1, after a breach of a substantive *Charter* guarantee has been established.[10] Vagueness then becomes a notion that will prevent the State from demonstrating that the breach is justified under s. 1. Vagueness can have two distinct roles under s. 1. First, it can be raised in relation to the requirement that limitations on *Charter* rights be "prescribed by law."[11] In that regard, an overly vague law is considered not to be a "law," and the Crown is thus denied access to justification under s. 1. Second, vagueness can acquire importance in the context of the *Oakes* test.[12] Since a vague law possesses the potential for being interpreted in an overly broad manner, the vagueness of a law can thus attract scrutiny under "minimal impairment."[13] The law is then seen as problematic because of its potential overbreadth on constitutionally protected freedoms. Gonthier J. explained the potential overlap between the concepts of vagueness and overbreadth by quoting a passage from a decision of the Ontario Court of Appeal: "Vagueness and overbreadth are two concepts. They can be applied separately, or they may be closely interrelated. The intended effect of a statute may be perfectly clear and thus not vague, and yet its application may be overly broad. Alternatively, as an example of the two concepts being closely interrelated, the wording of a statute may be so vague that its effect is considered to be overbroad."[14]

However, Gonthier J. added that the content of what is to be referred to as "the vagueness doctrine" (which he purported to define further in the decision), does not *per se* encompass those instances where a vague statutory formula is objected to for reasons related to overbreadth. He wrote: "For the sake of clarity, I would prefer to reserve the term 'vagueness' for the most serious degree of vagueness, where a law is so vague as not to constitute a 'limit prescribed by law' under s. 1 *in limine*. The other aspect of vagueness, being an instance of overbreadth, should be considered as such."[15]

Therefore, what is called the "vagueness doctrine" is limited to the classic concerns of "fair warning" and "law enforcement discretion." Concerns of overbreadth that can be triggered in the context of minimal impairment are not relevant *per se* under the vagueness doctrine. The applicability of the vagueness doctrine thus can be summarized as follows: "Vagueness may be raised under the substantive sections of the Charter whenever these sections comprise some internal limitation. For example, under s. 7, it may be that the limitation on life, liberty and security of the person would not otherwise be objectionable, but for the vagueness of the impugned law. The doctrine of vagueness would then rank among the principles of fundamental justice. Outside of these cases, the proper place of a vagueness argument is under s. 1 *in limine*."[16]

In *Nova Scotia Pharmaceutical,* the Court also purported to define the content of the vagueness doctrine. The two fundamental rationales of "fair notice" and "law enforcement discretion" were examined by Gonthier J. He first defined the rationale of fair notice as follows:

> Principles of fundamental justice, such as the doctrine of vagueness, must have a substantive as well as procedural content. Indeed the idea of giving fair notice to citizens would be rather empty if the mere fact of bringing the text of the law to their attention was enough, especially when knowledge is presumed by law. There is also a substantive aspect to fair notice,

which could be described as a notice, an understanding that some conduct comes under the law ...

The substantive aspect of fair notice is ... a subjective understanding that the law touches upon some conduct, based on the substratum of values underlying the legal enactment and on the role that the legal enactment plays in the life of the society.[17]

The content of the law enforcement discretion rationale was then expressed in the following manner: "A law must not be so devoid of precision in its content that a conviction will automatically flow from the decision to prosecute. Such is the crux of the concern for limitation of enforcement discretion. When the power to decide whether a charge will lead to conviction or acquittal, normally the preserve of the judiciary, becomes fused with the power to prosecute because of the wording of the law, then a law will be unconstitutionally vague."[18]

Gonthier J. then went a step further and purported to spell out a general test that, in his view, would encompass the two rationales he had just defined. This is something that had never been undertaken, either in Canada or in the United States.[19] Thus, the Court stated a general criterion for determining whether legislation is unconstitutionally vague. After mentioning that "the threshold for finding a law vague is relatively high,"[20] Gonthier J. stated the general standard as follows: "A vague provision does not provide an adequate basis for legal debate, that is for reaching a conclusion as to its meaning by reasoned analysis applying legal criteria. It does not sufficiently delineate any area of risk, and thus can provide neither fair notice to the citizen, nor a limitation of enforcement discretion. Such a provision is not intelligible, to use the terminology of previous decisions of this Court, and therefore it fails to give sufficient indications that could fuel a legal debate. It offers no grasp to the judiciary."[21]

Using this standard, a law will be upheld as soon as it possesses some element, minimal though it may be, to fuel a legal debate. This test, which has been followed ever since in the case law, is obviously very permissive.[22] As Peter Hogg points out, "almost any provision, no matter how vague, could provide a basis for legal debate."[23] All that is required by the test is simply that the law be "intelligible." If some element can be found in the law that provides a "grasp to the judiciary"[24] and allows speculation on its meaning, the law is deemed sufficiently precise. We realize that a great preference for flexibility over certainty is openly advocated through this standard of legal debate.

The object of this book is to discuss the application of the vagueness doctrine as well as its appropriate place in the context of the Canadian Constitution. Among other things, it examines the approach the Supreme Court of Canada has taken to vagueness through this standard of legal debate. In order for the doctrine to be viable, this primary test cannot be applied to every case. The book examines how the doctrine, which is still embryonic in Canada, can be developed to achieve its purposes of protecting adequately the rationales of providing fair notice to citizens and limiting law enforcement discretion. An approach that strikes a sensible balance between the two competing imperatives of certainty and flexibility is articulated.

The book is divided into four basic chapters: (1) a study of the principle of legality (which is closely connected to the rationale of fair notice); (2) an analysis of the principle of the rule of law (which is closely related to the rationale of limiting law enforcement discretion); (3) a detailed inquiry into the content of the vagueness doctrine; and (4) an examination of the appropriate place of the vagueness doctrine in the *Charter*. Chapters 1 and 2, which are more descriptive, will serve the purpose of introducing and strengthening the developments that will be articulated in Chapters 3 and 4.

It must be realized that vagueness is, as already mentioned, a new phenomenon in our constitutional framework. Moreover, there is no actual provision of the *Charter,* or of the *Constitution Act, 1867,*[25] expressly prohibiting vague legislation. The doctrine can be invoked as it is implicitly triggered by some of the provisions of the *Charter*.[26] We know that the two rationales of vagueness are fair notice and limitation of law enforcement discretion. Taken in the abstract, however, and outside any constitutional justification or support, these rationales are not initially or obviously compelling. In other words, the vagueness doctrine appears at first glance to have little legitimacy because its substantive rationales are not well understood and its constitutional bases are uncertain. It is important to realize, however, that the rationales underlying the doctrine can be traced to other principles that possess stronger roots in our legal tradition. In this regard, the principles of legality and the rule of law will be examined in Chapters 1 and 2.

The principle of legality, which translates the old maxim *nullum crimen nulla poena sine lege,* requires that penal laws be prospective only in reach. It therefore condemns the *ex post facto* application of penal law. This is done with the desire to avoid "unfair surprise" to citizens in a manner very similar to the first rationale of the vagueness doctrine. We recall that fair notice is a rationale of vagueness because vague laws can create "unfair surprise" for citizens who could not have foreseen that a law would apply to their situation. It is therefore useful to begin this book by examining the principle of legality in Chapter 1. Through the enforcement of this principle, we will see how courts are dedicated to protecting the ideal of fair notice in our legal tradition. This is especially important since legality now enjoys explicit constitutional recognition through s. 11(g) of the *Charter,* which provides that no one can be found guilty of an act unless at the time it "constituted an offence" under law. An examination of the principle of legality in Chapter 1 will therefore reinforce the constitutional legitimacy of the doctrine. It will justify treating concerns pertaining to fair notice as substantially compelling (in Chapter 3). Also, it will strengthen the bases of the doctrine and even broaden the number of situations where it can be invoked (in Chapter 4).

Along a similar line of thinking, Chapter 2 will examine the principle of the rule of law. This principle seeks to strike a balance between pre-established rules and grants of discretionary powers to law-enforcing authorities. It requires that discretion be granted with caution in order to protect citizens from arbitrary government. The parallel with the second rationale of the vagueness doctrine – that of limiting discretion in law enforcement – is obvious. An inquiry into the implications of this principle will therefore be very useful in better understanding the second rationale of the vagueness doctrine. As we will see in Chapter 2, the rule of law is expressly mentioned in the preamble to the *Charter* and has attracted considerable constitutional importance, especially in recent years. By exploring the rule of law's rejection of excessive discretion, Chapter 2 will show the importance of legal certainty in our legal and constitutional tradition. This will be useful to better understand the analysis in Chapter 3 on the contents of the doctrine. Moreover, an analysis of the rule of law will also foster a better understanding of the formal conditions under which the doctrine can be applied, as will be seen in Chapter 4.

Thus, Chapters 1 and 2 will introduce Chapters 3 and 4 by reinforcing the rationales of fair notice and law enforcement discretion through discussions of the principles of legality and the rule of law. It should be noted that, although legality will be presented mostly as associated with fair notice on the one hand, and the rule of law will be essentially affiliated with the limitation of law enforcement discretion on the other hand, these are not watertight compartments. In fact, it will be seen that the benefits of fair notice are quite often associated with the rule of law in the case law and the literature, while concerns about limiting discretion are also sometimes considered within the ambit of legality.[27] This interpenetration of the two concepts is quite understandable as they are both aimed at promoting certainty in the legal system. To some extent, legality can even be considered to be included in the broader principle of the rule of law.[28]

Chapter 3 will examine the actual content of the vagueness doctrine. First, through a brief overview of the American situation, we will see that the Supreme Court of the United States will protect citizens against vague laws in only a rather limited fashion. Thus, fair notice will be seen as being offended in American constitutional law only when the law touches upon some conduct usually perceived as "innocent." Meanwhile, the law enforcement discretion rationale will not provoke the invalidation of vague laws unless the law is viewed as a "catch-all," encouraging selective enforcement by the authorities.

The Supreme Court of Canada has defined the two rationales of vagueness restrictively, in a manner similar to the American situation. Thus, pursuant to *Nova Scotia Pharmaceutical,* the rationale of fair notice is seen as offended essentially if the law is detached from the "substratum of values" of society, while the law enforcement discretion rationale is viewed as protecting only against "catch-all" laws that could lead to automatic convictions once prosecution occurs. As dictated by the principles of legality and the rule of law (studied in Chapters 1 and 2), I will explain how a broader protection may be afforded to the two essential rationales of vagueness. I will also show how the Supreme Court of Canada's narrow definitions of the two rationales may be useful in making the requirement of precision fluctuate in certain cases.

In Chapter 3, emphasis will also be placed on the "legal debate" test, which is, as mentioned earlier, the permissive criterion developed in *Nova Scotia Pharmaceutical* to assess the validity of vague legislation. This test is not inspired by the American situation. It is a creation of the Supreme Court of Canada by which Gonthier J. sought to define in a comprehensive manner the threshold of constitutional validity that is to be applied to all laws, a thing that has never been attempted in the United States. It will be shown how this permissive test of legal debate, if applied indiscriminately to all cases, is likely to undermine the importance of legality and the rule of law. Consequently, the doctrine must inevitably be developed beyond this initial test. A series of factors is articulated in this book in order to help nurture the development of the vagueness doctrine in a manner consistent with the important concerns it seeks to balance. The minimal legal debate test may be appropriate in some cases where the legislative assembly cannot efficiently reach its objectives without considerable flexibility. In some other cases, however, a more demanding and elaborate test will inevitably have to be applied.

Chapter 3 will study some factors that can make the requirement of precision fluctuate depending on the circumstances, thus allowing courts to adequately balance the needs of the State against individual rights. Among these factors, the most important are: (1) the presence of a "substratum of values," (2) the likelihood of selective enforcement, (3) the necessity of resorting to vague legislation, and (4) the type of law involved.

Chapter 3 will also examine possible solutions towards greater precision that could help statutes comply with the constitutional requirements of the vagueness doctrine. First, it will examine the method that consists of adding words to the law through the judicial process. As will be argued, a difficulty with this approach is that it increases the burden of citizens who wish to know the law, by forcing them to search through volumes of reported decisions in addition to reading the statute. Moreover, an *ex post facto* application of the law can occur when a newly defined standard is applied to the accused in the case at bar. We will see that this undermines the principle of legality. Thus, whenever possible, it is preferable that the legal standard be spelled out in the statute itself rather than by the judiciary. The legislative assembly can make its rules more specific by articulating in greater detail the conditions under which they apply, but we will see that it can also resort to other methods. For instance, by providing illustrations of the law's applicability, its scope can be made more certain through the use of the principle of interpretation known as *ejusdem generis*. Another technique that will be examined in Chapter 3 is the potential usefulness of delegated legislation to specify the standards contained in the law.

The object of Chapter 4 will be to study the appropriate place of the vagueness doctrine in the *Charter* in order to determine its practical applicability in particular cases. Its object will also be to understand the influence the bases can sometimes have on the nature of the vagueness analysis on the merits. As already mentioned, the provisions that can render the doctrine applicable are essentially ss. 1 and 7, as well as other provisions that, much like s. 7, contain an "internal limitation." From this fragmented recognition of the vagueness doctrine can arise certain procedural as well as substantive problems, which will be addressed in Chapter 4.

As mentioned earlier, under s. 1 of the *Charter,* vagueness can become relevant in two different ways. First, it can be raised in relation to the requirement that limitations on *Charter* rights be prescribed by law. Second, vagueness can acquire importance under the "minimal impairment" branch of the *Oakes* test, after a breach to a substantive *Charter* guarantee has been demonstrated. A vague law, since it possesses the potential for being interpreted in an overly broad manner, may fail the test of "minimal impairment." In that sense, the concepts of vagueness and overbreadth are similar in some ways but also present some differences, which Chapter 4 will analyze.[29] The relationship between these first two bases of vagueness under s. 1, the "prescribed by law" and "minimal impairment" requirements, will be examined.

Chapter 4 also contains an analysis of other bases that have been recognized in substantive provisions of the *Charter*. Vagueness is normally applicable every time a provision of the *Charter* contains an internal limitation. For example, it is considered to be a "principle of fundamental justice" under s. 7. Some problems surrounding the applicability of the doctrine in the framework of s. 7, as well as in other provisions of the *Charter* containing an internal limitation, will be analyzed.

It will be realized that the vagueness doctrine currently does not have autonomous status. This means that there must always be some other *Charter* interest at stake in order for the precision of legislation to become relevant. Chapter 4 will explore the possibilities of a broader applicability of the doctrine in the future. The strong interpretative influence of the principles of legality and the rule of law will be helpful in that regard. In particular, we will see that ss. 7 and 11(g) can reasonably be interpreted in light of these principles as permitting an autonomous recognition of the vagueness doctrine in the future, or at least allowing its applicability in all penal matters. Finally, Chapter 4 will address the impact of constitutional bases on the severity of vagueness analysis. We will see that, especially due to the interplay between the concepts of overbreadth and vagueness, the requirement of precision can sometimes vary depending on the constitutional basis under which it is being analyzed.

1
The Principle of Legality

The principle *nullum crimen nulla poena sine lege* (no crime nor punishment without law) requires not only that punishments be based on laws but also that these laws be prospective in reach. As already mentioned, this is required in order to avoid individuals being the victims of "unfair surprise" as new standards are applied to their past conduct. The principle of legality has deep roots in our legal tradition, in addition to finding explicit support in the text of the Constitution. Section 11(g) of the *Canadian Charter of Rights and Freedoms* provides the following: "11. Any person charged with an offence has the right ... (g) not to be found guilty on account of any act or omission unless, at the time of the act or omission, it constituted an offence under Canadian or international law or was criminal according to the general principles of law recognized by the community of nations."

The principle expressed in s. 11(g) is enforced in many countries around the world, as well as in several international human rights law instruments. The principle was first stated in a significant manner in Article 8 of the *French Declaration of the Rights of Man, 1789:* "no one may be punished except by virtue of a law established and promulgated before the crime and legally applied."[1] It was later incorporated into the French Constitution of 1791.[2] The principle was stated as well in Germany by Article 116 of the Weimar Constitution[3] following the works of Feuerbach, who was the first to enunciate it as an apophthegm: "Nulla poena sine lege, nulla poena sine crimine, nullum crimen sine poena legali."[4] The United States also protects its citizens from *ex post facto* federal laws through Article 1, s. 9(3) of the Constitution. A similar prohibition is applicable to the individual states through Article 1, s. 10(1).[5] A number of other foreign countries also possess constitutional limitations of this nature.[6] The principle is also formulated at the international level in Article 11(2) of the *Universal Declaration of Human Rights,*[7] Article 7 of the *European Convention for the Protection of Human Rights and Fundamental Freedoms,*[8] and Article 15 of the *International Covenant on Civil and Political Rights.*[9]

Within the principle of legality, several different aspects contribute to upholding the "fair warning" ideal. First, legality requires that offences be defined by statutes, as opposed to being defined by courts. In Canada since 1955, s. 9 of the *Criminal Code* states that with the exception of criminal contempt of court, "no person shall be convicted ... of an offence at common law." This has at least two implications. First, it prevents the *ex post facto* creation of new crimes by judges. Second, it forbids convictions for common law crimes that, although established by precedent, have no statutory basis. Also, by way of s. 11(g) of the *Charter,* the protection of legality now goes a step further. Not only must convictions for offences be based on statutes, but these statutes must be prospective in reach. This means that not only courts but also legislatures must respect the need for providing "fair notice to the citizens" through the advance definition of offences.

The first part of this chapter will present the traditional antipathy towards *ex post facto* legislation. This will allow us to examine its inherent relationship with the concept of fair warning to citizens, common to the principle of legality and to the vagueness doctrine. We will see that whether the legal standard being applied to the legal subject is entirely created after the fact or derived from a vague law, concerns of unfair surprise come into play in both situations as the rule is being given a retroactive effect.

The analysis will then move on to the historical evolution that led to the disappearance of the judicial creation of offences in Great Britain, the United States, and Canada. The common law system is based on case-by-case adjudication involving rule making (or "rule declaring") by judges. When this method is applied to penal law, it offends the principle of legality because it implies that accused persons can be held liable for acts that had not yet been declared illegal at the time they were committed. Moreover, judicial decisions cause a problem of fair warning as it is difficult for citizens not accustomed to legal research to trace and analyze them. In that sense, we will see that a system of codified penal law is more respectful of the principle of legality.

This chapter will also explore the constitutional protection against *ex post facto* legislation. In that context, I will examine the scope of s. 11(g) of the *Charter,* which has been applied exclusively in relation to laws creating offences. The possibility of recognizing a broader applicability for this provision will also be touched upon, while keeping in mind that it is most naturally relevant in the context of penal law. I will focus mainly on the penal applications of s. 11(g) and study the impact of the fair warning rationale in that regard. I will also examine the impact of the exceptions to the *nullum crimen* principle allowed by s. 11(g) related to offences in international law. Finally, I will examine the reach of another possible basis for legality in the *Charter,* namely, s. 7.

"Fair Warning" and the Antipathy towards
Ex Post Facto Lawmaking

The antipathy towards retroactive lawmaking has very deep roots. The ancient Greeks believed that laws should have only a prospective reach.[10] Similarly, the Roman Civil Law *(Corpus Juris Civilis)* declared that statutes were to be construed to have only a prospective reach.[11] Retroactivity could be achieved only if the legislation expressly declared it. This Roman principle of interpretation was introduced into the common law of England through the writings of Bracton[12] and Coke.[13] It was also incorporated into civil law systems insofar as they were founded directly on Roman law.[14]

Ex post facto laws, especially in the penal context, offend society's most basic sense of justice and fairness. Thomas Hobbes considered that a retroactive law was simply not a law.[15] As pointed out by James Madison in *The Federalist*, "ex post facto laws ... are contrary to the first principles of the social compact, and to every principle of sound legislation."[16] Cicero called a retroactive measure an "abominable and monstrous wickedness."[17] This category of legislation is elsewhere described as "evil,"[18] and "a betrayal of what the law stands for."[19] In the same vein, Lon Fuller writes: "A retroactive law is truly a monstrosity. Law has to do with the governance of human conduct by rules. To speak of governing or directing conduct today by rules that will be enacted tomorrow is to talk in a blank prose."[20]

What is interesting for our purposes is that the main reason why *ex post facto* rule making is generally perceived as a reprehensible exercise of state power is that it does not provide fair warning to citizens as to what the law prescribes. The element of unfair surprise created by the application of a new law to past situations betrays the ethical integrity of the legal system. A basic sense of fairness implies that individuals should not suffer penalties for events that occurred prior to the enactment of the law. An *ex post facto* law obviously does not provide any notice as to its content since it does not even exist at the time the act is committed. The relationship to the vagueness doctrine is obvious. The advantage of prospective lawmaking (as of clear lawmaking)[21] is that citizens are provided with a fair opportunity to anticipate legal sanctions and adjust their conduct accordingly. It should be noted that what matters most to "notice" in that framework is not whether citizens have actually acquired knowledge of the law but whether they have had the opportunity to do so. It has long been considered to be important for the ethical integrity of a legal system that – even if citizens do not enjoy actual notice of the law – they at least have the opportunity to find out the extent of their right and obligation should they wish to do so. As Oliver Wendell Holmes eloquently stated in *The Common Law* while talking about the distinction between law and morality: "But while the law is thus continually adding to its specific rules, it does not adopt the coarse and impolitic principle that a man always acts at his peril. On the contrary, its concrete rules, as well as the general questions addressed to the jury, show that the defendant *must have had at least a fair chance* of avoiding the infliction of harm before he becomes answerable for such a consequence of his conduct."[22]

A well-established principle in our system states that "ignorance of the law is no excuse" *(ignorantia juris neminem excusat)*.[23] Thus, an individual who did not know that a particular offence stood in the books cannot escape conviction for lack of "notice." Although at first glance this principle may appear to betray the ideal of fair notice that lies behind the antipathy towards *ex post facto* legislation,[24] we realize that it penalizes only those citizens who neglect their duty to consult the law prior to acting. It would be cynical to deny that the law is, at least occasionally, consulted in advance by its subjects.[25] Responsible citizens who do consult the law, either directly or through legal counsel, prior to adopting a course of conduct that they suspect might come under law value the notion of fair notice associated with prospective (and clear) legislation. In fact, the *ignorantia juris* principle operates under the presumption that citizens will in fact consult the law. It is therefore a necessary corollary of that principle that citizens have at least the possibility of knowing the law.

In relation to the rationale of unfair surprise, it is important to keep in mind the entire framework of the legal system. At first glance, it might seem questionable in some cases to reject accusations merely on the basis that the accused did not have a fair opportunity to find out that his conduct might trigger legal liability, when we know that he probably would have acted the same way had the law been promulgated ahead of time. Consider, for example, the case of *R. v. Jacobson,*[26] in which the Saskatchewan Court of Appeal reversed a conviction for dangerous driving causing death on the basis that this offence had been enacted after the alleged conduct of the accused. It is very possible that the accused in *Jacobson* did not consult the law or seek legal advice prior to his actions. Consequently, his discharge may appear to be based on a pure technicality. However, in cases of *ex post facto* application of the law like this, it is important to keep in mind the entire framework of the legal system. By adopting reasoning based merely on the demands of justice *in the case at bar,* we run the risk of seeing the legislature act with carelessness in the future in its task of promulgating laws. If the practice of *ex post facto* lawmaking is not condemned, legislative assemblies might tend to neglect to update the body of positive laws, since any gap could always be filled *post hoc* through retroactive legislation. In other words, by allowing gaps to be filled *ex post facto,* we invite the lawmaker to leave more gaps, and the overall effect of this situation will be to substantially diminish the fair notice given to citizens. Cases of surprise that are genuinely unfair may multiply as a result of exaggerated permissiveness towards *ex post facto* legislation.

An analogy with this type of long-term reasoning can be drawn from the constitutional protection of privacy rights. In applying s. 8 of the *Charter,* which protects citizens against "unreasonable search or seizure," courts do not look only at protection of the accused's privacy rights but are also concerned with the preservation of privacy in society at large. For example, take the situation where narcotics are found in a private residence but the evidence is excluded at trial under s. 24(2) of the *Charter* because the police neglected to obtain a warrant prior to conducting the search.[27] Most often, substantive justice *in the case at bar* would require that the evidence be admitted because the accused is guilty of the crime, regardless of how the evidence was discovered. Nevertheless, the evidence is sometimes excluded because: (1) under s. 8 it is important that members of the public be protected from invasion of their privacy, and therefore releasing individuals who are guilty is necessary as it has the long-term effect of making the police more conscious of protecting the privacy rights of other "innocent" citizens; and (2) as stated in s. 24(2) of the *Charter,* the admission of the evidence would "bring the administration of justice into disrepute." In connection with the guarantee against "unreasonable search and seizure," LaForest J. stated the following in the recent case of *R. v. Edwards:* "The provision is intended to afford protection to all of us to be secure against intrusion by the state or its agents by unreasonable searches or seizures, and is not solely for the protection of criminals even though the most effective remedy will inevitably protect the criminal as the price of liberty for all."[28]

And further: "We exercise discretion to exclude evidence obtained by unconstitutional searches from being used against an accused, even when it would clearly establish guilt, not to protect criminals but because the only really effective safeguard for the protection of the constitutional right we all share is not to allow use of evidence obtained in violation of this public right when doing so would bring the administration of justice into disrepute."[29]

It is easy to see a similarity with the reasoning in cases of *ex post facto* legislation. Thus, in *Jacobson,* it may be true that the accused *in the case at bar* was probably not prejudicially affected by the fact that he had had no opportunity to find out the content of a law that was promulgated after his actions. However, the long-term effect of allowing such convictions would be to invite the legislature, and the courts, to be less cautious in providing fair warning to citizens. Interestingly, *ex post facto* laws can also "bring the administration of justice into disrepute," to use the terminology of s. 24(2), since their use betrays the ethical integrity of the legal system.

The Judicial Creation of Offences

As mentioned earlier, breaches of the principle of legality can take different forms. They can occur through the retroactive operation of a statute, but also through the creation of an offence by a court, without statutory basis. Before examining the phenomenon of retroactive statutes, let us focus on breaches of legality through the judicial process.[30]

The principle of legality, which stands for "the desirability in principle of advance legislative specification of criminal conduct,"[31] repudiates the historical methodology of the common law in penal matters. However, despite the British heritage from which Canadian and American justice systems spring, the *nullum crimen* principle has had major influence in these systems. In fact, even in Great Britain, criminal law has evolved over the last centuries to reduce and even practically eliminate judicial crime creation.

The Judicial Creation of Offences in Great Britain

Historically in Great Britain, felonies and misdemeanours were created by judges who acted without statutory support to protect the public interest. The common law tradition implied an assumption by judges that they had the power to create (or "declare") new offences on a case-by-case basis. The actions of citizens could retroactively be declared criminal if they were found by common law courts to be "public mischiefs" deserving punishment. In 1616, the Court of King's Bench made the following statement: "To this court belongs authority, not only to correct errors in judicial proceedings, but other errors and misdemeanours extra-judicial, tending to the breach of peace, or oppression of the subjects, or to any manner of misgovernment; so that no wrong or injury, either public or private, can be done, but that it shall be reformed or punished in due course of law."[32] And in 1774: "Whatever is contrary, bonos mores est decorum, the principles of our law prohibit, and the King's Court, as the general censor and guardian of the public manners, is bound to restrain and punish."[33]

Through the legal fiction of the "declaratory theory" of the common law, the offences thus created were said to have always been part of the law of England. The judges merely discovered them. However, as the decisions were being applied directly to the accused, their effect was, in fact, *ex post facto*. Examples include the crime of nudity in public, which was declared to be a misdemeanour in 1664.[34] In 1676, the crime of blasphemy was created.[35] Other examples include the crimes of forgery[36] and digging up of corpses (for scientific or other purposes),[37] declared in 1727 and 1788, respectively. In all these cases, the accused were convicted even though the law as previously stated by either statute or precedent contained nothing prohibiting their acts.

Over the years, the exercise of this power became narrower. As precedents accumulated, the need to create new offences gradually disappeared.

In addition, as Parliament increased its activity, opportunities for innovation by judges became less frequent. Originally, statutes were designed to address gaps in the common law. As Parliament grew in power, its activities increased and the role of creating new offences became predominantly legislative. A commission on the reform of criminal law even recommended, as early as 1879, that the lawmaking power of judges be eliminated and that only offences created by legislation remain:

> In bygone ages, when legislation was scanty and rare, the powers referred to may have been useful and even necessary; but that is not the case at the present day. Parliament is regular in its sittings and active in its labours; and if the protection of society requires the enactment of additional penal laws, Parliament will soon supply them. If Parliament is not disposed to provide punishments for acts which are upon any grounds objectionable or dangerous, the presumption is that they belong to that class of misconduct against which the moral feeling and good sense of the community are the best protection.[38]

The commission recommended the adoption of a code that would embody the whole of criminal offences, and the abolition of convictions based on judicially created offences. This recommendation was motivated by the desire to promote greater certainty and stability in the administration of criminal law. This now appeared to be possible, considering the growth of Parliament. However, the commission's position was not followed, as the authorities at the time felt the need to preserve the advantages associated with the elasticity of the common law tradition.[39] This is not to say that judicial crime creation was still common at the time. Although the exercise of this power was still possible, it had come to be viewed as something exceptional. Consider the following passage by J. Stephen in 1883: "Though the existence of this power as inherent in the judges has been asserted by several high authorities by a great length of time, it is hardly probable that any attempt would be made to exercise it at the present day; and any such attempt would place the bench in an invidious position."[40] And this other pronouncement made in 1884: "The great leading rule of criminal law is that nothing is a crime unless it is plainly forbidden by law. This rule is no doubt subject to exceptions, but they are rare, narrow, and to be admitted with the greatest reluctance, and only upon the strongest reasons."[41]

Therefore, although it was not totally abolished, there was an understanding towards the end of the nineteenth and the beginning of the twentieth centuries in England that if the judicial creation of offences was ever to be used, it had to be done with extreme care. The main concern being security and predictability, some of the elasticity of the common law had to be sacrificed, especially considering the fact that Parliament now had the means to adapt rapidly to the evolving needs of criminal law.

The case of *Rex v. Manley*[42] is one of very few remaining examples of clear judicial crime creation by an English court in the twentieth century. Elizabeth Manley was accused of having committed a "public mischief" in common law by reporting fictitious crimes to the police. She had complained to the police that a man, of whom she gave a description, had stolen her purse. It was later discovered that she had invented this story and that she had never been robbed. Her acts were obviously reprehensible since she wasted the time and energy of the police force, not to mention that an innocent man might have been falsely arrested. However, there was, at the time she acted, absolutely no provision in any penal statute that would prohibit such conduct, nor was there a judicial precedent to that effect. She had therefore not been given notice by law that her act would trigger penal liability. She was nonetheless convicted, as the court decided to create a new crime of knowingly reporting fictitious crimes to the police and to apply it to the accused.

The decision in *Manley* was widely criticized at the time,[43] but it left open the possibility of judicial crime creation should the need arise. Comforted by *Manley*, the House of Lords asserted the power to create another common law offence in *Shaw v. Director of Public Prosecutions*.[44] The accused had been charged with "conspiracy to corrupt public morals" because he had published a "Ladies Directory" in which he allowed prostitutes to advertise their services as an alternative to illegal street solicitation. Such publication was not prohibited by statute or even by the common law at the time, but the accused was nonetheless convicted through the use of the judiciary's residual power to create penal offences.[45] Similarly, in *Knuller v. Director of Public Prosecutions*,[46] the House of Lords upheld a conviction for having published classified ads by male homosexuals. The publication was found to be contrary to the common law of crimes as it had a tendency to "corrupt public morals," and the accused was convicted despite the absence of a statute or precedent criminalizing the conduct.

Despite cases such as *Manley*, *Shaw*, and *Knuller*, it remains doubtful whether courts can legitimately claim and exercise the power to create new offences in England. *Manley* has been at least implicitly repudiated since it was decided in 1933,[47] and all three decisions have been the object of severe criticism by commentators.[48] They are now viewed by many as relics. Even if a judge could still, strictly speaking, invoke the power, it is unlikely that it would be done convincingly outside of extreme circumstances. The consensus around the *nullum crimen* principle has reached such proportions among western legal scholars that it is likely to prevail over the traditional "elasticity" of the common law. Moreover, and perhaps more importantly, England has ratified and is now bound by the

European Convention on Human Rights (1950), which recognizes the principle of legality. Similar to s. 11(g) of the *Charter,* Article 7 of the *Convention* recognizes that:

1. No one shall be held guilty of any criminal offence on account of any act or omission which did not constitute a criminal offence under national or international law at the time when it was committed. Nor shall a heavier penalty be imposed than the one that was applicable at the time the criminal offence was committed.

2. This Article shall not prejudice the trial and punishment of any person for any act or omission which, at the time when it was committed, was criminal according to the general principles of law recognized by civilised nations.

Article 7 has been interpreted not only as prohibiting *ex post facto* legislation *per se* but also as preventing judges from expanding the realm of penal offences.[49] As leading authors on the *European Convention* point out: "Article 7 does not merely prohibit retrospective penal legislation; it also prohibits extension of the criminal law through interpretation by analogy. Indeed it may well be argued that it excludes any form of extensive application of criminal legislation."[50]

In fact, Article 7 protects the essence of the *nullum crimen* principle, and thus imposes upon member states the obligation to favour certainty over elasticity in the definition of crimes. Article 7 would most likely prohibit convictions like *Manley, Shaw,* or *Knuller,* as the principle of legality embodied in this provision is offended by the *ex post facto* application of new common law crimes to individuals. In fact, leading commentators on the *European Convention* recognize and have expressly suggested that the *Shaw* and *Knuller* decisions would not have stood the test of Article 7 had they been challenged at the European Community level.[51]

In defence of *Manley, Shaw,* and *Knuller,* the argument could be made that the crimes were not, strictly speaking, new crimes. They can indeed be viewed as merely new applications of the already existing common law crimes of "public mischief" or "corruption of public morals." Pursuant to this argument, conviction of the accused in these cases would not have an *ex post facto* effect. It is easy to see the weakness of this reasoning, however. Whether the crime is entirely new or whether it constitutes a particular application of the general standard of public mischief, for example, the effect is in practice very similar. In fact, all criminal laws are driven by the underlying purpose of preventing "public mischiefs." Moreover, Article 7 has been interpreted by the European Court as prohibiting convictions based on vaguely defined offences.[52] With a standard as general as "corrupting public morals," in *Shaw* and *Knuller,* and "public mischief" in *Manley,* there is little doubt that Article 7 and the *nullum crimen* principle it enshrines are being encroached on. Whether or not we consider the convictions to possess a basis in common law, the result is the same since these so-called bases are patently vague and general.[53]

The Judicial Creation of Offences in the United States
As in Great Britain, the evolution of the *nullum crimen* principle in the United States has not been straightforward. When independence was achieved by the thirteen British colonies of America to form the United States, two different series of legal values opposed each other in determining the content of a new criminal justice system. This new system was subject, on the one hand, to the strong influence of the British common law tradition, which was rather favourable to judicial crime creation. On the other hand, since the United States was a new country, having just liberated itself from colonialism, a sense of hostility towards authority could be felt in legal and political circles. In that regard, the Enlightenment school of thought was influential in pushing forward the virtues of legality and opposing them to the common law tradition.[54]

Enlightenment thinkers such as Montesquieu[55] and Beccaria[56] stressed the need to preserve a separation between the three levels of State authority. Thus, in order to ensure that neither the legislative, the executive, nor the judiciary gains excessive power, which would be potentially dangerous to individual liberties, their respective roles must be kept reasonably distinct. This idea of separation of powers derives from a contractual understanding of legitimate government. According to this view, individuals have surrendered their liberty to the State through a social compact for the benefit of society as a whole. Implicitly, this entails an obligation for the State to use punishment solely in accordance with laws enacted by the legislative branch. This satisfies the ethical concern that individuals be given advance notice of what is prohibited, as well as the institutional concern that rules be enacted essentially by the representatives of the people.

Despite the doctrinal influence of these concerns associated with Enlightenment theories, the early years of the American criminal justice system were marked by a domination of the traditional British common law approach.[57] In all thirteen original states, the prevalence of the common law heritage was recognized either by statute or by judicial decision. Most of the later states followed the same path. This implied not only the preservation of established British common law offences, as long as they were deemed applicable to local conditions, but also the subsistence of the judiciary's residual power to create new crimes. One fact that must not be overlooked in that regard is that in the United States, criminal law falls within the jurisdiction of the individual states. Early on, the separation of powers played a much larger role in the context of the federal Constitution than in the constitutions of the individual states. In addition, before the Civil War amendments, individual liberties were protected against federal but not against state powers. This may have contributed to the limited impact of the principle of legality on the early development of American criminal law.

At the legislative level, this early reluctance regarding the *nullum crimen* principle led to the rejection of codification initiatives.[58] At the jurisprudential level, several cases displayed a preference for the elasticity of the common law over the more secure but still unfamiliar and underdeveloped technique of advance legislative rule making. This concern for elasticity was expressed as follows by the Supreme Court of Pennsylvania in *Commonwealth v. Taylor:* "The malicious ingenuity of mankind is constantly producing new inventions in the art of disturbing their neighbours. To this invention must be opposed general principles, calculated to meet and punish them."[59]

Pursuant to this view, early American jurisprudence displayed little resistance towards *ex post facto* crime creation by judges. For example, in the case of *Pennsylvania v. Gillespie,*[60] an individual was convicted for having torn down an advertisement for public auction despite the fact that there was no statute or precedent criminalizing such conduct. The court relied on an analogy with the law of torts, which recognized the validity of claims for tearing down advertisements for private sales. Similarly, in *State v. Buckman,*[61] the accused was convicted for having put a dead animal in another person's well. Prior to the *Buckman* decision, this type of conduct had never been declared criminal, but the court nevertheless convicted the accused by making an analogy with the common law offence of selling unwholesome food or poisoning food or drink intended for human consumption.

At the doctrinal level, this same philosophy prevailed in the nineteenth century and during the first few decades of the twentieth century.[62] However, by the 1930s and 1940s, as legislative assemblies had increased the intensity of their activities and statutes started to cover criminal law in a comprehensive manner, commentators began stressing the importance of the *nullum crimen* principle. Up to that point, the judiciary's residual power had been a *mal nécessaire,* considering the incapacity of legislative assemblies to react in a timely manner to the evolving needs of criminal law. As the truth associated with this reality diminished, jurists could afford to devote greater attention to the principle of legality.

After the Second World War, the repugnance towards judicial crime creation became even more dominant in the United States. This came about as a reaction against undemocratic methods of government associated with foreign countries perceived as tyrannical. Thus, the infamous "principle of analogy" that prevailed in Germany under the Nazi regime of Adolf Hitler triggered an overall repugnance towards breaches to the principle of legality. The principle of analogy provided that: "whoever commits an act which the law declares to be punishable or which is deserving of punishment according to the fundamental idea of a penal law and sound perception of the people, shall be punished. If no determinate penal law is directly applicable to the action, it shall be punished according to the law, the basic idea of which fits best."[63]

This provision is quite similar to the philosophy that prevailed in cases such as *Manley, Shaw,* and *Knuller* in England, or *Gillespie* and *Buckman* in the United States. In a case such as *Gillespie,* for example, where the accused was convicted at the criminal level for having torn down an advertisement for public auction, the court's reasoning was very similar to the above-quoted Nazi principle of analogy. Considering that there was no statute or precedent indicating that it was criminal to tear down an advertisement for public auction, the individual was subject to an unfair surprise, as he had no way of knowing that the common law of torts would be extended to apply to his situation and used to convict him *ex post facto.* The effect of the Nazi episode was to show the tremendous abuses and injustices that could result from breaches of the principle of legality. Judges and commentators therefore began condemning judicial crime creation altogether, in order to protect citizens from threats of future despotism.[64]

As a result of this evolution, the judicial creation of new offences in the United States has practically disappeared. Although some rare examples of judicial innovation in the definition of crimes can still be identified,[65] the majority of authors and judges now view this power as being outside the courts' reach.[66] Although it has not been definitively put aside expressly by an authoritative judicial pronouncement, a consensus has grown among judges and commentators that American law now repudiates the judicial creation of offences.

The Judicial Creation of Offences in Canada

We recall that in Great Britain attempts were made during the nineteenth century to enact a criminal code. In 1879, a draft criminal code based upon the work of Sir James Fitzjames Stephen was proposed by a Royal Commission.[67] This code was an attempt to reduce the uncertainties associated with the scattered nature of criminal law, which was buried in numerous statutes and judicial decisions. The Stephens code purported to abrogate common law offences and to negate the residual power of judges to create new crimes. However, this draft code was never adopted in England. Expressing the reluctance of British authorities to depart from the common law tradition, Baron Parke formulated the following comments in relation to the proposed code: "My objection to the proposed measure is founded on the danger of confining provisions against crimes to enactments and repealing in this respect the rules of the common law, which are clear and well understood and have the incalculable advantage of being capable of application to new combinations of circumstances, perpetually recurring, which are decided, when they arise, by inference and analogy to them and upon the principles on which they rest."[68]

Thus, codification efforts failed in England and, up to the present day, this country's criminal offences remain scattered among over 200 statutes and numerous judicial decisions.[69] It is interesting to note that the work of the British Royal Commission of 1879 inspired Canadian authorities, who adopted our country's first criminal code in 1892. This code was indeed modelled on Stephen's *Digest of the Criminal Law* from England. Other sources include Burbridge's *Digest of the Canadian Criminal Law* of 1889 and several Canadian statutes.[70] However, the Canadian *Criminal Code* of 1892 did not expressly put aside common law offences or the judiciary's residual power to create new crimes, contrary to what the Stephens code attempted to do. As Sir John Thompson stated when introducing the Canadian *Criminal Code* bill in the House of Commons: "The common law will still exist and be referred to, and in that respect the Code ... will have that elasticity which has been so much desired by those who are opposed to codification on general principles."[71] Despite this preservation of common law crimes, legal certainty was greatly improved by the codification. As E.G. Ewaschuk, QC, notes: "Unlike the uncertainty that continued in Britain, the Criminal Code (Canada) proved invaluable to the judiciary and the legal profession, as well as the police and general public, in readily determining what the elements of various criminal conducts were and the applicable criminal procedures."[72]

Even though it was still technically possible for individuals to be convicted *ex post facto* for crimes that had not been previously declared criminal by legislation or precedent, such occurrences were very uncommon in Canada after 1892.[73] It was generally understood that a conduct was criminal only if it was contrary to Canadian law at the time it was committed. While the judiciary's residual power was not expressly taken away by legislation, the judiciary itself opted in favour of the *nullum crimen* principle. Consider, for example, the case of *R. v. Hastings*.[74] In this case, the Appeal division of the Supreme Court of New Brunswick refused to recognize the offence of indecent exposure since it had not been previously stated by legislation or precedent. Therefore, an accused who had been caught urinating in public could not be legally arrested.[75] Similarly, in *Frey v. Fedoruk*,[76] the Supreme Court of Canada declared that peeping through the window of a woman who was undressing at night was not a criminal offence as it had not been declared punishable in the past by either statute or precedent.[77] In *Frey*, Cartwright J., writing for a majority of the Court, rejected the traditional methodology of the common law in criminal matters. Speaking about the judiciary's residual power to create new crimes in British common law tradition, he commented:

> In my opinion, this power has not been held and should not be held to exist in Canada. I think it safer to hold that no one shall be convicted of a crime unless the offence with which he is charged is recognized as such in the provisions of the *Criminal Code*, or can be established by the authority of some reported case as an offence known to the law. I think that if any course of conduct is now to be held criminal, which has not up to the present time been so regarded, such declaration should be made by Parliament and not by the Courts.[78]

Thus, since 1950 and the Supreme Court's decision in *Frey*, the *nullum crimen* principle has prevailed in Canadian criminal law over the traditional elasticity of the common law. This choice was legislatively sanctioned in the 1955 revision of the *Criminal Code* when Parliament enacted what is now s. 9 of the current *Criminal Code*, which reads as follows:

> 9. Notwithstanding anything in this Act or any other Act, no person shall be convicted or discharged under section 730
>   (a) of an offence at common law,
>   (b) of an offence under an Act of the Parliament of England, or of Great Britain, or of the United Kingdom of Great Britain and Ireland, or
>   (c) of an offence under an Act or ordinance in force in any province, territory or place before that province, territory or place became a province of Canada, but nothing in this section affects the power, jurisdiction or authority that a court, judge, justice or provincial court judge had, immediately before April 1, 1955, to impose punishment for contempt of court.

Parliament went even further than the Supreme Court in *Frey* in that it not only prohibited judicial crime creation but also eliminated existing common law offences, with the exception of contempt of court.[79] Thus, most criminal offences in Canada are to be found in a single document, the *Criminal Code*. Other statutes complement the *Code* in defining other, somewhat more specialized criminal offences. Among these statutes are the *Customs Act*,[80] the *Food and Drugs Act*,[81] the *Income Tax Act*,[82] the *Competition Act*,[83] and the *Narcotics Control Act*.[84]

Interestingly, there seems to have been a fairly sustained willingness to protect the *nullum crimen* principle in Canada since Confederation. Unlike the British experience, where codification efforts failed and where modern examples of clear judicial crime creation can still be found in cases such as *Manley, Shaw,* and *Knuller,* we can observe in the history of the Canadian criminal justice system a sustained preference for the certainty associated with legislation. Even in the United States, often thought of as the sanctuary of individual rights and the separation of powers, we have seen that the *nullum crimen* principle, although relatively secure in recent years, has had a rather chaotic evolution. The failure of early efforts to codify American criminal law and the examples of cases such as *Gillepsie* and *Buckman* are evidence of confrontations between legality and the common law tradition in the United States.

This sustained willingness to protect *nullum crimen* within the Canadian experience may be explained in part by the coexistence of both the British common law system and the French civil law tradition in our country. As E.G. Ewaschuk, QC, notes while talking about the historical background of the *Criminal Code:* "The Canadian legal system is divided obviously into the common law and civil law traditions. Whereas the common law tradition is empirical in nature and tends to evolve on a case by case basis, the civil law tradition is *"a priori"* in nature and favours legislation in respect of all legal subject-matter. Given the blend of the Canadian legal systems, it is little wonder that in 1892 Canada enacted its own Criminal Code without much difficulty, contrary to what took place in Britain."[85]

The Canadian legal profession includes members who are familiar with both systems of law. Some jurists have received training in both civil law and common law, or have at least been indirectly exposed to both systems during the course of their careers. As Canadian jurists are relatively at ease with both systems of law, they have been able to blend these traditions' respective characteristics in framing our system of justice. In private law, where the rights of individuals are the object of a lesser intrusion by the State, authorities have simply allowed regional preferences to govern the choice of legal system. Thus, the civil law tradition prevails in Quebec with regard to private law because the legal profession in this province, under the influence of the French tradition, prefers to be governed by a code. In contrast, in all other provinces, the British common law system was chosen to govern relationships between individuals. With regard to criminal law, it is interesting to note that both traditions have had an influence. In order to secure greater predictability and fairness to individuals, it was decided that offences had to be codified, as in the French tradition. However, other components of criminal law, such as defences to prosecution, can still be governed by the common law as they do not represent the same unpredictable threat to individual liberty.[86]

The *nullum crimen* principle is therefore guaranteed under Canadian law in relation to the definition of offences. It is now entrenched in the Constitution by virtue of s. 11(g) of the *Charter,* which forbids *ex post facto* legislation. Section 11(g) does not – at least not expressly – prohibit prosecution for established common law crimes.[87] It protects the *nullum crimen* principle, however, insofar as it forbids crime creation by judges. In the same line, it can also operate to prevent the *ex post facto* conviction of an accused for an act that has been newly declared criminal as a result of a jurisprudential shift in interpretation.[88]

All this is not to say that Canada has an unblemished record in protecting the principle of legality. For example, consider the case of *R. v. Jobidon*,[89] in relation to which it could reasonably be argued that the Supreme Court of Canada ventured into the territory of judicial crime creation. The facts that gave rise to this case were simple, although tragic. Following a dispute in a bar, two individuals agreed to engage in a fistfight. As a result of the fight, one of the men died of a head injury. Jobidon was accused of manslaughter. In order for the accused to be convicted on such account, the conduct that led to the demise had to be unlawful in itself. In that regard, the Crown relied on s. 265(1)(a) of the *Criminal Code,* which provides that "a person commits an assault when ... *without the consent of another person,* he applies force intentionally to that other person" [emphasis added]. However, in the case at bar, the evidence was to the effect that there had been consent by the victim. Nevertheless, a majority of the Court led by Gonthier J. held the accused liable by resorting to the English common law, which denied the defence of consent in cases where serious bodily harm was either caused or intended.

This decision resulted in a breach of the principle of legality. While it is true, as the majority of the Court pointed out, that in relation to defences s. 8(3) of the *Code* declares the common law to be applicable, it must nonetheless be recognized that the common law was not used here to interpret such a common law defence. The absence of consent was expressly mentioned as an element of the offence in s. 265 (1)(a) of the *Criminal Code.* The common law was used here to discharge the Crown from proving this element of the *actus reus.* In other words, the common law was used to deny the application of an exculpatory element of the offence that had a statutory basis. As Sopinka J. points out in dissent:

> The effect of my colleague's approach is to create an offence where one does not exist under the terms of the *Code* by application of the common law. The offence created is the intentional application of force with the consent of the victim. I appreciate that my colleague's approach is to interpret the section in light of the common law but, in my view, use of the common law to eliminate an element of the offence that is required by statute is more than interpretation and is contrary to not only the spirit but also the letter of s. 9(a). One of the basic reasons for s. 9(a) is the importance of certainty in determining what conduct constitutes a criminal

offence. That is the reason we have codified the offences in the *Criminal Code*. An accused should not have to search the books to discover the common law in order to determine if the offence charged is indeed an offence at law.[90]

The effect of the *Jobidon* decision was, in fact, to create a new offence and to apply it *ex post facto* to the accused. Even though the accused in this case probably did not read the law before acting, the principle of legality and the ethical integrity of the criminal law nevertheless suffered a breach as a result of this unforeseeable conviction.[91]

Also, consider the recent case of *R. v. Cuerrier*,[92] which involved an accusation of aggravated sexual assault against an individual who had engaged in unprotected intercourse without revealing to his partners that he was HIV-positive. Under s. 265(3)(c) of the *Criminal Code,* consent to sexual activities is void if it is obtained by reason of fraud. The main issue was whether the failure to disclose his HIV-positive status amounted to fraud on the part of the accused since his partners indicated they would not have consented to unprotected sexual activities had they known about the illness. The Supreme Court concluded that the alleged conduct indeed constituted an aggravated sexual assault because the victims' consent was vitiated by fraud. Although the common law up to that time was to the effect that failure to disclose a venereal disease did not constitute fraud vitiating consent, a majority of four members of the Court led by Cory J. ruled that a legislative amendment enacted in 1983 had had the effect of broadening the notion of fraud to encompass the conduct of the accused. According to Cory J.'s interpretation, consent is vitiated if the fraud leads "to a significant risk of bodily harm."[93] According to McLachlin J. (as she then was), writing in a separate opinion (with Gonthier J. concurring), this new standard was unacceptable, as it injected uncertainty into the law:

> When is a risk significant enough to qualify conduct as criminal? In whose eyes is "significance" to be determined ...? What is the ambit of "serious bodily harm"? Can a bright line be drawn between psychological harm and bodily harm, when the former may lead to depression, self-destructive behaviour and in extreme cases suicide? The criminal law must be certain. If it is uncertain, it cannot deter inappropriate conduct and loses its *raison d'être*. Equally serious, it becomes unfair. People who believe they are acting within the law may find themselves prosecuted, convicted, imprisoned and branded as criminals. Consequences are serious and should not turn on the interpretation of vague terms like "significant" and "serious."[94]

McLachlin J. was concerned that the majority's interpretation did not give fair notice to citizens. In other words, she was concerned about the principle of legality. If the standard created by the majority was excessively vague, individuals might be unfairly "entrapped," as it would be impossible for them to foresee its ambit. In place of this standard of "significant risk of bodily harm," however, McLachlin J. offered an alternative solution that, quite interestingly, also appears in some measure repugnant to the *nullum crimen* principle. According to McLachlin J., the 1983 amendment *did not* have the effect of changing the conditions of fraud in relation to sexual assault. As she states, "for more than a century, the law has been settled; fraud does not vitiate consent to assault unless the mistake goes to the nature of the act or the identity of the partner."[95] She maintained that this had been the law since the 1888 decision of *R. v. Clarence,*[96] which in fact repudiated prior jurisprudence to the effect that failure to disclose a venereal disease amounted to fraud. Having said that, McLachlin J. insisted that the needs of society had evolved and concluded that "the common law should be changed to permit deceit about sexually transmitted disease that induces consent to be treated as fraud vitiating consent."[97] In other words, McLachlin J.'s opinion constituted a return to pre-*Clarence* jurisprudence.

The problem is that this new standard was to be applied to the accused in the case at bar. The creation of the new standard amounted in practice to the creation of a new criminal offence: engaging in sexual intercourse without revealing a venereal disease. Although this type of conduct is highly reprehensible, it was clearly considered not criminal prior to *Cuerrier*. In McLachlin J.'s own words, "for more than a century, the law has been settled; fraud does not vitiate consent to assault unless the mistake goes to the nature of the act or the identity of the partner."[98] Thus, an offence that was clearly new was being applied *ex post facto* to the accused, contrary to the *nullum crimen* principle enshrined in s. 9 of the *Criminal Code* and s. 11(g) of the *Charter*. The accused was the victim of unfair surprise as he had no prior notice that his conduct could be criminal. Notice, if any, was rather to the effect that failure to disclose venereal disease was *not* a fraud, pursuant to the *Clarence* decision (and subsequent jurisprudence), which had expressly repudiated this offence in 1888. Thus, this was not just statutory interpretation (which usually does not create problems amounting to unfair surprise).[99] This was in fact a *shift* in interpretation by which the accused had been unfairly trapped.

It must noted, however, that McLachlin J.'s opinion in *Cuerrier* is somewhat less problematic than *Jobidon* because in the former case, the Court simply changed its interpretation of the law, whereas in the latter case, McLachlin J. went further and contradicted the express terms of the statute by creating a new offence. Thus, in *Jobidon,* the fact that the Court created the offence of "intentional application of force with the consent of the victim" while the *Code*'s provision expressly excluded it makes it more problematic. In that case, the Court went much further than interpretation. It literally created an offence. Not only is a conviction under this offence problematic (1) in the case at bar (for the accused, Jobidon) because it is done *ex post facto* and therefore creates unfair surprise, but the standard also becomes problematic (2) when it is applied subsequently to other individuals because this offence was really created judicially and without statutory support, contrary to s. 9 of the *Criminal Code*.

At the same time, McLachlin J.'s opinion in *Cuerrier* presents only the first of the two defects that were present in *Jobidon*. While the new standard of fraud was problematic when applied to the accused in the case at bar because it was done *ex post facto*, the application of this new standard in the future is less problematic (although the notice could still be improved if the standard were contained directly in the statute). Interpretation can change over time, and this is generally legitimate. Thus, if the Court changes its interpretation and the offence becomes broader as a result, this rule can be applied in the future as long as it is not being applied in the case at bar or against an individual who acted before this shift in interpretation became operational.

The Constitutional Protection of Legality

We have just examined a manifestation of the *nullum crimen* principle, namely, that penal laws be promulgated by legislative assemblies rather than by common law courts. The rationale for this requirement of legality is that laws provide an advance warning to guide citizens' conduct and avoid the unfair surprise associated with *ex post facto* crime creation. But what if betrayals to the principle of legality come from a statute rather than from the operation of a judicial decision? The *Charter* has placed some limitations on the powers of Parliament and provincial legislatures to enact *ex post facto* statutes.[100] Section 11(g) of the *Charter* provides the following: "11. Any person charged with an offence has the right ... (g) not to be found guilty on account of any act or omission unless, at the time of the act or omission, it constituted an offence under Canadian or international law or was criminal according to the general principles of law recognized by the community of nations."

It will be useful at this point to assess the extent of the protection afforded by this constitutional provision.

The Limited Scope of Section 11(g)

The stated purpose of s. 11 in general is to protect "any person charged with an offence." Thus, s. 11(g) is designed at first glance to apply only to penal laws. Before examining the scope of this constitutional prohibition in relation to laws establishing offences, let us first examine the question of whether it could be applied to laws of a nonpenal nature.

Although the text of the provision appears to exclude this possibility and has been interpreted restrictively in that sense in the case law and in the literature,[101] the issue remains, in my view, debatable. This is especially true in light of the Supreme Court of Canada's recent jurisprudence granting an important status to the principle of the rule of law and other "unwritten principles" of the Constitution. As we will see later in greater detail, the rule of law might possess an independent status in Canadian constitutional law. Since the 1997 decision of the Supreme Court of Canada in the *Judges Remuneration Reference*,[102] it possesses at least the potential for "filling out gaps" in the express provisions of the Constitution.[103] In the *Judges Remuneration Reference*, the unwritten principle of judicial independence was used to broaden the scope of s. 11(d) of the *Charter*. Although this provision, by its express terms, appeared to apply only in penal matters, it was interpreted as also protecting the judicial independence of judges hearing cases in nonpenal matters. By the same reasoning, s. 11(g) could be rendered applicable to a broader range of statutes since *ex post facto* laws are viewed by many leading authorities as repugnant to the rule of law. In fact, several authors who have purported to describe the different elements protected by the rule of law include the requirement of prospectiveness of statutes as one of the chief concerns of the principle.[104] Therefore, the requirement of prospectiveness as an integral part of the rule of law could be a compelling standard in Canadian constitutional law, which could broaden the applicability of s. 11(g).[105]

We must, however, recall that the requirement of prospectiveness is most naturally applicable in penal matters. Although it is not necessarily viewed in the literature as confined to penal laws, the notion of unfair surprise offered as chief rationale for the principle is most applicable to penal offences. That is because it is the area of law that establishes the most direct link between command, act, and punishment in the governance of human conduct. It is the field where the individual is most directly confronted with the State and can be most vulnerable to its abuses. Also, the sanctions involved, especially in criminal legislation, are often very high and the stigma linked with conviction can be extremely important.[106]

Moreover, we must realize that some retroactive laws are not repugnant to the rule of law because they do not represent a threat from the State. These laws rather represent an intent by the legislature to give a benefit to individuals. That is the case, for example, with statutes seeking to remedy a particular defect or problem in the previous legislative scheme. This type of remedial legislation is not problematic even if it is retroactive insofar as it does not seek to coerce individuals. If a law does not create unfair surprise, its retroactivity raises no great controversy. As an example of a benevolent use of *ex post facto* legislation, Fuller gives the example of a law stating that no marriages would be valid unless a specific stamp provided by the State be affixed to the marriage certificate.[107] He speculates on what would happen if, due to material circumstances, several marriages were concluded without the special stamp between people and by a minister who know nothing of the law. In this type of circumstance, it would be in everyone's interest to allow this anomaly to be corrected by retroactive legislation. Although it may appear at first sight to betray the rule of law, common sense indicates that the rule of law is not aimed at preventing this type of *ex post facto* "remedial" law. As Fuller explains: "Situations can arise in which granting retroactive effect to legal rules not only becomes tolerable, but may actually be essential to advance the cause of legality. Like every other human undertaking, the effort to meet the often complex demands of the internal morality of law may suffer various kinds of shipwreck. It is when things go wrong that the retroactive statute often becomes indispensable as a curative measure; though the proper movement of law is forward in time, we sometimes have to stop and turn about to pick up the pieces."[108]

In other circumstances, the legislature has no choice in order to achieve its aims but to enact retroactive statutes. As stated by Peter W. Hogg: "A taxation law is often made retroactive to budget night, when the law was publicly proposed; otherwise, there would often be room for avoidance action by taxpayers during the hiatus between the budget and the enactment of the law ... The power to enact retroactive laws, if exercised with appropriate restraint, is a proper tool of government."[109]

Thus, not all *ex post facto* laws are illegitimate. In the example given by Hogg of a tax law made retroactive to budget night, the technique is acceptable as it is necessary to avoid economic disorder. Moreover, the situation arguably complies with fair warning to a certain extent, since citizens have been notified, at least informally, through the prior ministerial announcement. Even though the warning is not ideal, this defect is counterbalanced by the competing pressing objective the State is attempting to reach.[110]

One must therefore be careful before applying s. 11(g) to nonpenal *ex post facto* laws, especially when the legislature has a strong reason for using retroactivity. The concerns identified above should be kept in mind by the courts in applying this provision. A nonpenal law might render s. 11(g) applicable mainly if it creates an unfair surprise for the individual – a surprise equivalent in its operation and consequences to the surprise that would be triggered by an *ex post facto* penal law.[111]

Section 11(g) in the Penal Context

The main rationale against *ex post facto* legislation, the desire to avoid unfair surprise, is most naturally applicable in the area of penal law. It is in that context that it is most often explained and defended. Blackstone states that retroactive penal law is "cruel and unjust,"[112] while Hall goes so far as to maintain that "there has probably been no more widely held value-judgement in the entire history of human thought than the condemnation of retroactive penal law."[113]

What types of penal law provisions are within the realm of s. 11(g)? Very little attention has been devoted thus far towards this question in the case law and the literature. To this day, the most substantial doctrinal analysis of the subject is found in an article published in 1996 by François Chevrette and Hugo Cyr.[114] In this article, the authors purport, *inter alia,* to determine the meaning of the notion of "offence" (in French, "infraction") for the purpose of applying s. 11(g).

First, as Chevrette and Cyr point out, s. 11(g) not only prevents the conversion of a past behaviour into a totally new offence but also protects an accused against amendments that have the effect of expanding the reach of an offence to his past conduct.[115] The example is given of a prohibition on acquiring a type of narcotic for the purpose of trafficking, purchases for personal use not being prohibited. If the law subsequently eliminates the requirement that the purchase be for trafficking purposes, such law could not be applied to an individual who, prior to the enactment of the law, had bought the substance for personal consumption only. It is easy to see how the unfair surprise created by this type of situation affects the individual in the same manner as if a totally new infraction had been created. In the same line of reasoning, the suppression of a defence would not be applicable to an accused who had committed an offence prior to such suppression. Again, eliminating the defence has the potential for generating unfair surprise as it equates in practice to the creation of a new offence.[116]

Chevrette and Cyr note, however, that s. 11(g) does not work to ensure the accused the benefit of the least severe of two legal regimes. In other words, if after the commission of the offence the law is rendered *less* severe, either through a change in the offence or its abrogation, the accused does not have a constitutional right to benefit from the new law.[117] He can still be prosecuted under the old law. We can see once again the influence of the fair warning rationale that lies behind the guarantee against *ex post facto* legislation. Obviously, the fact of applying to an accused the law that stood when the offence was committed does not create unfair surprise. By denying the accused the benefit of the new law, all that is accomplished is preventing a "good surprise" from applying to the accused's situation.

With the underlying rationale of fair warning in mind, Chevrette and Cyr also maintain that s. 11(g) will not apply in most cases regarding modifications to the rules of evidence and procedure.[118] Such rules govern the judicial process, which takes place in the present. They do not operate in the past, although they change for the future some of the rules applicable to a past conduct.[119] Therefore, applying new rules of procedure and evidence as soon as they are enacted does not amount to retroactivity. It does not impair the fair warning that must be given to citizens as to what is prescribed by law.

As Chevrette and Cyr further explain, the inapplicability of s. 11(g) to laws of evidence and procedure is not without exceptions. Thus, the authors rightfully maintain that legal presumptions should be within the realm of s. 11(g).[120] Thus, acts generating presumptions should be considered as elements of an "offence" for the purpose of applying this provision. The reason is that fair warning becomes involved whenever legal presumptions are attached to the accused's past behaviour. For example, s. 82(2) of the *Criminal Code* provides for the offence of possessing an explosive substance "for the benefit of, at the direction of or in association with a criminal organization." Suppose Parliament were in the future to enact a provision stating that the presence of a particular criminal organization's logo on the accused's clothing creates a presumption that this individual is acting for the benefit of that organization at all times. Pursuant to s. 11(g), this presumption could not be made retroactive. It could not be made applicable to an individual charged under s. 82(2) who was arrested with explosives prior to the enactment of this new provision. As Chevrette and Cyr maintain, "the accused could have adjusted his conduct had he known that his action would later trigger a presumption against him [translation]."[121] It is the same idea that leads the authors to add that s. 11(g) does not prevent a previous conviction for a crime from being considered in relation to a newly enacted offence of repetition for the same crime. As the authors put it, "it is difficult to maintain that the accused might have abstained from committing the first theft had he known he could become a recidivist [translation]."[122]

Finally, as an exception to the nonapplicability of s. 11(g) to evidence and procedure, Chevrette and Cyr maintain that it should apply to modifications to the burden of proof.[123] Normally the burden of proving every element of an offence rests on the prosecution. Occasionally a law will state that once certain elements are proven, the burden of proof regarding the other elements will be altered or shifted onto the accused. Interestingly, this opportunity for applying s. 11(g), which involves to a significant degree the presumption of innocence guaranteed by s. 11(d), does not really involve concerns of fair warning. As the authors point out, it would be "difficult ... to argue that an individual would not have acted a certain way, had he known that proof of this behaviour in a subsequent penal prosecution would be facilitated [translation]."[124] However, modifications to the burden of proof call upon such fundamental values that s. 11(g) would be applicable to prevent their retroactive operation. As the authors note, "the burden of proof is perceived in penal law as such a fundamental rule that a shift or an alleviation of it, applicable to an act done before the enactment of the law operating it, would also betray the spirit of s. 11(g) [translation]."[125]

The Exceptions Allowed by Section 11(g)

During the constitutional discussions that led to the adoption of the *Constitution Act, 1982*, s. 11(g), then s. 11(e), did not refer to "international law" or to the "general principles of law recognized by the community of nations." The provision simply stated that "anyone charged with an offence has the right ... not to be found guilty on account of any act or omission that at the time of the act or omission did not constitute an offence."[126] After interventions by Jewish organizations, the provision was changed to ensure that prosecutions of war criminals would be constitutionally possible. The final provision is as follows: "11. Any person charged with an offence has the right ... (g) not to be found guilty on account of any act or omission unless, at the time of the act or omission, it constituted an offence under Canadian *or international law or was criminal according to the general principles of law recognized by the community of nations*" [emphasis added].

In 1987, Parliament enacted s. 7(3.71 to 3.77) of the *Criminal Code*, under which individuals can be prosecuted for war crimes or crimes against humanity. In the case of *R. v. Finta*,[127] this provision was challenged on the basis of, *inter alia*, s. 11(g), as it was being applied to a Nazi military officer in relation to acts committed during the Second World War in Europe. It is interesting that the majority did not rely on the exception of "international law" or "general principles of law recognized by the community of nations" to uphold the validity of the legislation against the claim of retroactivity. The majority of the Supreme Court confessed that the law was retroactive since the alleged actions were not yet considered criminal by international law or by the "general principles of law" at the time they were committed.[128] It is true that the acts were "illegal" in the sense that they could trigger *collective* responsibility under international law, but they were not "criminal" because they could not yet cause *individual* responsibility.[129] However, the Court decided that s. 11(g) was not violated because the alleged acts were so genuinely wrong that it would go against the interests of justice not to prosecute them. Through this reasoning, the statute was held not to be illegitimately retroactive. In support of this view, Cory J. cited an extract from an article by Hans Kelsen. The most telling part of this extract is the following:

> [As] the persons who committed these acts were certainly aware of their immoral character, the retroactivity of the law applied to them can hardly be considered as absolutely incompatible with justice. Justice required the punishment of these men, in spite of the fact that under positive law they

were not punishable at the time they performed the acts made punishable with retroactive force. In case two postulates of justice are in conflict with each other, the higher one prevails; and to punish those who were morally responsible for the international crime of the Second World War may certainly be considered as more important to comply with than the rather relative rule against ex post facto laws, open to so many exceptions.[130]

Following the extract by Kelsen, Cory J. concluded that the provisions' retroactivity did not violate ss. 7 or 11(g): "The approach of Professor Kelsen seems eminently sound and reasonable to me. I would adopt it as correct and apply it in reaching the conclusion that the provisions in question do not violate the principles of fundamental justice."[131]

The *Finta* case is worth noting in that it illustrates a tendency by courts to allow breaches of the principle of legality more easily when conduct that is genuinely wrong is at stake. Other examples of this tendency can be found in decisions from other jurisdictions. Consider, for example, the decision *C.R. v. United Kingdom,* rendered in 1995 by the European Court of Human Rights.[132] Until 1992, rape within marriage was not a criminal offence in England.[133] In November 1989, while the accused was separated from his wife but not yet legally divorced, he broke into her house one evening and attempted to rape her. He invoked the long-standing exemption for marital rape before the House of Lords, but the Court finally decided to abolish this exemption and convicted the accused retroactively.[134] He applied for relief to the European Court of Human Rights and argued that his rights under Article 7 of the *European Convention* – which is almost the same as s. 11(g) of the *Charter* – had been violated as a result of this *ex post facto* conviction. It is plain that at the time the accused committed the offence, the law of England did not render his conduct criminal. However, the complaint was rejected by the Court, which argued that this change in the criminal law was foreseeable. As Rosalyn Higgins wrote, the Court in this case was "undoubtedly affected by the subject matter."[135] The similarity with *Finta* is obvious. The European Court's decision was criticized by commentators as breaching the principle of legality,[136] but it can be explained by a tendency, legitimate or not, to allow prosecution when, as in *Finta,* the acts committed are highly reprehensible morally and socially.

In the United States, the case of *Dobbert v. Florida*[137] offers another illustration of this tendency. When the state of Florida enacted a law imposing the death penalty for murder in late 1972, it made the act apply retroactively to murders committed when a previous capital punishment statute, which had been invalidated earlier that same year,[138] was in force. Thus, the accused, who had committed his offence early in 1972, was convicted and sentenced to death under a statute enacted several months later.

Dobbert complained that this new standard was being applied retro-actively to his situation, but the United States Supreme Court upheld the conviction, arguing that he had been given sufficient warning by the old – since struck down – statute that his conduct could lead to capital pun-ishment.[139] Confronted with this *ex post facto* application of the law, the dissenting judges in the case declared that the majority's opinion was "an archaic gargoyle" compromising "a majestic bulwark in the framework of our Constitution."[140] However, it is probable that the decision was influ-enced in part by the "genuinely horrifying tale of petitioner's torture and murder of his own children,"[141] which had led to this particular conviction.

Upon examination of these cases where the principle of legality appears to have been breached, we must realize, however, that the convictions were never entered in total absence of fair warning. In would be wrong to consider that legality was totally ignored. It would be more accurate to say that the *nullum crimen* principle's severity was altered. Indeed, some kind of warning, although deficient, was in fact given to the individuals in these cases. Thus, in *Finta,* while the acts could not provoke *personal* penal liability when they were committed, they could still provoke *collective* responsibility, and the accused had therefore received at least some form of legal signal that his acts were in conflict with the law. Similarly, in the *Marital Rape Case,* the disappearance of the marital rape exemption could have been foreseen since, as argued by the House of Lords, the Law Com-mission had already recommended its abolition.[142] As for the *Dobbert* case, a certain warning was indeed provided by the old capital punish-ment statute as it was in the books prior to its invalidation by the Florida Supreme Court. While all these warnings were not ideal, and probably would not have been sufficient to maintain the accusations if less tragic circumstances had been involved, it must nonetheless be recognized that the courts at least attempted to find a reasonable source of warning in sup-port of their decisions. This was done in order to comply to a certain extent, at least in appearance, with the principle of legality.

The Role of Section 7 in Relation to *Ex Post Facto* Laws

The primary constitutional protection of legality in Canada emanates, of course, from s. 11(g) of the *Charter.* However, another basis for denying the *ex post facto* operation of a statute can be s. 7 of the *Charter.* According to the residuary theory of s. 7, this provision contains a general principle in relation to which the rights enshrined in ss. 8 to 14 are simply examples or illustrations.[143] Section 7 could therefore provide an additional basis under which *ex post facto* legislation could be prohibited whenever life, liberty, or security of the person is compromised.

The antipathy towards retroactivity in the context of s. 7 was considered by the Supreme Court of Canada in the case of *R. v. Gamble.*[144] In this case, the appellant had been convicted in 1976 of first-degree murder following the killing of a police officer by her accomplice during a robbery. The law under which the accused was convicted had been enacted several months after the commission of the act. This law required only that the prosecution prove that the accused had been a "party to the offence." Under s. 21 of the *Criminal Code*, an individual is a "party to the offence" (murder) if he "does or omits to do anything for the purpose of aiding any person to commit it" (s. 21[1][b]), or if he was engaged in an unlawful purpose with another person and "knew or ought to have known that the commission of the offence [of murder] would be a probable consequence of carrying out the common [unlawful] purpose" (s. 21[2]). However, under the law that stood at the time the act was committed, the Crown would have had to prove much more, namely, that the accused by her "own act caused or assisted in causing the death of a police officer" (s. 214[2] of the *Criminal Code*, R.S.C. 1970, c. 34, as amended by S.C. 1973-74, c. 38). In addition, under the law that stood at the time of the murder, the appellant could have been eligible for parole after ten years, while under the new law she could be eligible only after twenty-five years of imprisonment. Mrs. Gamble was thus convicted under the new law of first-degree murder without the possibility of parole before twenty-five years. The accused could not challenge this retroactive conviction at the time because this was before the enactment of the *Charter*, and the statute that operated the transition provided for the application of this new law to past conducts.

After having served more than ten years of her sentence, the appellant argued before the Supreme Court of Canada that she should now be eligible for parole. The *Charter* was now in force, and she argued successfully that continuing to deny her the possibility of parole violated her s. 7 rights. Since she had been sentenced under a law that was enacted after the murder, continuing to deny her parole would offend the "principles of fundamental justice."

It is interesting to note that the Court did not rely on s. 11(g) to condemn the *ex post facto* application of the penal statute but relied instead on s. 7. This was done because there was a dispute in the case as to the retroactive application of the *Charter* itself since the conviction had taken place in 1976, six years before the *Charter* came into force. It would have been difficult to rely on s. 11(g), which protects against retroactive *convictions* because this right is normally exercised at the time of the trial. The opportunity for the application of s. 11(g) was in the past, before the enactment of the *Charter*, and it would have been difficult to apply it without giving it a retroactive effect. Thus, Gamble's conviction could not be reversed by resorting to s. 11(g). In contrast, the rights guaranteed by s. 7 can be continuous in time. Thus, the condition of the sentence providing for the accused's ineligibility for parole before twenty-five years was held to be a violation of s. 7. Gamble was deprived of her "liberty" in a manner inconsistent with the "principles of fundamental justice" because the sentencing order pursuant to which she was currently denied parole emanated from the application of a retroactive law.[145]

Conclusion

As legality stands for the desirability of advance rule making to guide citizens' conduct in order to avoid unfair surprise, it encompasses an antipathy towards judicial crime creation, as well as a rule proscribing *ex post facto* penal legislation.

The judiciary's power to create new offences has gradually disappeared over the years, partly because of the increased activity of legislative assemblies and partly because of a desire by judges and academics to avoid uncertainty in the law. Under the influence of the civil law tradition, which forms part of Canada's legal heritage, our legal history has been marked by a predominance of values associated with legality, especially in the area of penal law. An understanding of the dangers associated with judicial crime creation has led Canadian authorities to make clear jurisprudential, legislative, and constitutional choices to preserve individual liberties. In this regard, the recent encroachments on legality brought about by the *Jobidon* and *Cuerrier* decisions must not be taken lightly. Judicial crime creation, as benign as it might sometimes seem when viewed in isolation, can lead to long-term uncertainty in the law and to the multiplication of cases where the accused is subject to unfair surprise.

This chapter has also enabled us to take a closer look at the issue of *ex post facto* legislation. We saw that the objections against retroactivity are essentially the desire to avoid unfair surprise to citizens. This standard, finding support under ss. 7 and 11(g) of the *Charter,* is aimed primarily at laws creating offences retroactively. It will be interesting to see in the future whether the constitutional principle of the rule of law can broaden the scope of these protections beyond the area of penal law.

We saw that the rules against *ex post facto* legislation are subject to some exceptions, some of which are more acceptable than others. Thus, retroactive laws of a nonpenal nature are generally seen as less problematic, especially when they do not have the effect of subjecting individuals to unfair surprise. Also, the technique of *ex post facto* lawmaking is viewed as acceptable when its use is justified by the imperative demands of practicality, as in the case of tax laws being made retroactive to budget night.

Other limitations on legality are more debatable. Recall the controversial tendency by courts, displayed, *inter alia,* by the *Finta* case, to uphold significant restrictions to legality in cases involving highly reprehensible conduct. This will prove particularly interesting in the context of the inquiries in later chapters regarding the content of the void-for-vagueness doctrine in Canadian constitutional law. This is especially true considering that Gonthier J. in *Nova Scotia Pharmaceutical* placed great emphasis on the "substratum of values" involved in a particular legislative scheme to explain how the fair warning rationale is to be assessed.[146] The extent to which this may imply an approach similar to the one that prevailed in *Finta, Dobbert,* and the *Marital Rape Case* will be examined in Chapter 3.

Another relevant question to be addressed, which involves concerns of retroactivity as well as vagueness, is related to the approach that is often taken by courts to remedy the alleged vagueness of a law. When Canadian courts are confronted with a vague law, they will sometimes try to render it more specific through judicial interpretation instead of striking it down.[147] This technique appears satisfactory at first glance, considering that from the moment the law is interpreted authoritatively, it will cease to present the risk of arbitrary enforcement, which satisfies the second rationale of the vagueness doctrine. However, the fair warning given to citizens through this type of reasoning has some defects because it renders the research task more complex for individuals who wish to know the law.[148] Moreover, when this new standard is applied immediately to the accused in the case at bar, it triggers concerns of retroactivity. This can be unacceptable, especially in the context of penal law, in a manner very similar to the one discussed in the present chapter regarding *ex post facto* judicial crime creation. After all, if a court is able to articulate standards to govern more precisely the application of a vague law, why could the legislature not have done it in the first place? This would have the advantage of rendering legal rules more accessible to citizens, not to mention that it would eliminate the period of uncertainty between the time that a law is enacted until the time it is authoritatively interpreted. Until a law has been interpreted conclusively by the Supreme Court of Canada or at least by the Court of Appeal of a province, there is indeed great uncertainty regarding the scope of a vague law. This can cause problems of fair warning as well as arbitrary enforcement, issues that will be examined in a subsequent chapter.[149]

2
The Rule of Law

Under the Canadian vagueness doctrine, laws must be sufficiently precise for two reasons: (1) they must provide "fair notice" to citizens, and (2) they must limit the arbitrary power of law-enforcing authorities. The study undertaken in the first chapter (on the principle of legality) has laid the groundwork with regard mainly to the first rationale, as it assessed the extent to which *ex post facto* rule making that creates "unfair surprise" for citizens is unacceptable under our Constitution. This chapter does the same in relation to the second rationale, that of limiting discretion in law enforcement. Without directly addressing the issue of discretion in relation to vague laws (a study that will be undertaken in a subsequent chapter), this chapter examines the principle of the rule of law that favours pre-established rules over grants of discretionary power to law-enforcing authorities as a means of protecting individuals from arbitrary government.

It is well known that State authority can be exercised through various combinations of rules and discretion. In a legal system such as ours, why push forward the rule of law to require that discretion be minimized to the benefit of rules? After all, discretion allows for better and more adapted solutions in particular cases.[1] Thus, for individuals whose concerns are limited only to reaching the most "perfect" solution to the problem at stake in every case, rules can sometimes be seen as an obstacle because the generalizations they contain are inevitably imperfect.[2] This view in favour of greater discretion is, however, in disharmony with some of the other requirements of justice, such as personal freedom, predictability, and equal treatment. It is the essence of the rule of law to ensure that the blessings of liberty be secured against arbitrary State power.

The rule of law, by expressing a preference for rules over discretion, contributes to reducing arbitrariness in the legal system. Rules have the advantage of enhancing predictability in the administration of justice. Citizens can therefore plan their lives and adjust their behaviour in advance. Without the predictability of rules, a sword of Damocles hangs over personal freedom. Although rules are not the only precondition of personal freedom, they play an important role as they reduce the influence of arbitrary decision making on the deception of people's expectations.

Moreover, evenhandness in the administration of justice is better served by rules than it is by discretionary powers. Indeed, rules have some binding effect upon the authority that enforces them. Discretion, on the other hand, allows for the legal standard to fluctuate more easily depending on who applies it, but also depending on who it is being applied to. In that regard, the importance of rules is not to be overlooked as they provide greater support to the notion of equal treatment. In an article published in 1989, Justice Antonin Scalia of the United States Supreme Court metaphorically captured the issue as follows: "Parents know that children will accept quite readily all sorts of arbitrary substantive dispositions – no television in the afternoon, or no television in the evening, or even no television at all. But try to let one brother or sister watch television when the others do not, and you will feel the fury of the fundamental sense of justice unleashed."[3]

Therefore, by promoting evenhandness in the administration of laws, as well as predictability, rules help to eradicate the disadvantages of arbitrariness. Thus, personal freedom enjoys a greater degree of protection from Leviathan through the delicate compromise of the rule of law.

Of course, the opposition between rules and discretion does not reflect watertight compartments. Indeed, most standards in a legal system cannot be clearly classified as being either rule or discretion. There is, in fact, a whole spectrum of standards between the two opposite poles. Most legal provisions will involve both to a certain degree. In that framework, the rule of law is a principle that pushes us towards the rule end of the rule-discretion spectrum. It is a driving force, inciting the legislature to aim for settled standards instead of granting arbitrary powers. This does not mean that all discretion is to be avoided. The rule of law is a flexible notion, not an absolutist doctrine. Discretion is often very useful and even necessary to achieve legitimate State objectives. Generally speaking, though, a law will be in greater harmony with the rule of law if its discretionary aspects are minimized to the advantage of standards expressed by rules.

The preamble to the *Canadian Charter of Rights and Freedoms* states that "Canada is founded upon principles that recognize the supremacy of God and the rule of law." Thus, since 1982 the text of our Constitution acknowledges expressly the importance of the rule of law. This principle was already implicitly part of Canadian constitutional law through the preamble to the *Constitution Act, 1867,* which refers to our Constitution as being "similar in principle to that of the United Kingdom." Given this reality, an analysis directed at the appropriate scope of the rule of law in Canada becomes relevant. This chapter seeks to reach a better understanding of this principle in the Canadian constitutional context.

The first part of the chapter examines the status of the rule of law in Canada. We will see that in recent years there has been an evolution in the jurisprudence of the Supreme Court tending to give an important status to "unwritten" constitutional principles, including the rule of law. This analysis will be useful not only in determining the circumstances under which the principle can be invoked but also in indicating that it must be considered seriously as a constitutional doctrine, especially since 1982.

The discussion then moves on to present the substantive content of the rule of law resulting from the few decisions of the Supreme Court that have purported to define it. As this jurisprudence is still embryonic, the scope of the principle remains uncertain in Canada, thus inviting us to look further afield for answers.

I then attempt to deepen the understanding of the principle expressed in the preamble to the *Charter* in light of academic literature on the rule of law. This will lead to considering it more appropriate in Canadian constitutional law to associate procedural limitations on State power – instead of substantive limitations – with the principle of the rule of law. Thus, the rule of law will not prevent the State from reaching its policy objectives, but will require that the influence of arbitrary power and discretion be limited in that process.

The chapter ends with an attempt to determine the appropriate threshold that should be associated with the rule of law in the Canadian constitutional context. The rule of law stands for a preference for rules over discretion. Despite the fluidity of the concept, it is important to determine the point at which grants of discretion become contrary to the rule of law. As some policy objectives require greater discretion than others, it is inappropriate to state a fixed and rigid level of compliance. Instead, a flexible standard inspired by the philosophy behind s. 1 of the *Charter* must be articulated. With these concerns in mind, I will suggest that the appropriate standard should be whether a grant of discretion was "reasonably necessary" to reach the particular legislative objectives. This standard, if applied carefully, will ensure a delicate balance between the interests of the State and the constitutional principle requiring that citizens be ruled by law.

Status of the Rule of Law in Canada

Avenues to Be Considered

Where is the rule of law located in the hierarchy of legal norms? The way in which it can influence the outcome of cases depends in part on the strength it is given in relation to other legal rules or principles. The main avenues to be considered regarding this issue can be grouped in three main categories.

First, the rule of law can be seen as a principle of administrative law requiring that all government powers emanate from the law. Statutes are interpreted and common law principles are developed as far as possible in compliance with the rule of law. According to this conception, however, the rule of law does not have a constitutional status.

This is how the rule of law was seen by A.V. Dicey.[4] This nineteenth-century British commentator saw the rule of law as requiring that the exercise of arbitrary power be avoided by forcing the government to seek legal authorization for its actions.[5] According to Dicey, the rule of law also serves to protect equality before the law. The law should be applied to everybody the same way, and no one should be exempt from compliance with it.[6] These requirements are not aimed at invalidating legislative enactments that might betray rule of law values. As seen by Dicey, the rule of law prevails as a persuasive argument in court only so far as the government has acted without legislative authorization.

This point is further emphasized by Dicey's insistence on the fact that the sovereignty of Parliament is not limited by the rule of law. According to him, Parliament has the "right to make or unmake any law whatever."[7] The British Parliament was (and in a sense still is)[8] unconstrained by the rule of law or any other constitutional norm. It is important to realize that there is no written constitution in Great Britain. In fact, this reality was even part of Dicey's very definition of the rule of law.[9] Thus, what the British call "constitutional law" originates from the common law. The limits imposed by this "constitution" are, from a hierarchical standpoint, closer to what we refer to in Canada as "administrative law" than "constitutional law." They act as common law standards and principles of interpretation to determine the powers of government, but they do not prevail over the legislature's will.

The second type of status the rule of law can be given is that of a relevant principle in constitutional interpretation. In that sense, it could be used to clarify the meaning of other constitutional provisions. In this regard, it is important to recall that the rule of law is included in the preamble to the *Charter* as well as implicitly derived from the preamble to the *Constitution Act, 1867*. Principles of statutory interpretation suggest that preambles have no direct legal force but may be used to interpret the actual provisions of regular statutes.[10] Peter W. Hogg has expressed the view that this type of reasoning also applies to the use of preambles to constitutional documents such as the *Charter*.[11]

As an example of such a use of the rule of law, let us examine how it could be useful in the interpretation of s. 12 of the *Charter*, which provides that "everyone has the right not to be subjected to any cruel and unusual treatment or punishment." In the United States, one of the criteria for determining whether a punishment is cruel and unusual with regard to the Eighth Amendment is the question of whether it is imposed in an "arbitrary manner."[12] In Canada, however, in the case of *R. v. Smith,*[13] Lamer J. and Dickson C.J. refused to recognize the relevance of this criterion of "arbitrariness" in the interpretation of s. 12 of the *Charter.*[14] On the other hand, in separate opinions, McIntyre J. (dissenting),[15] as well as LeDain[16] and Wilson[17] JJ., were in favour of recognizing the importance of this criterion. The outcome of this controversy has not yet been settled by the Supreme Court of Canada, but the principle of the rule of law could play in favour of McIntyre, LeDain, and Wilson JJ.'s interpretation as far as the prevention of arbitrary decision making is concerned.

The third way to view the status of the rule of law is to give it an autonomous status in constitutional law. According to this conception, endorsed by Patrick J. Monahan, the rule of law could be used independently to render legislation invalid.[18] This option rejects the relevance of the distinction made by some authors between a constitutional "provision" and a constitutional "principle."[19] According to these authors, constitutional "principles" such as the rule of law cannot be used to strike down legislative enactments because of the text of s. 52 of the *Constitution Act, 1982,* which states that "any law that is inconsistent with the *provisions* of the Constitution is ... of no force or effect" [emphasis added].[20] Therefore, these authors see the rule of law (apart from its potential use as a tool of constitutional interpretation) as a mere requirement of legality similar to Dicey's conception described earlier.[21] The rule of law would therefore provide a protection against arbitrary State power, but only as long as the legislature did not give its assent to such power.

According to Professor Monahan, however, the latter position is unsatisfactory because it provides an insufficient protection to the rule of law. According to him, in order to be effective, the rule of law must bind not only the government but also the legislature. When the government acts arbitrarily, whether with or without statutory authorization, the result is the same for the citizens involved. Holding otherwise might allow the government to do indirectly what it cannot do directly. Thus, when the government wishes to act arbitrarily but is prevented from doing so because of a lack of express statutory authorization, all it would have to do is cause the legislature to grant it such power by statute.[22] As a matter of administrative law, the subsequent government actions would be legal, although no less arbitrary. This is precisely the problem allowed by the British conception of the rule of law advanced by Dicey that Monahan's argument attempts to remedy. Thus, even if Parliament were to grant the government the power to act, these entities would still have to respect the rule of law. According to this conception, the rule of law would have independent constitutional status.[23]

It is important to try to determine the appropriate status of the rule of law in Canada for at least two reasons, one formal and one substantive. The formal and most obvious reason is that we ought to be able to know under what circumstances this principle can rightfully be invoked in adjudication. Indeed, it must be determined what norms can be influenced or overridden by the rule of law. The substantive and more subtle reason is that the status of the rule of law can have an impact on the actual persuasive weight it possesses once its application is admitted. For example, let us imagine that the rule of law were recognized as a principle having an independent constitutional status, as Monahan suggests. Needless to say, it would still be possible to use it for "inferior" purposes such as mere constitutional interpretation or as a common law principle. What is interesting, however, is that since it would have been granted such a high status, we can reasonably believe that the rule of law would have more persuasive weight in the cases where it is only being used for "inferior" purposes such as constitutional interpretation. For instance, we referred earlier to the possible use of the rule of law to interpret s. 12 of the *Charter*. In the event that the rule of law were considered only as a tool of constitutional interpretation, we have seen that it could be used to favour the inclusion of "arbitrariness" as a criterion for determining whether a punishment is cruel and unusual. However, the persuasive weight of such an argument would probably be increased if the rule of law were recognized as also having the potential to strike down legislation independently.

Having presented the main possibilities regarding the status of the rule of law, let us now examine the Supreme Court's jurisprudence to determine what approach is currently favoured. Although the Court has not yet ruled clearly and conclusively on the issue, we will see that it appears to favour an answer that lies in the middle ground between the second option (constitutional interpretation) and the third option (autonomous status).

Status of the Rule of Law in Supreme Court Jurisprudence

Since the rule of law is not mentioned in a specific provision of the Constitution, but rather is included through the preambles of both *Constitution Acts,* it is considered to be an "unwritten principle" of the Constitution. (The rule of law is, in fact, included expressly in the preamble to the *Charter,* and could therefore be considered as one of the most "written" of those "unwritten" principles.) Since there are not many cases directly addressing the issue of the status of the rule of law *per se,* jurisprudence on the status of "unwritten principles" of the Constitution in general will be helpful to us.

One of the first significant cases in the Supreme Court of Canada dealing with the rule of law is *Roncarelli v. Duplessis*.[24] The facts that gave rise to this case were rather simple. Quebec Premier Maurice Duplessis had ordered the liquor commission to suspend Mr. Roncarelli's liquor permit to punish him for having posted bonds for Jehovah's Witnesses arrested for distributing pamphlets in breach of municipal bylaws. As a result, Mr. Roncarelli was forced to cease operating the restaurant he owned. The Supreme Court held that the licence revocation for such reasons irrelevant to the statute was an abuse of power that was inconsistent with the rule of law, even though the text of the statute apparently gave complete discretion to the liquor commission to revoke licences. Since the statute did not expressly allow for such irrelevant reasons to serve as grounds for licence revocation, it was interpreted through the rule of law as not granting such power to Premier Duplessis.[25]

We realize that it was from a merely legal (as opposed to constitutional) standpoint that the rule of law was used to overrule Premier Duplessis's decision. The Court's reference to the rule of law in *Roncarelli* as being a "fundamental postulate of our constitutional structure"[26] is therefore not to be regarded as meaning that it was used constitutionally, in the sense of overriding legislation. This reference to the Constitution in *Roncarelli* can be seen as bearing more resemblance to the British constitutional understanding of the rule of law as Dicey describes it.

The next case is the well-known *Reference Re Resolution to Amend the Constitution*.[27] This case is not related directly to the principle of the rule of law, but it is nonetheless interesting for our purposes because both the majority and the dissenting opinions contain some comments on the unwritten principles of the Constitution, including the rule of law. As we will see, these comments point in opposite directions, which makes them even more interesting from an analytical standpoint. Let us consider first the following passage from the majority decision:[28]

> What is stressed is the desire of the named provinces "to be federally united ... with a Constitution similar in Principle to that of the United Kingdom" ... What is then to be drawn from the preamble as a matter of law? A preamble, needless to say, has no enacting force but, certainly, it can be called in aid to illuminate provisions of the statute in which it appears. Federal union "with a Constitution similar in Principle to that of the United Kingdom" may well embrace responsible government and some common law aspects of the United Kingdom's unitary constitutionalism, such as the rule of law.[29]

Several elements emerge from these comments. First, the rule of law is recognized as being included in the preamble to the *British North America Act* through the words "with a Constitution similar in Principle to that of the United Kingdom." Second, the authority of this principle is rather limited, as the Court seems to indicate that the status of the rule of law is that of a principle of common law or, at most, a tool to interpret the provisions of the *B.N.A. Act,* like any other preamble to a statute. The comments expressed by the dissenting judges (Martland and Ritchie JJ.) on this point are much more generous. Let us consider the following passage:

> On occasions, this Court has had to consider issues for which the *B.N.A. Act* offered no answer. In each case, this Court denied the assertion of any power which would offend against the basic principles of the Constitution ...
>
> It may be noted that the above instances of judicially developed legal principles and doctrines share several characteristics. *First,* none is to be found in express provisions of the *British North America Acts* or other constitutional enactments. *Second,* all have been perceived to represent constitutional requirements that are derived from the federal character of Canada's Constitution. *Third,* they have been accorded full legal force in the sense of being employed to strike down legislative enactments. *Fourth,* each was judicially developed in response to a particular legislative initiative in respect of which it might have been observed ... that "There are no Canadian constitutional precedents addressed directly to the present issue."[30]

Note that the dissent does not refer expressly to the rule of law. This extract is nonetheless interesting in that it stands in contrast with the position of the majority with regard to the status of the unwritten principles of the Constitution that can be traced back to the preamble (such as the rule of law). Indeed, the dissenting judges seem to be willing to give these principles an autonomous status similar to the one Professor Monahan defends. This is especially clear in light of their statement that these principles "have been accorded full legal force in the sense of being employed to strike down legislative enactments."

The status of the rule of law began rising in the jurisprudence of the Supreme Court in 1985 with the case of the *Reference Re Manitoba Linguistic Rights.*[31] The question in this case was whether the Court should render invalid most legislation in the province of Manitoba on the grounds that it was not published in both official languages despite a requirement to that effect in s. 23 of the *Manitoba Act, 1870.*[32] For the first time in the jurisprudence of the Supreme Court of Canada, the principle of the rule of law lay at the core of a constitutional decision. The Court confessed that most of Manitoba's legislation was unconstitutional, but decided to suspend its invalidity for a period of time to allow for the laws to be translated. This extraordinary remedy was motivated by a desire to avoid the legal chaos that might have resulted if such a large part of the province's legal order had suddenly disappeared. In that instance, the rule of law in a "law and order" perspective not tolerant of anarchy played a large part in supporting the Court's reasoning.[33] The importance of the principle of the rule of law was acknowledged extensively by the Court in the *Manitoba Language Reference*. The following comments are germane in that regard:

> Additional to the inclusion of the rule of law in the preamble of the *Constitution Acts* of 1867 and 1982, the principle is clearly implicit in the very nature of a Constitution. The Constitution, as the Supreme Law, must be understood as a purposive ordering of social relations providing a basis upon which an actual order of positive laws can be brought into existence. The founders of this nation must have intended, as one of the basic principles of nation building, that Canada be a society of legal order and normative structure: one governed by the rule of law. While this is not set out in a specific provision, the principle of the rule of law is clearly a principle of our Constitution.[34]

This passage outlines the importance of the rule of law as a principle of our Constitution, but it does not take a stand with regard to its appropriate status. By looking further in the decision, however, we can see that the Court seems to be implying a willingness to grant the rule of law an independent status. Indeed, the Court in the *Manitoba Language Reference* cited the passage I referred to earlier from the dissenting judges in the *Patriation Reference* concerning the importance of unwritten principles of the Constitution.[35] Moreover, the Court added emphasis in the citation to the statements according to which "none [of these principles] is to be found in express provisions of the *British North America Acts* or other constitutional enactments" and "they have been accorded full legal force in the sense of being employed to strike down legislative enactments."

Note that the Court did not refer to the passage by the majority in the *Patriation Reference* in which the status of the rule of law had appeared to be diminished.[36] Yet the latter passage was the one that had referred expressly to the rule of law, contrary to the passage from the dissent in the *Patriation Reference*. The *Manitoba Language Reference* therefore seems to express a preference for the more liberal way the dissenting judges had commented on the status of the unwritten principles of the Constitution in the *Patriation Reference*.

It is uncertain, however, whether this decision could serve as a solid basis for declaring that the rule of law can strike down legislation on its own. Indeed, one could emphasize the fact that the rule of law was, in fact, used in the *Manitoba Language Reference* to preserve the validity of legislation, not to strike it down. Moreover, this case could be seen as merely using the rule of law to interpret restrictively s. 52 of the *Constitution Act, 1982* as not mandating statute invalidations that would be detrimental to the rule of law. Its use would therefore be limited to interpretative purposes, as had been stated by the majority in the *Patriation Reference*.

Nonetheless, the reference to the passage of the dissent from the latter decision, and especially the extra emphasis placed by the Court on the statement that "they have been accorded full legal force in the sense of being employed to strike down legislative enactments" is at the least indicative of a willingness on the part of the Court to strengthen the status of the rule of law.

The Court further affirmed the status of unwritten principles of the Constitution in the case of *OPSEU v. Ontario (A.G.).*[37] A statute restricting the political activities of civil servants in Ontario was challenged on several grounds, including that it constituted a breach of freedom of expression. The appellants could not rely on s. 2(b) because the activities in litigation had all taken place before the enactment of the *Charter.* Nonetheless, the Court recognized the possibility of invoking a right of discussion and debate derived from the preamble to the *Constitution Act, 1867.* In that sense, a majority of the Court[38] led by Beetz J. gave its approval to a statement made some thirty years earlier by Abbott J. in *Switzman v. Elbling.*[39] That statement suggested the existence of an implied bill of rights rendering Parliament incompetent to "abrogate th[e] right of discussion and debate."[40] Beetz J. concluded that this right was part of the fundamental structure of our Constitution, and that "the legislative bodies in this country must conform to these basic structural imperatives and can in no way override them."[41] Although this right of free speech was deemed not to have been breached in the case at bar, the decision appears to stand for the position that some unwritten constitutional principles could have an autonomous status.

Even if no mention of the rule of law was made in the *OPSEU* case, we can safely speculate that this kind of reasoning might be applicable to such a fundamental principle as the rule of law. The fact that the rule of law is indeed among these "basic principles of the Constitution" (and perhaps the most important one) follows from the comments of the Court in the *Manitoba Language Rights Reference.*[42]

The inclusion of unwritten norms in Canada's Constitution was further confirmed by the Supreme Court in the case of *New Brunswick Broadcasting Co. v. Nova Scotia (Speaker of the House of Assembly).*[43] In this case, s. 2(b) of the *Charter* had been raised by the broadcaster in an attempt to force the House of Assembly to allow their legislative proceedings to be filmed. Against this claim, the House of Assembly successfully invoked a parliamentary privilege allowing them to maintain decorum during the proceedings. This privilege was said to be part of the Constitution through the preamble to the *Constitution Act, 1867.* Section 52(2) of the *Constitution Act, 1982* could have been an obstacle to this recognition of status since it refers to a series of documents (and not to any unwritten principles) as being "include[d]" in the Constitution of Canada. However, the Court led by McLachlin J. decided that the use of the word "includes" in s. 52(2) implied that the list was not exhaustive.[44] It was thus possible to recognize the constitutional status of an unwritten principle such as the parliamentary privilege and to use it to preclude the application of s. 2(b) of the *Charter.*

This case confirms the tangible constitutional status that can be possessed by some unwritten principles such as the rule of law. However, much as in the *Manitoba Language Reference,* the principle in question is being used to uphold the validity of State action rather than strike it down. Although demonstrative of a strong status granted to an unwritten constitutional principle, the *New Brunswick Broadcasting* case can hardly be read as granting this kind of norm autonomous status, with the power to invalidate legislation. On the other hand, in a paradoxical manner, the unwritten principle in *New Brunswick Broadcasting* can be said to have been given an even greater status than the one of striking down legislation, namely, the power to prevent the application of a constitutional enactment such as the *Charter.* In that way, parliamentary privilege is being given a "supra-constitutional" status. Note that the same type of comment could have been made with regard to the *Manitoba Language Reference,* where the rule of law was used to suspend the application of the *Manitoba Act, 1870,* although in the latter case the suspension was only for a limited period.

This jurisprudential evolution of the status of these unwritten principles culminates in the comments of Lamer C.J., speaking for a majority of six members of the Supreme Court in the case of the *Judges Remuneration Reference.*[45] This case involved a series of challenges to provincial legislation attempting to reduce the salaries of the judiciary as part of a broader plan to cut down on governmental expenses. The arguments were framed by the parties in large part in relation to s. 11(d) of the *Charter,* which guarantees judicial independence to a certain extent.[46] However, the Court's analysis of s. 11(d) is preceded by a discussion on the unwritten principles of the Constitution, which include the protection of judicial independence.[47]

With regard to unwritten norms generally, the Court insists upon the importance of identifying their source prior to granting them constitutional recognition.[48] This is motivated by a desire to promote legal certainty and defend the legitimacy of constitutional judicial review. This way, it can be assured that the Canadian evolution "which [has] culminated in the supremacy of a definitive written constitution"[49] will not be undermined. A legitimate way to identify those unwritten norms is through the use of the preamble.[50] In that sense, the preamble "serves as the grand entrance hall to the castle of the Constitution."[51] With regard to the case at bar, judicial independence is recognized through the preamble to the *Constitution Act, 1867.*

Concerning the legal status of unwritten principles contained in the preamble, Lamer C.J. made very revealing observations that are worth reproducing here at length:

> Although the preamble has been cited by this Court on many occasions, its legal effect has never been fully explained. On the one hand, although the preamble is clearly part of the Constitution, it is equally clear that it "has no enacting force": *Reference re Resolution to Amend the Constitution,* [1981] 1 S.C.R. 753, at p. 805 (joint majority reasons). In other words, strictly speaking, it is not a source of positive law, in contrast to the provisions which follow it.
>
> But the preamble does have important legal effects. Under normal circumstances, preambles can be used to identify the purpose of a statute, and also as an aid to construing ambiguous statutory language: *Driedger on the Construction of Statutes* (3rd ed. 1994), by R. Sullivan, at p. 261. The preamble to the *Constitution Act, 1867,* certainly operates in this fashion. However, in my view, it goes even further. In the words of Rand J., the preamble articulates "the political theory which the Act embodies": *Switzman, supra,* at p. 306. It recognizes and affirms the basic principles which are the very source of the substantive provisions of the *Constitution Act, 1867.* As I have said above, those provisions merely elaborate those organizing principles in the institutional apparatus they create or contemplate. As such, the preamble is not only a key to construing the express provisions of the *Constitution Act, 1867,* but also invites the use of those organizing principles to fill out gaps in the express terms of the constitutional scheme. It is the means by which the underlying logic of the Act can be given the force of law.[52]

As we can see, the Court confirms the judgment of the majority in the *Patriation Reference* to the extent of negating a positive legal "enacting force" to the preamble. However, the preamble is seen as being more than a mere tool of interpretation for the provisions of the Constitution. Its potential use to "fill out gaps" implies the possibility of broadening the scope of actual provisions of the Constitution beyond what the text purports to protect. In other words, the unwritten principles, although they do not have an entirely autonomous status, can be used to expand the reach of constitutional provisions.

For example, with regard to judicial independence, the Court noted in the *Judges Remuneration Reference* that ss. 96 to 100 of the *Constitution Act, 1867* offer a partial protection. Section 11(d) of the *Charter* adds to this protection, but its application is limited to courts exercising jurisdiction over offences. We are therefore left with a scheme according to which judicial independence receives only a partial protection through the provisions of the Constitution. In that framework, the preamble is used to complete the picture by expanding the reach of s. 11(d) so that it covers the independence of all courts, regardless of their jurisdiction.[53]

Note that this type of reasoning does not give a completely autonomous status to unwritten principles such as the rule of law in the sense of giving them the power to strike down legislation on their own. A concrete basis is still required in the actual provisions of the Constitution, but the preamble allows us to apply some of these provisions in a more liberal manner. The status of unwritten principles therefore seems to lie in a middle ground between that of a principle of interpretation and an independent constitutional requirement. It goes further than a tool of interpretation because it allows courts to bend fairly dramatically the actual words of constitutional provisions. However, since there still needs to be an anchor point in the provisions to frame a constitutional argument, the principles are not totally autonomous.

The reasoning behind the *Judges Remuneration Reference* was confirmed in the decision of the Supreme Court of Canada in the *Quebec Secession Reference*,[54] where emphasis was again placed on the importance of underlying constitutional principles, including the rule of law. In that case, the Court had to decide whether the province of Quebec had the right to secede unilaterally from the rest of Canada. In a unanimous decision, the Court held that there was no unilateral right to secede, but that an obligation would rise for the rest of Canada to negotiate secession with Quebec if a clear majority of Quebecers voted in a referendum on a clear question in favour of secession.[55] This solution was articulated by resorting to five fundamental unwritten principles of the Constitution, identified as the rule of law, federalism, democracy, constitutionalism, and respect for minority rights.[56] These principles allowed the Court to "fill the gap" in the text of the Constitution (in particular Part V of the *Constitution Act, 1982*), which was silent on the question of secession. In that regard, the justices confirmed the gap-filling potential of unwritten principles that had been put forth in the *Judges Remuneration Reference*.[57]

Thus, upon examination of all these cases, the *Judges Remuneration Reference* (confirmed by the *Quebec Secession Reference*) seems to stand out as representing a sensible and balanced solution to the controversy surrounding the use of unwritten constitutional principles in general. However, other cases, such as *OPSEU*, may lead us to believe that, regarding some of these principles, like the right of "discussion and debate," their status may be even greater, going so far as to maintain that "quite apart from *Charter* considerations, the legislative bodies in this country must conform to these structural imperatives and can in no way override them."[58] Similarly, we may note that the *Quebec Secession Reference* contains comments that seem to suggest that in certain circumstances, unwritten principles could be autonomous. Consider in that regard the following passage: "Underlying constitutional principles may in certain circumstances give rise to substantive legal obligations (have 'full legal force,' as we described it in the *Patriation Reference, supra,* at p. 845), which constitute substantive limitations upon government action. These principles may give rise to very abstract and general obligations, or they may be more specific and precise in nature. The principles are not merely descriptive, but are also invested with a powerful normative force, and are binding upon courts and governments."[59]

We see that the Supreme Court again grants support to the view that had been expressed by the dissenting judges (Martland and Ritchie JJ.) in the *Patriation Reference* regarding the "full legal force" some unwritten principles may have. Does this mean that some of these principles can be autonomous in the sense of being able to strike down laws without any textual support? Although the Court is not clear on that, it remains a possibility. In particular, the rule of law might be one of these principles possessing an independent constitutional status for several reasons. First, several comments in the *Manitoba Language Reference* indicate the fundamental character possessed by the rule of law in the context of our Constitution.[60] Second, in the same case (where the rule of law is directly in question), the Court cites the passage from the dissent in the *Patriation Reference* concerning the status of unwritten constitutional principles, and puts extra emphasis on the statement that "they have been accorded full legal force in the sense of being employed to strike down legislative enactments."[61] Third, the rule of law possesses several anchor points in provisions of the *Charter,* such as ss. 7,[62] 9,[63] and 11(g).[64] Indeed, these provisions are all aimed at promoting legality and at eradicating arbitrariness in a manner similar to the rule of law. They are indicators of the intolerance our Constitution has towards breaches of the rule of law. Fourth, not only is the rule of law recognized in both preambles but it is recognized *expressly* in the preamble to the *Charter.* This element may suggest that the rule of law is more than an unwritten principle, as this passage from the *Judges Remuneration Reference* seems to indicate: "The express provisions of the Constitution should be understood as elaborations of the underlying, unwritten, and organizing principles found in the preamble to the *Constitution Act, 1867.* Even though s. 11(d) is found in the newer part of our Constitution, the *Charter,* it can be understood in this way, since the Constitution is to be read as a unified whole. An analogy can be drawn between the express reference in the preamble of the *Constitution Act, 1982* to the rule of law and the implicit inclusion of that principle in the *Constitution Act, 1867.*"[65]

What this passage seems to imply is that while the rule of law was only an unwritten principle before 1982, it is now fully recognized by the

Constitution. In the same manner, judicial independence was only an unwritten principle before 1982 and now possesses an autonomous status through s. 11(d).

Moreover, it is worth noting that Lamer C.J.'s general comments (quoted above at length)[66] about the use of the preamble to "fill out gaps in the express terms of the constitutional scheme" contain explicit mention of the 1867 preamble only, and no mention of the 1982 preamble. Is this reality explainable only by the fact that it was the preamble to the *Constitution Act, 1867* that was at stake in the case at bar, or is it a deeper indication of a willingness to treat the preamble to the *Constitution Act, 1982* differently because of its express reference to the rule of law?

While this question remains unanswered, we may safely conclude that the rule of law possesses a strong status in Canadian constitutional law. It can be used to at least broaden significantly the impact of constitutional provisions purporting to protect particular aspects of the rule of law by filling out the "gaps" in the text of the Constitution. As mentioned earlier, the strong status of the rule of law can be used not only to increase the number of situations in which it is applicable but also to render the rule of law argument more compelling whenever it is applied.[67]

Possible Reasons behind the Jurisprudential Evolution

Since the coming into force of the *Constitution Act, 1982,* there has been an evolution in the way the Supreme Court sees the unwritten principles of the Constitution such as the rule of law. Indeed, with regard to the status they are given, the Court seems to have switched from a limited approach to a more interventionist view.

This change of attitude can be explained in part by reasons that reveal the fundamental turn Canadian constitutional law has taken since 1982. Indeed, the existence of substantive limits on legislative authority contained in the *Charter* have made Canadian courts more comfortable with the exercise of a more active and creative role in judicial review.[68]

With regard to the rule of law in particular, it is now, of course, expressly recognized in the preamble to the *Constitution Act, 1982*. This can make courts more comfortable with giving it tangible legal effect in constitutional adjudication. Prior to 1982, the constitutional source of the rule of law was found in the words "with a Constitution similar to that of the United Kingdom." This recognition through the preamble to the *Constitution Act, 1867* could not give the rule of law more than a weak status for two reasons. The first and obvious one is that the reference was only implicit. The second and more subtle reason is that by deriving the rule of law from the Constitution of the United Kingdom, it logically had to remain tied to the British constitutional meaning of the rule of law as described by Dicey. Recall that according to Dicey, Parliament remains sovereign at all times, and the rule of law is merely a principle of common law precluding arbitrary action by the government. This was indeed the way the rule of law was used in the *Roncarelli* case, under the *B.N.A. Act*.[69] With an express reference to the rule of law in the preamble to the *Charter,* Canadian courts now have more leeway to define it independently from the British conception described by Dicey. The rule of law's status may therefore now evolve more freely, unfettered by its British counterpart.

In relation to the substantive content of the rule of law (i.e., what values it protects), we can presume that a slight departure from Dicey's writings is permitted as well since Canadian courts are no longer tied to British constitutional law in that regard. A substantive analysis of the theory of the rule of law in general derived from the literature will therefore be useful in guiding the courts in determining what meaning it should be given in the Canadian constitutional context. Before we begin such an analysis, however, we will examine the few decisions from the Supreme Court of Canada that have purported to give some definition of the rule of law.

Content of the Rule of Law in Supreme Court Jurisprudence
Unfortunately, the Supreme Court of Canada has attempted to define the scope of the principle of the rule of law only rarely, and then only in a rather broad and general fashion. Let us nonetheless begin by examining these cases that include some discussion of the meaning of the rule of law.

Recall the case of *Roncarelli,* in which Premier Duplessis had revoked Mr. Roncarelli's liquor licence because he had provided bail for some Jehovah's Witnesses accused of distributing religious literature. Recall also that the statute in question apparently gave the administration discretion to revoke liquor licences. It was, however, interpreted as not allowing decisions that breached the rule of law, in relation to which the Court made the following comments: "That an administration according to law is to be superseded by action dictated by and according to the arbitrary likes, dislikes and irrelevant purposes of public officers acting beyond their duty, would signalize the beginning of disintegration of the rule of law as a fundamental postulate of our constitutional structure."[70]

This broad statement was the only account of the notion in the Supreme Court jurisprudence until the *Patriation Reference,* in which a slightly more detailed definition was given. Although the rule of law was not directly involved in the case at bar, the majority opinion of the Court contained the following comment: "The 'rule of law' is a highly textured expression, importing many things which are beyond the need of these reasons to explore but conveying, for example, a sense of orderliness, of subjection to known legal rules and of executive accountability to legal authority."[71]

The rule of law was given further attention by the Court in the case of the *Manitoba Language Reference*. Recall that the question in this case was whether the Court should declare invalid most of Manitoba's legislation on the grounds that it was not published in French as well as in English despite a constitutional requirement to that effect in the *Manitoba Act, 1870*. The Court confessed that the failure to publish the laws in French rendered them unconstitutional, but decided to maintain their validity for a period of time to allow the government to translate them. This remedy was motivated by a need to avoid the legal chaos in the province that might have followed such a wholesale declaration of invalidity. The prospect of such chaos was seen as repugnant to the rule of law, which the Court attempted to partially define: "The rule of law, a fundamental principle of our Constitution, must mean at least two things. First, that the law is supreme over officials of the government as well as private individuals, and thereby preclusive of arbitrary power ... Second, the rule of law requires the creation and maintenance of an actual order of positive laws which preserves and embodies the more general principle of normative order. Law and order are indispensable elements of civilized life. 'The rule of law in this sense implies ... simply the existence of public order.'"[72]

The first element expresses without further clarification the same concern for precluding the influence of arbitrary power that previous cases had already identified. The second element, however, bore the most relevance to the case at bar. Thus, a "law and order" perspective of the rule of law that does not tolerate anarchy played a large part in supporting the Court's reasoning to temporarily uphold the validity of Manitoba's legislation. This aspect had already been recognized as being part of the rule of law in the *Patriation Reference*, which referred to a "sense of orderliness" in the passage already cited.[73]

Later, in the case of *Nova Scotia Pharmaceutical*,[74] the Court underlined a link between the rule of law and the theory of vagueness. The Court seized this opportunity to state its understanding of the rule of law in reference to a European author writing on the similar doctrine of "État de droit":

J.-P. Henry, "Vers la fin de l'État de droit?" (1977), 93 *Rev. dr. publ.* 1207 gives the following definition of the *"État de droit"* at p. 1208:

[Translation] In theoretical terms, the État de droit is a system of organization in which all social and political relations are subject to the law. This means that the relations between individuals and authority, as well as relations between individuals themselves, are part of a legal interchange involving rights and obligations.

... At the core of the "État de droit," as under the rule of law, lies the proposition that the relationship of the State to the individuals is regulated by law.[75]

This aspect of the rule of law, which remains rather general, can be added to the first two components that had been identified in the *Manitoba Language Reference*. In the *Judges Remuneration Reference,* the Court stated again this third element of the rule of law, according to which "the exercise of all public power must find its ultimate source in a legal rule."[76] Finally, in the *Quebec Secession Reference,* the Court confirmed once again the first two elements identified in the *Manitoba Language Reference* as well as the third one invoked in later cases, which states that "the relationship between the State and the individual must be regulated by law."[77]

As this overview of the case law indicates, the rule of law according to the Supreme Court stands for the general idea that our society is characterized by the existence of an organized legal order, the content of which is preferably determined by laws as opposed to arbitrary powers. Considering that the rule of law is an important constitutional principle with the potential to have significant legal effects in adjudication, it is of the utmost importance to analyze this idea more deeply. Hopefully, a study of the literature that will be dedicated to scrutinizing the essence of the rule of law will shed light on the appropriate meaning of this principle in the context of our Constitution.

The Rule of Law in the Literature

As Madame Chief Justice Beverley McLachlin wrote in 1992, "the term 'Rule of Law' means many things to many people."[78] In fact, the expression has been widely used in the literature, with a broad variety of meanings. Such a free use of the expression "rule of law" has diluted its meaning to the extent that "just about every political ideal which has found support in any part of the globe during the post-war years"[79] has been associated with it at one time or another. Of course, the more content we inject into the concept of the rule of law, the less likely it is that a consensus will be reached on its legitimacy.

When the concept is viewed in the abstract, as a political ideal, debates can go on forever as to its appropriate meaning because no one has the authority to determine the right answer. In fact, there is no clear-cut answer in the abstract. In the context of the Canadian Constitution, however, the rule of law loses its abstraction and becomes a constitutional principle expressly affirmed in the preamble to the *Charter.* As has been seen thus far, the rule of law is a notion that can have a legal impact in Canadian constitutional adjudication. Given this reality, the courts have the responsibility to determine the meaning that ought to be given to the concept of the rule of law in the context of our Constitution.

There are two main streams of thought as far as defining the rule of law is concerned. The first can be said to be rather formal, the second more substantive.[80] The formal rule of law is represented by the expression

"government by law, not by individuals." Although several distinct requirements can be associated with this version of the rule of law, as identified by authors like John Rawls,[81] Joseph Raz,[82] or Lon Fuller,[83] they can
be summarized by a general attitude purporting to address the opposition
between rules and discretion in the legal system. The focus is located in
this opposition between law and arbitrary power. As far as determining
the rights and obligations of both the government and the individual is
concerned, pre-established standards set by the representatives of the people (i.e., laws) are to be favoured over arbitrary powers.

This formal version does not attempt to control what the State does. In
other words, the State is free to pursue whatever objective it wishes. The
control is merely aimed at the means employed to reach the objective. The
State's ability is limited by this version of the rule of law only insofar as
the substantive aims must be achieved through laws, as opposed to arbitrary decisions. Of course, this so-called formal version of the rule of law
is not totally free of substantive content. In fact, its underlying purpose
remains to protect personal freedom and other related values.[84] This is not
to say that these substantive values are protected at large by the rule of
law, but merely that it is to a certain extent for the sake of these values that
the formal rule of law requires rules as opposed to discretion.

The formal rule of law is thus concerned only with a rather narrow
realm of elements. It does not represent all that is to be included in the
ideal political system. It is presented as only one of the several qualities a
system may possess.[85] This version does not negate other valuable ideals
such as democracy and fundamental human rights, but neither does it purport to protect them.[86] It has been noted that undemocratic political systems can still be perfectly compatible with the formal rule of law,[87] just as
systems sanctioning gross human rights violations may comply with it.[88]

This leads us to the substantive version of the rule of law. This conception accepts the safeguards of the formal rule of law, but seeks to expand
its reach to the protection of other values like democracy and substantive
human rights. This view is put forward by authors like Michael Moore[89]
and Ronald Dworkin,[90] under the influence of the writings of John
Locke.[91] As a particularly liberal illustration of this line of thinking, let us
consider the following approach to the rule of law taken by the International Congress of Jurists in 1959: "The function of the legislature in a free
society under the Rule of Law is to create and maintain the conditions
which will uphold the dignity of man as an individual. This dignity requires not only the recognition of his civil and political rights but also the
establishment of the social, economic, educational and cultural conditions which are essential to the full development of his personality."[92]

This extract is an unusually inclusive approach to the rule of law. Most
views, even if they are substantive, are usually narrower. However, the

inclusion of requirements oriented towards the control of State policy is characteristic of the substantive version of the rule of law. This version purports to give a more complete answer to the orientation a legal and political system should take towards the ideal situation. Although this may be ideologically commendable, it stretches the notion to a degree that fails to attract consensus among commentators. Indeed, while most authors agree that the rule of law includes at least the formal requirements, the inclusion of other values is more controversial.[93] Quite apart from the problem of definition, when the rule of law is understood as a substantive limitation on State power, it attracts far less support as an ideal.[94]

As the substantive rule of law is more uncertain as a concept and controversial as an ideal, I will focus mainly on the formal version as being the appropriate understanding of the rule of law as used in the preamble to the *Charter*. This is not to say that substantive elements viewed by some authors as being part of the rule of law are not part of Canadian constitutional law in general. For example, Canadian authorities have chosen to include some democratic rights in ss. 3 to 5 of the *Charter,* as well as some fundamental rights and freedoms in ss. 2 and 7 to 15. It can therefore be said that the latter elements are constitutionally protected in Canada, whether or not we agree with the appropriateness of such protection as a matter of policy. However, I will not consider these substantive rights as being within the realm of the principle of the rule of law.

When it comes to defining the expression "rule of law" as used in the preamble that shall be granted the status described earlier, great care must be taken. We are concerned here with the analysis of the rule of law as used in the preambles to the 1867 and 1982 *Constitution Acts,* where it can have a legal impact in constitutional adjudication. In this framework, defining the rule of law is an exercise of constitutional interpretation that allows for less leeway than if it were treated merely as a political ideal. Although we do not want the rule of law to be an empty shell, neither is it appropriate to grant it an overly important content, especially considering the fact that it is only an unwritten principle of the Constitution. I will therefore propose that the content of the rule of law, in the context that concerns us, represents only formal requirements. This reliance on the formal rule of law is safer because it represents the conception that is the most widely accepted, allowing us to presume that it is used in that sense in the Canadian Constitution.

Even in countries where it is not recognized as a constitutionally protected principle, the rule of law standing as a preference for rules over discretion is widely accepted as an ideal in the literature.[95] Most commentators agree that the philosophy surrounding the ideal is a step in the right direction.[96] Of course, this is not to say that the system of the rule of law is perfect. No system can be perfect. Often the rule of law can miss the point. Thus, even if efforts are made to enact more definite rules, arbitrary considerations will still often continue to influence legal decisions. Sometimes, judges may even pretend to follow a rule, when in fact they purposely (or subconsciously) base their decision on personal preferences. Also, in cases where the judge does render a decision bound by strict rules, these rules may sometimes not serve justice as well as discretion would have served it in that particular case. However, the rule of law is the best system we have been able to develop. A system based solely on discretion could not work in our society. The determination of the rights and obligations of citizens cannot be left to discretion alone. Consider the following description of how Louis IX dispensed justice in France centuries ago:

> Louis IX of France, Saint Louis, was renowned for the fair and evenhanded manner in which he dispensed justice. We have the following account from The Life of Saint Louis written by John of Joinville ...
>
>> In summer, after hearing mass, the king often went to the wood of Vincennes, where he would sit down with his back against an oak, and make us all sit round him. Those who had any suit to present could come to speak to him without hindrance from an usher or any other person. The king would address them directly and ask: "Is there anyone here who has a case to be settled?" Those who had one would stand up. Then he would say: "Keep silent all of you, and you shall be heard in turn, one after the other."
>
> The judgements there pronounced, under the oak tree, were regarded as eminently just and good – though as far as I know Louis IX had no particular training in the customary law of any of the counties of France, or any other legal training.[97]

Obviously, we could not rely on such a system based solely on discretion in today's society. Contemporary social relations are far too complex and numerous for us to expect that grievances and disagreements involving individuals and the State could be resolved simply by deciding what is "just" or "unjust." As Professor Walker rightfully argues, "we need the rule of law especially in an age of transformation, precisely because we cannot agree on ends, or on what constitutes justice, right and wrong."[98] Saint Louis might have been able to dispense justice in a satisfactory manner because the problems arising at the time were far more simple and involved a much smaller number of actors. Moreover, it was by chance that Louis IX was such a wise and just adjudicator. Had he been a leader with less talent or virtue, the situation would not have sounded as good as described above. Therefore, because of practical considerations existing especially in contemporary society, the rule of law serves as a necessary (although imperfect) safeguard in our quest for justice.

The Threshold of the Rule of Law in Canada

Having established the importance of the rule of law as representing a striving for rules in a legal system, we may now address the following issue: when can it be said that the law relies too much on discretion? We must realize that in Canada the rule of law is now, as seen earlier, a standard that possesses a strong constitutional status. It is a standard against which the validity of legislation can be assessed, either directly according to some authors, or at least through its potential to "fill out gaps" in the provisions of the Constitution.[99] We must therefore attempt to provide a picture of what is expected from the State to satisfy the principle of the rule of law.

Fixed Standard versus Balanced Approach

There are two types of approaches that can be taken to determine the constitutional threshold of conformity with the rule of law. I shall begin by dismissing the inappropriate option, which purports to establish a "fixed" standard, before examining the more appropriate "balanced" approach.

Under the fixed-standard approach, the minimum degree of precision required is the same for all laws. For example, one could declare that on a scale of "one" to "ten," "one" being absolute discretion and "ten" being a perfectly fixed rule, the rule of law requires at least a "five." The "five" represents the fixed standard against which all laws are to be measured. The level of scrutiny is therefore the same whether the law creates a criminal offence or establishes a mere administrative standard that has little impact on citizens, for example. The scrutiny is also the same regardless of the fact that some legislative objectives are more difficult to achieve than others without resorting to vague statutory language. This way of settling on a particular point on the rule-discretion spectrum is unsatisfactory because it provides a rigid and artificial solution. It does not take into account the many factors that come into play in legislative drafting and law enforcement, and the necessity to balance them against citizens' interests. It ignores the fact that uncertainty in some types of laws can be more problematic than in other laws. It also ignores the fact that some laws deal with subject matters that require more discretion in enforcement than others.

This fixed-standard approach was unfortunately favoured by the Supreme Court of Canada with regard to the void-for-vagueness doctrine in the case of *R. v. Nova Scotia Pharmaceutical Society*.[100] In this case, the Court led by Gonthier J. set out a general test for determining whether legislation is unconstitutionally vague. It was decided that all laws would satisfy the threshold of constitutional validity if they provided a "basis for legal debate": "A vague provision does not provide an adequate basis for legal debate, that is, for reaching a conclusion as to its meaning by reasoned analysis applying legal criteria. It does not sufficiently delineate any area of risk, and thus can provide neither fair notice to the citizen, nor a limitation of enforcement discretion. Such a provision is not intelligible, to use the terminology of previous decisions of this Court, and therefore it fails to give sufficient indications that could fuel a legal debate. It offers no grasp to the judiciary."[101]

All that is required is that a law provide some standard, minimal though it might be, in order to fuel a legal debate. In other words, what the Court says is that if a law ranks at about "two" or higher on our imaginary scale, it is constitutionally valid. That same standard is made applicable to all laws. This approach is, with respect, unsatisfactory to the extent that it uses the same fixed number for the evaluation of all laws. It ignores the "strive" character of the rule of law and fails to take into consideration the need to balance the various governmental and individual interests arising in different legislative frameworks.[102] Ironically, we could say that the Court is being too precise when setting the threshold of constitutional validity with regard to the vagueness doctrine. Indeed, it would have been more appropriate for the Court to be flexible with regard to the issue at stake rather than setting a general criterion such as legal debate.

In the *Nova Scotia Pharmaceutical* case, the fixed-standard approach was used to set a very low threshold of evaluation. But a higher standard is not appropriate either if it is not flexible. As an example of such a standard, let us consider the following statement by Friedrich A. Hayek: "When the administration interferes with the private sphere of the citizen ... the problem of discretion becomes relevant to us; and the principle of the rule of law, in effect, means that the administrative authorities should have no discretionary powers in this respect."[103]

The only limitation Hayek brings to this very broad statement is that discretionary powers will be tolerated "only when ... it is a question of preserving liberty in the long run, as in the case of war."[104] This fixed standard for the rule of law is as inappropriate as the criterion set out in the *Nova Scotia Pharmaceutical* case because it ignores the need to balance the constraints faced by the State against individual interests. The appropriate approach as far as setting a threshold is concerned must take into consideration the constraints the legislature faces when attempting to state rules. Therefore, if the use of discretion is justified by impediments outside the control of the law-making body, it is to be accepted more easily than if arbitrary considerations are allowed to influence the enforcement of the law without any apparent reason.

With these concerns in mind, let us now focus on the appropriate approach as far as setting the threshold of conformity with the rule of law:

the "balanced" approach. This approach must necessarily take into consideration the particular reality emanating from our constitutional context while respecting the need to balance conflicting interests within the rule of law. In that regard, the jurisprudence surrounding the interpretation of s. 1 of the *Charter* provides an interesting point of reference for our problem.[105] Canadian courts have in recent years become accustomed to reconciling societal concerns with compelling individual interests through s. 1 of the *Charter*. This is not to say that the threshold of conformity should necessarily follow the same lines dictated by the *Oakes* case[106] and subsequent cases on the matter, but rather that a philosophy similar to the one prevailing under s. 1 could be useful with regard to the rule of law.

Although it has been modulated to some extent in recent jurisprudence,[107] the test relative to s. 1 under the *Oakes* case is relatively severe. We recall that the Crown must demonstrate that the limitation to the particular right or freedom at stake satisfies four requirements: (1) the objective of the law must be sufficiently important; (2) there must be a rational link between the means taken by the State and its objective; (3) the State must use "less drastic means" to reach its objective; and (4) the restriction must not be disproportionate with regard to the legislative objective.[108]

Should justifications for grants of statutory discretion follow the same guidelines? Probably not. It is important to keep in mind two elements when selecting the appropriate stringency of the test that will determine whether the rule of law is complied with. The first consideration is related to the status of the rule of law in the Canadian Constitution. As seen earlier, the rule of law is not protected by a particular constitutional provision. Therefore, the philosophy behind s. 1 of the *Charter* should not be applied with all its strength in relation to a mere constitutional "principle" such as the rule of law. However, especially since the *Manitoba Language Reference* and the *Judges Remuneration Reference*, we have seen that the unwritten principles of the Constitution are to be accorded a strong legal status. They can be used to "fill out gaps" in the actual provisions of the Constitution. With regard to the rule of law, it can be recalled that it might even possess a greater status than other unwritten principles, considering its inherent importance and its express inclusion in the preamble to the *Constitution Act, 1982*. Moreover, the principle possesses several anchor points in the actual provisions of the *Charter*, namely ss. 7, 9, and 11(g). The rule of law will therefore be used in adjudication in conjunction with these *Charter* provisions to interpret them or to "fill out gaps" they may contain. In the latter regard, the rule of law may be considered to be indirectly included in the provisions of the Constitution. These considerations can militate towards the creation of a standard for the rule of law that is close to, although not as severe as, the *Oakes* test.

The second relevant aspect that should determine the appropriate intensity of the requirements associated with the rule of law is related to practicality. Many statutes – in fact, a majority of statutes in Canada – involve grants of discretion.[109] A large number of them might be challenged successfully if we were to adopt a standard of conformity with the rule of law as strict as the one dictated by the philosophy behind the *Oakes* test. It would be very onerous to the legislature if courts were to require wholesale legislative redraftings to ensure compliance with the rule of law. It would also create serious institutional concerns if courts became too activist in that direction. Therefore, those demands of practicality must always be considered, *inter alia,* before defining the appropriate constitutional threshold of conformity with the rule of law.

These considerations related to practicality as well as to the status of the rule of law are enlightening. They invite us to seek a threshold of conformity that is somewhat close to the *Oakes* test without being as severe. What is needed is a standard that has the potential for affording the rule of law the constitutional protection it deserves, considering its status and its value, without unduly burdening the State.

As far as the comparison with s. 1 is concerned, the analogy is mainly to the "rationality" and the "less drastic means" elements, namely, steps 2 and 3 of the *Oakes* analysis. Since steps 1 and 4 focus their attention on the legitimacy of the law's objectives, they are not appropriate for our purposes because the rule of law must remain a formal requirement that does not discriminate among substantive policies.[110] The appropriate test would therefore embody to a certain extent the philosophy behind steps 2 and 3 to require that discretion be rationally related to the State objectives (step 2) and that it be reasonably necessary in that regard (step 3).

With all these considerations in mind, we must now attempt to define the appropriate threshold of conformity with the rule of law in the Canadian constitutional context.

The Balanced Criterion of "Reasonable Necessity" as the Threshold of the Rule of Law

An interesting view on the rule of law was advanced in 1968 in the *Report of the Royal Commission, An Inquiry into Civil Rights,* chaired by J.C. McRuer, then Chief Justice of the High Court of Justice of Ontario.[111] The report studied the rule of law in relation to the legal system of Ontario and made the following observations concerning the need to limit discretionary powers:

(1) No ... [discretionary] power should be conferred unless it is necessary and unavoidable to achieve the social objective or policy of the statute. It ought not to be conferred where rules or standards for judicial application can be stated.

(2) Where ... [a discretionary] power is necessary and unavoidable, the power should be no wider in scope than is demanded to meet the necessity.[112]

This criterion of "necessity" for the rule of law brings to mind the following passage from Aristotle's *Politics:* "Rightly constituted laws should be the final sovereign; and personal rule, whether it be exercised by a single person or a body of persons, should be sovereign only in those matters on which law is unable, owing to the difficulty of framing general rules for all contingencies, to make an exact pronouncement."[113]

Essentially, this idea of necessity is attractive. Although these extracts may sound somewhat severe if taken literally and therefore need to be qualified and further explained in the following paragraphs, they indicate a valid approach to the rule of law in the context of our Constitution. In that regard, and in light of what will be said below, we can state that the use of discretion will be in conformity with the constitutional requirements of the rule of law in Canada if it is "reasonably necessary" to reach the particular legislative objective.

In determining whether a discretionary power is "reasonably necessary," it is essential to take into consideration the nature of the statutory provision at stake. Some legislative objectives require more discretion than others to be carried out effectively. The *McRuer Report* expresses the issue in the following terms:

> In determining whether a particular existing power or a proposed power is or will be an unjustified encroachment on civil rights under the principles we have stated, the social policy of the statute must be examined. The policy of the statute determines what power will be required to carry it out effectively. The policy must be analysed in detail to determine whether a power of any kind is required, and if so the characteristics it should possess. [However], [n]o general formula for the abstract analysis of the infinite variety of social policies that may be the subject of legislation can possibly be laid down.[114]

Interesting illustrations are given in the *McRuer Report* to show the difference between necessary and unnecessary grants of discretion. The *Provincial Auctioneers Act*[115] is used to demonstrate the case of a statute using unnecessary discretion. The Minister of Agriculture can grant licences to qualified individuals under the *Act* to sell purebred livestock by public auction. Then, s. 4 of the *Act* provides the following: "4. The Minister may revoke any licence under this Act at any time for any cause appearing to him sufficient."

It seems that the purpose of this statute is to ensure that purebred cattle auctioneers are competent, honest, and responsible. However, the law allows for revocation of the licence at the total discretion of the Minister. The revocation of an individual's licence to practice his profession can have a critical impact on his life. As demonstrated by *Roncarelli,* overly wide grants of discretion can lead to abuse of power in that context. As it is rightfully argued in the *McRuer Report,* this wide grant of discretion in s. 4 of the *Act* is unnecessary since it would be reasonably possible to set out some standards to guide the Minister's decision without compromising the legislative objectives.[116] The following redrafting is then suggested: "4. The Minister may at any time revoke an auctioneer's licence if in his opinion, (a) the conduct of the auctioneer establishes that he is not a responsible person in whom the public can place trust, or, (b) the auctioneer is not competent to act as an auctioneer of purebred cattle."[117]

Or even more precisely: "4. The Minister may at any time revoke an auctioneer's licence if in his opinion, (a) the auctioneer has made fraudulent or false representations in the course of his business as an auctioneer, has abused a confidence imposed in him by a vendor or purchaser at an auction conducted by him, or has failed to carry out an undertaking given by him to a vendor or purchaser at an auction, or (b) the auctioneer is not competent to act as an auctioneer of purebred cattle."[118]

Because of the nature of the objectives of the *Act,* we see that it is possible to draft provisions that leave less room for arbitrariness without undermining the legislative policy. However, other types of statutes may not allow this kind of redrafting to diminish discretion without compromising efficacy. Thus, as a legitimate grant of discretion, the *McRuer Report* contains the example of s. 13 of the *Public Works Act,*[119] which states: "13. The Minister may for and in the name of Her Majesty purchase or acquire and, subject as hereinafter mentioned, may without the consent of the owner thereof enter upon, take and expropriate any land he deems necessary for, (a) the public purposes of Ontario; or (b) the use or purposes of any department of the government thereof."

This provision grants wide and important discretionary powers to the Crown for expropriation, but unlike in the case of the *Provincial Auctioneers Act,* it is not possible to articulate more precise rules. There is an almost infinite number of purposes for which a particular property may be required.[120] The grant of discretion in this case is believed to be necessary, and therefore not repugnant to the rule of law.

One of the virtues of this criterion of necessity is that it manages to draw a line of conformity with the rule of law while taking into account the need to balance the interests of both the State and the individual. It is not a strict and settled requirement of clarity in the abstract. Thus, a law allowing a high degree of discretion could be valid while another law containing less discretion could be invalid at the same time. What matters is not the degree of discretion in the abstract but the extent to which the grant of such discretion was necessary to reach the legislative objectives.

Within this framework, the rule of law is still only a formal limitation on the exercise of State power. It does not prevent the achievement of any legislative objectives since only the use of "unnecessary" discretion is problematic. Only if discretion is granted while there was not an honest difficulty with resorting to rules does the law become suspect.

Softening the Impact of "Necessity"
Even if it represents only a formal limitation, this criterion of necessity may appear as a harsh requirement on the exercise of State authority to the extent that it requires substantial efforts on the part of the legislature to comply with the rule of law. The role of the State is obviously very complex in determining the rights and obligations of its citizens. As Gonthier J. noted in the *Nova Scotia Pharmaceutical* case:

> The modern State intervenes in almost every field of human endeavour, and it plays a role that goes far beyond collecting taxes and policing. The State has entered fields where the positions are not so clear-cut; in the realm of social or economic policy, interests diverge, and the State does not seek to enforce a definite and limited social interest in public order, for instance, against an individual. Often the State attempts to realize a series of social objectives, some of which must be balanced against one another, and which sometimes conflict with the interests of individuals. The modern State, while still acting as an enforcer, assumes more and more of an arbitration role.[121]

These were among concerns that prompted Gonthier J. to express a deferential view towards the legislature in the context of the void-for-vagueness doctrine.[122] With that in mind, let me add a few notes of caution to my analysis to ensure that the criterion of necessity will not represent an undue burden on the State but rather a sound and realistic approach to assessing the validity of legislation against the rule of law in the Canadian constitutional context.

First, "necessity" is not to be regarded as a strict and inflexible requirement. Courts should not declare legislation to be contrary to the rule of law simply because they can imagine a legislative formula that would still be as efficient while triggering less uncertainty. In other words, there should be judicial deference towards the legislative choice.[123] If the legislature could reasonably have believed that a certain amount of discretion was needed, the courts should not substitute their own judgment, although they might disagree with the legislative choice. Thus, the criterion is more one of "reasonable necessity" rather than pure necessity. Similarly, it is not because a legislative provision is merely ambiguous that it will be considered constitutionally problematic. Ambiguity is an inevitable problem in legislative drafting and the legislator often cannot foresee in advance the many problems involved in statutory interpretation. It is only when it is reasonably clear when the law is enacted that its vague terms create an unnecessary degree of uncertainty that the statute will be constitutionally suspect.

Second, it is important to note at this stage that the rule of law is designed primarily for laws that have an important coercive aspect.[124] Laws are coercive when the legislature purports to directly affect the citizen's rights and obligations.[125] The more closely a law affects citizens' rights and obligations, the more the rule of law will be important. The most flagrant example is the field of criminal law, because it entertains a direct relation with citizens' conduct, and also because of the severe penalties it can involve. Although coercive laws are the ones that citizens are most aware of, many legislative enactments in Canada have little to do with coercion. For example, laws structuring municipalities or creating school boards, or laws providing for the internal organization of administrative agencies or for nominations of public service executives contain provisions designed to "administer" the State without interfering directly with the rights of private citizens. The principle of the rule of law is less important in relation to these laws, and a greater judicial deference is appropriate in this regard.[126]

The difficulty of applying of the rule of law to legislation that has little or no coercive aspect is emphasized in the Canadian context by our constitutional reality. As we have seen earlier, although the rule of law does not seem to have totally independent constitutional status in Canada, its influence can be important when applied in conjunction with existing constitutional provisions. It is interesting to note that provisions purporting to protect aspects of the rule of law in the *Charter* – mainly ss. 7, 9, and 11(g) – are concerned with highly coercive laws (mostly penal laws). This reinforces the view that the reasonable necessity criterion should be applied to the rule of law with regard to laws that are essentially coercive in our constitutional context. Whether the rule of law could be used to broaden the scope of *Charter* provisions so that less coercive laws would have to comply with it is uncertain.[127] However, if the rule of law ever does apply to such less coercive laws, the threshold of validity would have to be lower than the one of reasonable necessity.

The preceding discussion is illustrated by a recent decision by Campbell J. of the Ontario General Division in the case of *Ontario Public School Boards' Assn. v. Ontario (A.G.)*.[128] The province, in a desire to restructure its school boards, enacted the *Fewer School Boards Act*,[129] which granted many discretionary powers to the administration (the Education Improvement

Commission) in order to operate the transition. This statute was challenged on the grounds that it was inconsistent with the rule of law. It is interesting to see how the requirement was treated on the merits in this case. Indeed, while the court recognized that "the Act could be much more explicit as to the discretionary basis on which its enormous powers should be exercised,"[130] Campbell J. nonetheless upheld the legislation while giving a rather narrow definition of the rule of law: "The rule of law, in this context, simply means that the law in question must be a constitutionally valid statute regularly passed by the appropriate level of government and that the courts retain the power to protect the liberties of anyone whose rights may be infringed by the operation of the legislation."[131]

While the court did not outline expressly the noncoercive character of the statute, it can seriously be doubted that the same attitude towards the rule of law would have prevailed if a criminal statute had been at stake, for example. The *Fewer School Boards Act,* although it will ultimately have an impact on citizens' lives, does not put the State in direct confrontation with the individual. The exercise of the discretion remains impersonal. Risks of abuse are therefore less present. This case is an illustration of the narrow approach to the rule of law, requiring much less than reasonable necessity in situations where a rather noncoercive statute is involved.[132]

We may note that even though the court in *Ontario School Boards* advocated a narrow approach in relation to this noncoercive statute, it does not mean that the rule of law can have no relevance whatsoever in such a context. In fact, Campbell J. even suggested that a particular provision of the *Fewer School Boards Act* might be inconsistent with the rule of law. Section 349(2) of the *Act* states that "in the event of a conflict between a regulation made under this Part and a provision of this Act or of any other Act or regulation, the regulation made under this Part prevails." This provision, known as a "Henry VIII clause," could be repugnant to the rule of law as it places the executive above the legislative assembly in an arbitrary manner. As Campbell J. noted: "This power is constitutionally suspect because it confers upon the government the unprotected authority to pull itself up by its own legal bootstraps and override arbitrarily, with no further advice from the Legislative Assembly, and no right to be heard by those who may be adversely affected by the change, the very legislative instrument from which the government derives its original authority."[133]

This betrayal of the rule of law is so flagrant that it might be unconstitutional even though the law is rather noncoercive. However, Campbell J. chose not to rule definitively on that particular issue since no attempt had yet been made by the Ontario government to exercise that breathtaking power.

Thus, when an important violation occurs, the rule of law can still be applied to laws that have only little or no impact in the direct coercion of individuals. However, the standard of reasonable necessity will prove most appropriate for laws that have a greater coercive dimension. The more closely and directly individuals are confronted with legislative enactment, the more it will be appropriate to apply the standard of reasonable necessity. I will come back to this issue in the next chapter in relation to the content of the vagueness doctrine.

Conclusion

This chapter has examined the possible scope that might be given to the principle of the rule of law in the context of our Constitution. By taking into consideration the text, structure, and history of our constitutional documents, as well as relevant jurisprudence and literature, this chapter has drawn some conclusions as to the appropriate scope of the principle in Canada.

As to content, the rule of law is destined to apply mostly to coercive laws. It constrains legislatures to strive for rules and to limit discretion to what is reasonably necessary to achieve State objectives in order to limit the influence of arbitrary power. This is the core of the rule of law in Canada. Considering the fact that it is a constitutional principle affirmed in the preamble to the *Charter*, it may be possible to use it independently to strike down legislative enactments or at least to "fill out gaps" in the express provisions of the Constitution. This means that even if the need to limit arbitrary power and discretion to what is reasonably necessary is not found to be a constitutional requirement *per se*, the rule of law will at least be a powerful tool for interpreting and expanding the scope of existing constitutional provisions.

In the context of this study of the vagueness doctrine, the inquiry conducted in this chapter will play a fundamental role in succeeding chapters. We know that one of the two rationales for requiring that laws be sufficiently precise is the concern for limiting discretion in enforcement. When taken in isolation and outside of any constitutional imperatives, the weight and scope of this rationale in relation to vagueness might be difficult to assess. Thus, having examined the different implications surrounding the principle of the rule of law in this chapter, we will be able to better understand the substantive content of the vagueness doctrine as well as its appropriate place in Canadian constitutional law.

3
The Content of the Vagueness Doctrine

This chapter examines the content of the vagueness doctrine in constitutional law. According to this theory, vague laws are considered problematic because they do not provide "fair notice" to citizens regarding the legal consequences of their actions, and also because they increase the discretionary power of law-enforcing authorities. In other words, vague laws are repugnant to the principle of legality and to the rule of law.

As part of this larger study of vagueness, the analysis in earlier chapters focused on the principle of legality and on the rule of law. Chapter 1 examined the principle of legality, which has long been part of our system of law and is now constitutionally entrenched through s. 11(g) of the *Charter of Rights and Freedoms*. The study considered the phenomena of judicial crime creation and retroactive legislation. We saw that these are repugnant to legality, mainly because they create "unfair surprise" for citizens. Similarly, vague laws failing to provide fair notice offend legality and are in that sense constitutionally problematic. In Chapter 2, in an attempt mainly to understand the "law enforcement discretion" rationale of the vagueness doctrine, we saw that the rule of law requires governments to limit the influence of arbitrary power in the legal system. We saw that this principle enjoys a high status in Canadian constitutional law, and it was argued that it requires that discretion be limited to what is "reasonably necessary" in relation to the legislative matter in question.

With this framework, this chapter will examine the actual content of the vagueness doctrine. Considerable emphasis will be placed on the scheme of analysis developed by the Supreme Court in the *Nova Scotia Pharmaceutical*[1] case, which provides a major frame of reference for this study. In that case, the Court purported to define in a fairly complete manner the constitutional theory of vagueness. We will see that the approach it has taken amounts to setting a rather permissive threshold of validity against which vague laws will be assessed. As this may constitute an insufficient protection of legality and the rule of law in certain cases, we will see how the doctrine could evolve towards greater requirements of certainty without depriving governments of the flexibility they may require to efficiently reach their policy objectives.

This chapter has two major parts. The first part will explore the American version of the vagueness doctrine; the second, more substantial part will study its Canadian counterpart.

The void-for-vagueness doctrine has existed in the United States since the beginning of the twentieth century. A study of the American theory will provide us with an interesting frame of reference that will foster a better understanding of the operation of the Canadian doctrine, especially in relation to its two rationales, fair notice and law enforcement discretion. We will see that the Supreme Court of the United States is usually hesitant to invalidate uncertain legislation. Although many cases in the past have invoked vagueness to strike down legislative provisions, a closer look reveals that many decisions were motivated by extraneous constitutional concerns. The remaining cases reveal that American courts will protect citizens against vague laws only in a rather limited fashion. Thus, fair notice will be seen as being offended in American constitutional law only when the law touches upon some conduct usually perceived as innocent. Meanwhile, the law enforcement discretion rationale will not provoke the invalidation of vague laws unless there is reason to believe that discretion will be exercised selectively by the authorities. In an attempt to illustrate this reality, I will compare two lines of cases that are very revealing of the attitude of the Supreme Court of the United States: cases dealing with public morals and cases involving vagrancy or other "street-cleaning" statutes.

The analysis will then move on to the content of the Canadian vagueness doctrine. I will first examine the rationale of fair notice as understood by the Supreme Court of Canada in *Nova Scotia Pharmaceutical*. Essentially, fair notice will be satisfied if citizens are subjectively conscious of the content of the law. The analysis is therefore based on the community's "substratum of values" rather than on the actual text of the statute. This resembles the American version of notice. I will attempt to show the impact of the Supreme Court's reasoning concerning the "substratum of values" issue. More specifically, I will examine whether this notion can be sufficient to invalidate laws independently, regardless of the text's precision. I will also ask to what extent vague laws can offend fair notice even if they do not create problems in terms of substratum of values. This will lead to the conclusion that in the context of vagueness, the issue of substratum of values identified by the Supreme Court will be a factor among others that can make the requirement of precision fluctuate in certain cases.

Next, I will focus on the Supreme Court's analysis of the law enforcement discretion rationale. In *Nova Scotia Pharmaceutical*, the second rationale of vagueness is seen as a guarantee against statutes that are so broad that they can lead to automatic convictions once prosecution occurs. Once again, a similarity with the American situation can be seen, which, as we recall, seeks under its second rationale to protect citizens against "catch-all" laws encouraging selective enforcement. It will be argued that in Canada, the rule of law militates in favour of a broader protection of the law enforcement discretion rationale. This view is confirmed implicitly in the case of *R. v. Morales,*[2] which I will discuss. The *Morales* case will also be useful in underlining the importance of the legislative context in determining whether a law adequately limits law enforcement discretion.

Next I will examine the threshold of constitutional validity against which vague laws are assessed. This is obviously an important question. In its embryonic jurisprudence on the subject of vagueness, the Supreme Court of Canada has stated a general standard pursuant to which laws will be upheld as soon as they provide a sufficient "basis for legal debate." This approach is very permissive towards the legislator since any law that is not totally unintelligible will satisfy this standard of legal debate. This permissive test, if applied invariably in all cases, will afford a rather poor protection to the rationales of fair notice and law enforcement discretion. Standards of constitutional validity taking sensible account of these important concerns must be developed. The minimal legal debate test may be appropriate in some cases where the legislative assembly cannot efficiently reach its objectives without considerable flexibility. In some other cases, however, more elaborate and demanding standards will be appropriate. I will examine some factors that can make the requirement of precision fluctuate depending on the circumstances, thus allowing courts to more adequately balance the needs of the State against individual rights.

Next, I will examine possible solutions towards greater precision that could help statutes comply with the constitutional requirements of the vagueness doctrine. First is the controversial technique that consists in remedying vague laws through judicial interpretation. I will argue that a difficulty with this approach is that it increases the burden of citizens who wish to know the law, by forcing them to search through volumes of reported decisions in addition to reading the statute. Moreover, an *ex post facto* application of the law can occur when a newly defined standard is applied to the accused in the case at bar. Thus, whenever possible, it is preferable that the legal standard be spelled out in the statute itself rather than by the judiciary. The extent to which this can be done will be examined. The legislative assembly can make its rules more specific by articulating in greater detail the conditions under which they apply, but we will see that it can also resort to other methods. For instance, by providing illustrations of the law's applicability, its scope can be made more certain through the use of the principle of interpretation known as *ejusdem generis.* Another, more innovative technique is to resort to delegated legislation to specify the standards contained in the law after a hearing held by administrators.

Finally, I will provide an illustration of how this overall approach to dealing with vagueness operates in practice. Up to that point, the analysis will have been conducted essentially in abstract terms. Two related cases from the Supreme Court of British Columbia will help us better understand the practical operation of the doctrine as this study will have been portraying it. In these cases, which will be referred to as *Canadian Bar Assn. No 1*[3] and *No. 2*,[4] legislative provisions that imposed a tax on legal services were challenged on grounds of vagueness. In the first case, Mr. Justice Lysyk invalidated a provision taxing legal services unless they had no "connection to British Columbia." Following the invalidation of this standard, the law was redrafted by the provincial legislature to better comply with fair notice and limit law enforcement discretion. It will be noted that the "connection to British Columbia" standard was not totally unintelligible, and would probably have been upheld by the Supreme Court of Canada pursuant to the legal debate test. However, the law was invalidated by resorting to an arguably higher threshold, and the result was beneficial to legality and the rule of law. We will see that the legislature was able to articulate a more precise standard without compromising its policy objectives. It resorted to the principle *ejusdem generis* and granted regulation-making powers to the government in order to better reconcile the needs for certainty and flexibility. The statute was ultimately upheld by Madame Justice Humphries in *Canadian Bar Assn. No. 2*.

The American Vagueness Doctrine

The American vagueness doctrine, much like its Canadian counterpart, requires that legislation reach an adequate level of precision in order to sustain constitutional validity. The two rationales behind this requirement are the same as in Canada, namely, that citizens be given adequate warning as to what the law prescribes and that discretion in law enforcement be limited. These requirements are embodied in the Fifth and Fourteenth Amendments to the Constitution of the United States, which both provide that no one can be deprived of "life, liberty, or property, without due process of law." Before examining the content of the vagueness doctrine in Canada, it would be useful to first describe the scope and meaning of its American counterpart. In fact, we will see that the Canadian theory, as developed by the Supreme Court, borrows many concepts from the American void-for-vagueness doctrine, which makes its consideration even more relevant in the context of this study. In particular, we will see that in *Nova Scotia Pharmaceutical,* the Supreme Court of Canada's definition of the two rationales of vagueness is almost directly imported from the United States. Thus, in order to fully understand the Canadian theory, and in particular the role of the two rationales of vagueness, let us consider at this point the American version of the vagueness doctrine.

Substantive Due Process: The "False" Vagueness Cases

Before going any further, it is important to realize that in the United States (as in Canada, for that matter), constitutional requirements of precision in statutes are primarily of a procedural nature. This means that they are directed at the form of the law rather than at its content or substance.[5] In other words, the State is not barred through these standards from reaching its substantive policy objectives. All that is required is that the legislature respect some formal standards of precision. In that sense, it must be noted that the true content of the vagueness doctrine is not reflected by all the cases where uncertainty in a statute has been invoked as part of the basis for a decision of constitutional invalidity. This calls upon the distinction between procedural ("true") vagueness cases and substantive ("false") vagueness cases. A fairly large number of declarations of invalidity based on the vagueness doctrine can be found in the volumes of reported decisions in the United States since the beginning of the twentieth century.[6] However, this does not necessarily mean that the precision of legislation *per se* as a way of protecting legality and the rule of law has been the Supreme Court's essential concern in all of these cases. In fact, an overview of the jurisprudence on vagueness shows that the Court has frequently been motivated, at least partially, by other considerations when invalidating laws on grounds of vagueness. In such situations, substantive due process interests were, in fact, the main concern, instead of the procedural due process values that characterize the basic theory of vagueness. Over the years of constitutional adjudication, the Supreme Court of the United States has focused on areas such as economic regulation and civil liberties (mainly free speech) with a varying degree of scrutiny, and vagueness cases have certainly been influenced by that phenomenon. I will discuss briefly these "false" vagueness cases, in order to remove them from the further analysis regarding the "true" protection afforded by the two rationales of vagueness.

The interpretation of the American due process clauses has given rise to great controversy, especially in the early twentieth century. Due process was first understood as protecting only procedural interests,[7] but the Court gave it substantive content in 1897 with its decision in *Allgeyer v. Louisiana*.[8] In the years that followed, especially since the famous 1905 decision in *Lochner v. New York*,[9] the Court used the due process clause to review the wisdom of legislation in the economic sphere. Many statutes were struck down by a Court favouring economic *laissez-faire*. In 1937, following pressures by the executive, the Court abandoned that attitude in *West Coast Hotel v. Parrish*.[10] A year later, the Court expressed its intention to defer to the legislature in the field of regulatory legislation.[11] With this historical framework in mind, it is interesting to note that the void-for-vagueness doctrine was developed by the Court during the same time period. The vagueness theory came to the forefront at the same time as substantive (economic) due process.[12] In that sense it was inevitable to find economic concerns in early vagueness decisions. In fact, the laws held void for uncertainty before 1937 were exclusively regulatory and economic control statutes.[13]

While the early vagueness cases appeared generous in the way they protected the ideals of legality and the rule of law through a requirement of high precision, it is more probable that the invalidations were motivated by substantive economic reasons. Consider, for example, the statute struck down in *United States v. Cohen Grocery Co.*,[14] which made it unlawful to willfully "make any unjust or unreasonable rate or charge in handling or dealing in or with any necessaries." It was held to be too vague, although it is not really more indefinite than the subsequently upheld enactment making it unlawful to sell goods at "unreasonably low prices" with intent to hurt competitors. The latter statute was upheld by the Court in *United States v. National Dairy Products Corp.*,[15] only this was in 1963 while the *Cohen Grocery* case was decided in 1921. As some commentators have noted, it would be wrong to consider the early vagueness decisions as reflecting an enthusiastic commitment to the ideals of legality and the rule of law. In these cases, vagueness was in fact used as a "buffer zone"[16] for economic interests that might have been seen as insufficient on their own to trigger constitutional invalidity.[17]

Since the 1937 crisis, the Court's focus has shifted towards protecting the civil liberties guaranteed by the Constitution with greater scrutiny. Among the substantive interests receiving heightened attention by the Court, freedom of speech has been dominant.[18] Many vagueness decisions involving statutes dealing with speech have openly advocated a higher requirement of precision.[19] In analyzing these cases on their merits, one must not confuse them with the "true" vagueness cases (i.e., the ones not involving any substantive guarantee of the Constitution, such as freedom of speech). Failing to do that might lead to a false belief that the procedural due process concerns of vagueness (legality and the rule of law) are given a broad protection. Even if the cases involving the First Amendment still talk about concerns of "notice to citizens" and protection against "arbitrary enforcement," it is not with the purpose of protecting them *per se* in the procedural sense.

The real concern here is one of overbreadth. When a statute purports to regulate activities that are within its legitimate reach but in fact reaches into protected speech, such a statute has the defect of overbreadth.[20] A law need not be vague in order to be overbroad, but vague laws dealing with speech often do represent a potential overreaching on protected expression.[21] Not only can this overreaching be achieved through selective enforcement against unpopular views[22] but it can also occur because of the deterrent effect such a law might have on citizens who are uncertain as to the scope of the prohibition.[23] This "chilling effect" causes citizens to "steer far wider of the unlawful zone,"[24] and protected speech is therefore inhibited.[25] This resembles the concern of notice that characterizes procedural due process vagueness, but one must realize that clear notice is encouraged in the sphere of expression not so much because of a wish to avoid unfair surprise but more with the purpose of giving "breathing space" to First Amendment freedoms. By the same token, the elimination of a potential for arbitrary enforcement of the law is pursued in cases of free speech not so much for classic vagueness reasons but to prevent overbreadth on protected expression.[26]

The "buffer zone" character of vagueness in cases where other pressing substantive concerns are involved is further highlighted in the way the standing or "scope of review" issue was treated by the Court in these cases. As a rule, in American constitutional adjudication, one may not challenge a law that is constitutional as applied to one's situation on the grounds that it might be applied unconstitutionally to others.[27] In principle, vagueness cases are no exception to this rule. In true procedural due process vagueness cases, a litigant to whom the law clearly applies may not challenge it "on its face" simply because it might be vague in the hypothetical situation of another person.[28] However, the Court does make an exception to that rule in cases of First Amendment overbreadth.[29] We recall that an overbroad law is drafted in a way that reaches both protected and unprotected activity. In cases of First Amendment overbreadth, the invalidation of the law "on its face" (regardless of the facts of the case) is permitted for the following reason: The Court fears that if it simply carves away the invalid applications of the law through case-by-case judicial invalidations, it will leave citizens uncertain as to the legitimate scope of the law. The Court fears that by trying to remedy the overbroad law in the traditional way, it will create a problem of vagueness. A chilling effect on protected speech would therefore occur, and the law would still be overbroad because citizens uncertain as to the legitimate scope of the law would engage in auto-censorship.[30]

As we can see, the fear of a judicially created vagueness lies behind the special standing exception in First Amendment overbreadth cases. Similarly, when vagueness is present on the face of a law regulating speech, the same concerns of "chilling effect" and overbreadth come into play to relax the standing requirements.[31] Thus, in cases of vagueness related to the First Amendment, a litigant's challenge may succeed even if the law could have been constitutionally applied to his situation.[32] For our purposes, the modification of the standing requirement is interesting in that it confirms the view that First Amendment vagueness cases have more to do with overbreadth than with vagueness. The substantive interests that drive these cases are so compelling for the Court that they manage to relax the issue of standing, something that is not possible in pure procedural due process vagueness cases.

This view is further confirmed when we adopt a historical perspective on the relationship between vagueness, standing, and the substantive concerns. When we look at cases from the early part of the twentieth century, it is interesting to note that the standing requirement was being treated differently in cases of vagueness because the substantive concerns of the Court were not the same.[33] As an example of a vagueness decision involving speech decided before the mid-thirties, consider the case of *Fox v. Washington (1915)*.[34] The defendant was charged under a statute that prohibited the distribution of any writing "having a tendency to encourage or incite the commission of any crime, breach of the peace, or act of violence, or which shall tend to encourage or advocate disrespect for law." The Court refused to examine the vagueness of the statute "on its face" and its potential for overreaching on protected freedoms because the defendant's publication, which encouraged indecent exposure, was interpreted as being clearly within the scope of the law.[35] On the other hand, in a case of economic regulation such as *Connally v. General Construction Co. (1926)*,[36] the Court saw no problem in invalidating "on its face" a statute that might have had many valid applications. The law made it unlawful for a contractor to pay his employees "less than the current rate of per diem wages in the locality where the work is performed." The statute might have been vague in some situations, but as one commentator has noted, "if the contractor was paying twenty cents a day less than the lowest wage in the vicinity there would be a clear violation of the statute."[37] Nonetheless, the Court struck down the statute "on its face" in *Connally* without considering whether it would have been possible to preserve some of its valid applications.[38]

Interestingly, we see that even at the beginning of the twentieth century the scope of review ("on its face" or "as applied") constituted a clear signal that the Court's concerns in vagueness cases were substantive rather than procedural. As economic *laissez-faire* values were more important at the time than freedom of expression, the contrast reflected by the treatment of standing was as telling then as it is in the Court's current attitude. In these lines of cases, vagueness was not and still is not an important concern *per se* but only a "buffer zone"[39] for the protection of substantive interests.

Illustrations of "True" Vagueness Cases
Having underlined the relatively poor guidance that can be derived from vagueness cases driven by substantive concerns, we now direct our attention to so-called "true" vagueness cases.[40] To illustrate how the American void-for-vagueness doctrine is treated in practice, it will be useful to compare two particular lines of cases that are revealing of the orientation of the Supreme Court's jurisprudence. These are cases dealing with so-called street-cleaning statutes and cases of public morals legislation. A brief description of the two lines of cases is appropriate, as it will allow us to refer to them more easily later on.

*"Street-Cleaning" Statutes (*Papachristou *and* Lanzetta*)*
"Street-cleaning" statutes are generally vagrancy-type legislation such as the following ordinance struck down in *Papachristou v. City of Jacksonville:*[41]

> Rogues and vagabonds, or dissolute persons who go about begging, common gamblers, persons who use juggling or unlawful games or plays, common drunkards, common night walkers, thieves, pilferers or pickpockets, traders in stolen property, lewd, wanton and lascivious persons, keepers of gambling places, common railers and brawlers, persons wandering or strolling around from place to place without any lawful purpose or object, habitual loafers, disorderly persons, persons neglecting all lawful business and habitually spending their time by frequenting houses of ill fame, gaming houses, or places where alcoholic beverages are sold or served, persons able to work but habitually living upon the earnings of their wives or minor children shall be deemed vagrants and, upon conviction in the Municipal Court shall be punished as provided for Class D offenses.[42]

This type of legislation can have several interrelated purposes. First, it is aimed at preventing future criminality by targeting behaviours that can be perceived as potentially leading to crime or indicating the imminence of the commission of a crime.[43] Second, these statutes can be used to "clean the streets" of people who are perceived as "undesirables."[44] For example, in the Jacksonville ordinance cited above, "dissolute persons who go about begging," "common drunkards," and "disorderly persons" are descriptions aimed at eliminating "undesirables." The two concerns often overlap because "undesirables" are generally perceived as having behaviour that can indicate future criminality. What vagrancy laws and similar types of legislation do is define offences in terms that are very vague and broad so that the police are given a dictatorial power to arrest.[45] Prosecutions often lead to automatic convictions under these statutes because of the broad language of the law. Since no particular offence is designated, it is very difficult for an accused to make an adequate defence in court.

The case of *Lanzetta v. New Jersey*[46] contains another example of this type of legislation designed to prevent future criminality by targeting "undesirables" in vague terms. Here, the statute held to be void for vagueness punished any person who, having been convicted of a crime or at least three disorderly offences, was not engaged in any lawful occupation and was "known to be a member of a gang." The State Courts had defined the word "gang" as meaning a company of persons acting together for some purpose "usually criminal" or going about together or acting in concert "mainly for criminal purposes."[47] The Supreme Court probably saw in this statute a "blanket authority to law enforcement officers to incarcerate unemployed ex-convicts."[48] Thus, the statute was invalidated in *Lanzetta* for reasons similar to those for invalidating the vagrancy ordinance in *Papachristou*. In fact, they were both "street-cleaning" statutes aimed at preventing future criminality by targeting "undesirables."[49]

Later we will come back to *Papachristou* and *Lanzetta* and compare them with another line of cases (that of public morals statutes) in an attempt to understand the practical implications of the two rationales of the vagueness doctrine (i.e., fair warning and law enforcement discretion).

Public Morals Statutes (Roth and Rose)
Quite differently from its attitude in cases of "street-cleaning" statutes, the Supreme Court tends to tolerate the use of vague terms in statutes dealing with public morals. Many of these laws target sexual matters. They are aimed at punishing sexual behaviours or sexual illustrations that are deemed particularly reprehensible by society. Since a wide variety of situations have the potential of offending the moral values of society in sexual matters, such legislation often uses vague terms, such as "indecent" or "obscene." The Court usually upholds these statutes, arguing that it would be impossible for the legislature to draft more precisely.

The case of *Roth v. United States*[50] is a good example of the tendency of the Court to uphold this kind of legislation. In *Roth,* a California statute punished the production or distribution of any "obscene" writing, picture, or print. The Court defined obscenity as follows: "Whether to the average person, applying contemporary community standards, the dominant theme of the material taken as a whole appeals to the prurient interest."[51] So defined, the Court held that obscenity was outside the protection of the First Amendment and sufficiently precise to meet the requirements of the void-for-vagueness doctrine.[52] Note that the concept of obscenity was further developed by the Court in *Memoirs v. Massachusetts*[53] and *Miller v. California,*[54] always with the purpose of making the definition more precise and manageable. With that process of interpretation, the Court was able to avoid the problem of vagueness and the statutes were upheld.

Another good example of the upholding of legislation addressing public morals is the case of *Rose v. Locke*.[55] The challenged statute provided that "crimes against nature, either with mankind or any beast, are punishable by imprisonment in the penitentiary not less than five (5) nor more than fifteen (15) years." In the case at bar, the defendant was convicted of having forced his victim to submit to cunnilingus. In light of unclear and inconsistent court decisions of different states on the matter,[56] cunnilingus was held to fall within the prohibition of "crimes against nature." Again, as in the *Roth* case, the objectively imprecise words of the statute were insufficient to trigger constitutional invalidity.

At first glance, one could argue, for example, that the expression "crimes against nature" upheld in *Rose* was not any more precise than the word "gang" that led to the invalidation of the statute in *Lanzetta*. Admitting that more legislative precision was impracticable without compromising the objectives of the public morals statutes,[57] the same argument could be made with regard to the crime-prevention purposes of the "street-cleaning" statutes.[58] In order to understand the underlying reasons for the Court's decisions, it is essential to pursue the analysis a little further. This will be accomplished by taking a closer look at the extent to which the Court is willing to protect the two rationales of the vagueness doctrine (i.e., legality and the rule of law).

The Two Rationales of the American Vagueness Doctrine

Fair Warning

One of the two basic concerns of the void-for-vagueness doctrine is to ensure that citizens are given fair warning of what is prescribed by law.[59] The constitutional legitimacy of this concern is derived from a general ideal of fairness protected by procedural due process.[60] It is important to realize, however, that the Supreme Court's protection of this concept of fair warning has become somewhat detached from its classical meaning. Naturally understood, the requirement of fair warning in relation to vagueness would require that the law itself be precise enough to reasonably guide citizens in their conduct: "That the terms of a penal statute creating a new offense must be sufficiently explicit to inform those who are subject to it what conduct on their part will render them liable to its penalties is a well-recognized requirement, consonant alike with ordinary notions of fair play and the settled rules of law; and a statute which either forbids or requires the doing of an act in terms so vague that men of common intelligence must necessarily guess at its meaning and differ as to its application violates the first essential of due process of law."[61]

The fair warning rationale, as protected by the vagueness doctrine in the United States, is not as straightforward as this classic judicial statement might seem to indicate. John Calvin Jeffries Jr., a leading commentator on vagueness in the United States, notes that the "core concept of notice"[62] is not so significantly related to the precision of the language used in the statute (or in the judicial decisions interpreting it) but rather to "whether the ordinary and ordinarily law-abiding individual would have received some signal that his or her conduct risked violation of the penal law."[63] In other words, the focus is not so much on the language of the law as it is on the values and habits of the community. If a law regulates conduct that is generally perceived as triggering risks of legal liability, the fair warning rationale is not really a concern. But if the vagueness of a law gives it a reach so great as to prohibit acts that are generally perceived as innocent, then the concern of notice becomes relevant.

It is interesting to note that this concept of fair warning can be offended even if a law is quite specific. In fact, Jeffries uses the example of *Lambert v. California*,[64] which is not a vagueness case, to illustrate his conclusion on the actual content of the fair warning rationale. In this case, the Supreme Court of the United States invalidated a Los Angeles ordinance that made it criminal for any person convicted of a felony to remain in the city for more than five days without satisfying certain registration procedures. This requirement is rather unusual. The reasons given by the Court for invalidating the legislation (even though the text was clear on its own) were expressed as follows by Justice Douglas:

> Her default was entirely innocent ... We believe that actual knowledge of the duty to register or proof of the probability of such knowledge and subsequent failure to comply are necessary before a conviction under the ordinance can stand. As Holmes wrote in The Common Law, "A law which punished conduct which would not be blameworthy in the average member of the community would be too severe for that community to bear." ... Its severity lies in the absence of an opportunity either to avoid the consequences of the law or to defend any prosecution brought under it. Where a person did not know of the duty to register and where there was no proof of the probability of such knowledge, he may not be convicted consistently with due process. Were it otherwise, the evil would be as great as it is when the law is written in print too fine to read or in a language foreign to the community.[65]

As the requirement of registration was highly unusual, the fair warning given by the Los Angeles ordinance was defective as its existence might very well have been unknown by the majority of citizens. With this particular concept of fair warning in mind, it becomes easier to understand the different treatment by the Court of the "street-cleaning" statutes on the one hand and the public morals legislation on the other. When a conduct is socially seen as innocent, and therefore perceived by the average citizen as not triggering penal liability, the rationale of fair warning comes into play with greater intensity. It is revealing that this type of "innocent" conduct often falls under the breadth of typical "street-cleaning" statutes. For example, the "common night walkers" or "persons able to work but habitually living upon the earnings of their wives" targeted by the Jacksonville ordinance in *Papachristou*[66] are not generally perceived by the population as being in conflict with the law. Note that the two latter prohibitions do not use a language that is particularly vague. They are nonetheless unconstitutional in that they contribute to giving the statute a very large breadth, thus reaching too far into "innocent" conduct. This concern was openly expressed by Justice Douglas, who delivered the opinion of the Court in *Papachristou*:[67] "The Jacksonville ordinance makes criminal activities which by modern standards are normally innocent ... these activities are historically part of the amenities of life as we have known them."[68]

The same type of concern can be expressed about the statute struck down in *Lanzetta*.[69] Since the State Court definition of "gang" included persons acting together for some purpose "usually criminal" or "mainly for criminal purposes," some activities that were not criminal could have fallen within the meaning of the statute. As the Supreme Court said, "so defined, the purposes of those constituting some gangs may be commendable."[70] In that sense, the statute failed to give the kind of notice that is the most important. Since the purposes of the gang may have been innocent, a citizen would have had no reason to think that belonging to this gang might trigger penal liability. This corresponds to the "core concept of notice" that Jeffries identified as being protected by the vagueness doctrine.

On the other hand, it is easy to see how the statutes regulating public morals involved in the *Roth*[71] and *Rose*[72] cases were less problematic with regard to the fair warning rationale. The acts involved in these cases would most likely have been perceived by the average citizen as involving the risk of legal sanctions. The defendants could therefore not claim that punishment under these statutes would create a true surprise for the accused. For example, in *Rose,* even if the prohibition of "crimes against nature" was probably even more vague than the "gang" standard in *Lanzetta*, the defendant could not claim that the average citizen at the time would not have suspected that forcing someone to submit to cunnilingus might trigger some kind of legal liability. By the same token, even if the "obscene material" rule in *Roth* could be seen as establishing a very fuzzy line, any individual who treaded close to that line could not argue that he had no clue he was entering into dangerous territory.

Law Enforcement Discretion

The second major concern generally identified as a rationale for the vagueness doctrine is the desire to prevent the arbitrary enforcement of laws.[73] This rationale is derived from the ideal of the rule of law,[74] which is, as we saw earlier, especially compelling in the area of coercive legislation. Thus, for example, when a criminal offence is defined in vague terms, the citizen's liberty is subject to the discretion of law enforcement. This reality is problematic because it is arbitrary. Of course, discretion is often necessary in the administration of justice, and must certainly not be seen as plainly illegitimate. What the "arbitrary enforcement" rationale of the vagueness doctrine is designed to eradicate is the *unnecessary* granting of discretion.

What I have just stated is the natural understanding of the arbitrary enforcement rationale under the rule of law. It must be noted, however, that American courts are only partially committed to the defence of this concern. They will find the rationale to be offended in practice mainly in cases where there is a probability of selective enforcement. If "undesirables" are likely to be targeted by law-enforcing authorities and if convictions will almost automatically follow decisions to prosecute because of the breadth (or "catch-all" character) of the law, such a law will be constitutionally vulnerable. On the other hand, the vagueness doctrine will rarely protect against the mere existence of unnecessary discretion, despite the fact that it may be inconsistent with the rule of law. In other words, even if the person who enforces the law is likely to base his decisions on arbitrary considerations such as his personal preferences, the arbitrary enforcement rationale will not be seen as offended in the United States. The important thing is that the law not be a catch-all designed to be selectively enforced and leading to automatic conviction when prosecution occurs. As a consequence of this practice, discretion given to the judiciary is generally perceived as less suspect because courts operate in the public eye and therefore are perhaps less likely to let their decisions be influenced by discriminatory considerations. On the other hand, police officers and prosecutors operate informally. They do not have to give reasons for their decisions. The abuse of discretionary power given to them is often hidden and can more easily be based on "evil" purposes.[75]

The "selective enforcement" criterion of the void-for-vagueness doctrine is openly recognized by the Court as being part of the broader "antiarbitrary" rationale. Understandably, "the 'worst case' breakdown of the rule of law is not random whim or caprice but hidden bias and prejudice."[76] In the United States, the law enforcement discretion rationale of the vagueness doctrine does not in practice often reach any further than this core concept of selective enforcement. Indeed, it is revealing to see that the laws that are the most vulnerable under the vagueness doctrine are those that fall within the category of "street-cleaning" statutes. These laws are generally local ordinances prohibiting loitering and vagrancy in terms so broad and encompassing that the police can arrest almost anyone who is perceived as an "undesirable."[77] Consider the cases of *Papachristou*[78] and *Lanzetta*[79] referred to earlier. Not only did the provisions challenged in these two cases allow selective enforcement, they encouraged it. These "street-cleaning" statutes were aimed especially at certain categories of individuals and were therefore vulnerable under the core meaning of the arbitrary enforcement rationale (i.e., risks of selective enforcement). In *Lanzetta*, the statute was believed to have been drafted in broad terms to "grant a blanket authority to law enforcement officers to incarcerate ex-convicts."[80] As for *Papachristou*, the variety of broad terms used in the ordinance were especially designed to serve as a catch-all giving dictatorial power to the police to arrest the deemed "undesirables." In practice, these kinds of vagrancy ordinances are often enforced against the poor[81] or against racial minorities.[82] Thus, it is probably not a coincidence that the defendants in *Papachristou* were two black men and two white women riding together in a car on the city's main thoroughfare.[83] On the other hand, the statutes challenged in *Roth*[84] and *Rose*[85] did not have these characteristics. For example, in *Roth* the vague prohibition of the legislation ("obscene material") may have given discretion to law enforcement authorities or to judges and juries to create their own standards. However, that arbitrariness did not threaten to become discriminatory, nor did it lead one to believe that it was designed to be a catch-all promoting dictatorial and selective enforcement by the authorities.

Only in exceptional cases will the Court invalidate a law for vagueness solely on the basis that it permits arbitrary (but not discriminatory) enforcement. A rare example of this is the case of *Giacco v. Pennsylvania*.[86] Here, the Court invalidated a statute that gave absolute discretion to juries to assess costs against defendants acquitted of misdemeanours. The statute had been construed by the State Courts as requiring that the defendant be guilty of "some misconduct."[87] The Supreme Court struck down the legislation since it "contain[ed] no standard at all."[88] The property rights of the defendant were at the mercy of the jury, which could create its own standards for decision. Note that the statute's flaw was not the risk of selective enforcement but only the more neutral risk of arbitrary enforcement. The legislation in *Giacco* was not of the "street-cleaning" type giving a dictatorial power to police officers. There was no reason to believe its enforcement would be guided by "evil" purposes. Still, the discretionary power given to the jury was not compatible with the principle of "government by law" and the statute was declared unconstitutional.

As noted, the approach in *Giacco* is not usually the one that, despite its merit, is favoured by the Supreme Court of the United States. As further manifestation of this reality, consider the case of *Jordan v. De George,*[89] which will conclude my observations on the American situation. The federal statute challenged in this case provided for the deportation of aliens having been convicted more than once of a "crime involving moral turpitude." The respondent had been convicted twice of conspiracy to defraud the United States of taxes on alcohol. The indefiniteness of the expression "crime of moral turpitude" made it difficult to know what Congress meant, but the statute was held valid by a majority of the Court. Alcohol tax fraud was found to fall within the statutory language since "a crime in which fraud is an ingredient involve[s] ... moral turpitude."[90]

The majority, led by Chief Justice Vinson, did not examine in great detail how the rationales of fair warning and arbitrary enforcement were satisfied in this case. It was sufficient to say that "the language conveys sufficiently definite warning as to the prescribed conduct when measured by common understanding and practices."[91] Note that the core concern of fair warning that I earlier identified as being protected (i.e., if the average citizen would have had reasons to avoid the conduct) was not offended in *Jordan* because, obviously, to be a "crime of moral turpitude" a conduct has to first qualify as a crime (assuming that this crime was itself defined with sufficient precision). With regard to the arbitrary enforcement rationale, nothing indicated that the law was designed to be a catch-all serving as a tool to give administrative officials dictatorial power to deport aliens on a discriminatory basis. In other words, the statute did not present the flaws that characterize vagrancy-type legislation or other "street-cleaning" statutes. The partial protection of legality and the rule of law I identified earlier were not triggered by the statute, nor was any substantive concern such as freedom of speech involved. The statute was therefore upheld. At the same time, important concerns regarding legality and the rule of law were being defeated.

It is important to realize that deportation has very severe consequences in the life of an individual, perhaps even more than criminal penalties. In enacting the statute involved in *Jordan,* it is not hard to imagine that Congress could have been more specific without compromising its purposes. It could have enumerated the categories of crimes it was aiming at, instead of using the vague expression "crimes involving moral turpitude." This would have provided a better warning to citizens and, perhaps even more significantly, it would have been more consistent with the rule of law. Even though the enforcement of the statute is not likely to be guided by "evil" purposes, it still permits judges to create their own standards according to their personal preferences. As Justice Jackson points out in dissent: "how many aliens have been deported who would not have been had some other judge heard their cases, and vice versa, we may only guess. That is not government by law."[92] In that sense, the dissent in *Jordan* is in the same line as *Giacco:* it seeks to protect citizens from arbitrary government, which complies in a more complete manner with the ideal of the rule of law.

The Content of the Vagueness Doctrine in Canada

As we know, vagueness as a constitutional vice is a recent phenomenon in our country. The case that stands out as the authority on the matter is the 1992 decision of the Supreme Court of Canada in *Nova Scotia Pharmaceutical.* In this unanimous decision, the Court commented substantially (which it had never done in the past)[93] on the two rationales of vagueness, namely, the desire to provide "fair notice to citizens" and to avoid the arbitrary enforcement of laws. It also elaborated a test, which I will refer to as the "legal debate test," to determine whether a piece of legislation is unconstitutionally vague. These notions will be presented and commented upon below in an attempt to discover their implications and assess their merit in relation to the problem of vagueness.

The Rationale of Fair Notice

Normally understood, fair notice seeks to ensure that citizens are able to determine the extent of their legal rights and obligations. Vague laws offend the principle of legality mainly because they create unfair surprise for individuals. The problem is similar to the one discussed in Chapter 1 regarding *ex post facto* laws. Thus, when a law is overly vague, its interpretation amounts to a newly created standard. This resembles retroactivity if this standard is applied to a set of facts that took place in the past, as citizens are then unfairly trapped.

The Supreme Court's Account of Fair Notice:
The "Substratum of Values" Issue
In the context of the vagueness doctrine, the text of the statute must be precise enough to allow a citizen *who reads it* to know with a reasonable degree of approximation what is forbidden and what is not. This is, as mentioned earlier,[94] the classic understanding of fair notice as related to the vagueness doctrine. In the *Nova Scotia Pharmaceutical* case, however, the Supreme Court of Canada stated a quite different understanding of the concept of fair notice.

According to Gonthier J., writing for the Court, the fair notice rationale has two components, one formal and the other substantive. The formal aspect is related to the knowledge citizens have of the actual text of the statute.[95] This relates to the question of whether the accused has actually read the law. As Gonthier J. reasoned, this formal notice is not of primary importance considering the principle that "ignorance of the law is no excuse."[96] We therefore usually presume that this requirement is satisfied. The main component of the notice rationale according to the Supreme Court lies in its substantive aspect. The question is whether citizens have been warned or are conscious of the reprehensible nature of a particular course of conduct, regardless of whether they have actually read the text of the statute. Gonthier J. explains the issue as follows:

> There is also a substantive aspect to fair notice, which could be described as a notice, an understanding that some conduct comes under the law. Jeffries, *supra,* calls this the "core concept of notice" (p. 211).
>
> Let me take homicide as an example. The actual provisions of the *Criminal Code* dealing with homicide are numerous (comprising the core of ss. 222-240 and other related sections). When one completes the picture of the *Code* with case law, both substantive and constitutional, the result is a fairly intricate body of rules. Notwithstanding formal notice, it can hardly be expected of the average citizen that he know the law of homicide in detail. Yet no one would seriously argue that there is no substantive fair notice here, or that the law of homicide is vague. It can readily be seen why this is so. First of all, everyone (or sadly, should I say, almost everyone) has an inherent knowledge that taking the life of another human being is wrong. There is a deeply-rooted perception that homicide cannot be tolerated, whether one comes to this perception from a moral, religious or sociological stance. Therefore it is expected that homicide will be punished by the State. Secondly, homicide is indeed punished by the State, and homicide trials and sentences receive a great deal of publicity.
>
> I used homicide as an example, because it lies so at the core of our criminal law and our shared values that substantive notice is easy to demonstrate. Similar demonstrations could be made, at greater length, for other legal provisions. The substantive aspect of fair notice is therefore a subjective understanding that the law touches upon some conduct, based on the substratum of values underlying the legal enactment and on the role that the legal enactment plays in the life of the society.[97]

Therefore, the primary method of knowing whether substantial fair notice is satisfied is based on a study of the "substratum of values" underlying the legal enactment. As Gonthier J.'s illustration indicates, the provisions of the *Criminal Code* on homicide are not problematic in relation to fair notice because as a matter of values, most people perceive the act of killing another person as being wrong and expect it to be punished by law. Note that when the legislative provision is not based on any "substratum of values" shared by the community, the requirement of notice can be satisfied if the State has compensated for this weakness by attracting people's attention to the content of the provision.[98] For example, as Gonthier J.

explains, publicity and advertisement related to demerit points and driver's licence suspensions allow for such provisions to satisfy substantive notice despite the weakness of the link with the "substratum of values" of society.[99]

Thus, the Supreme Court links the fair warning rationale to the presence of a "substratum of values," or its equivalent through advertisement of the law, as far as they indicate that citizens are subjectively conscious of the reprehensible character of a conduct. Note that this view is quite different from the traditional view of fair notice as related to vagueness. Pursuant to the traditional view, the relevant question is whether the vagueness of the text will prevent a citizen reading the law from understanding its implications. However, with the Supreme Court's view, the question is whether the community is subjectively conscious of the prohibition, regardless of the statute's precision and regardless of whether citizens have actually read it.

It is interesting to note that the Supreme Court's account of the fair notice rationale is very similar to the American situation described earlier. We recall that the main aspect of fair warning, as enforced by the Supreme Court of the United States under the due process clauses, refers to the protection of what can be perceived as innocent conduct. The main question with regard to fair notice is whether the conduct for which the accused is being prosecuted is viewed by the average citizen as triggering risks of legal liability.[100] Contrary to the Supreme Court of Canada in *Nova Scotia Pharmaceutical,* the Supreme Court of the United States has never made a clear statement to that effect, and generally describes notice by referring to its classic conception. However, as we have seen by comparing cases of "street-cleaning" statutes (*Papachristou* and *Lanzetta*) with cases of public morals legislation (*Roth* and *Rose*), the general attitude of the Supreme Court of the United States in cases of vagueness is to uphold laws that possess a sufficient link to the "substratum of values" of society, as Gonthier J. would put it in the Canadian context.

In light of this similarity between the approaches taken by the Supreme Court of Canada and the Supreme Court of the United States, it is revealing that when Gonthier J. explained the fair warning rationale in *Nova Scotia Pharmaceutical,* he in fact referred to the article written by John Calvin Jeffries Jr. in the United States, in which this "core concept of notice" is discussed.[101] In his leading article published in 1985, Jeffries points to the case of *Lambert v. California,*[102] which I described earlier, as being the best illustration of the type of fair warning that is currently protected under the due process clauses.[103] We recall that in *Lambert,* an unusual Los Angeles ordinance transforming into a crime a failure to satisfy certain registration procedures had been struck down by the Supreme Court of the United States because such conduct "would not be blameworthy in the average member of the community."[104] Fair warning was offended because the conduct did not have any foundation in the "substratum of values" of the community, and therefore the accused could hardly have been conscious of the illegal character of his acts.

Understanding the Roles of the "Substratum of Values" and
Fair Notice in Relation to Vagueness
What conclusions should be drawn from the Supreme Court of Canada's approach to fair warning in terms of the "substratum of values" in *Nova Scotia Pharmaceutical?* First, could it allow the invalidation of a law on the sole ground that it is detached from the "substratum of values" of society, even if it is not lacking in precision as in *Lambert* in the United States? This question is a delicate one. There are many statutes in the books that do not reflect the values of society at large, and of which average citizens are unaware. Does Gonthier J. mean to say that all these statutes will be invalid unless the government compensates for this weakness by calling the public's attention to these laws through publicity and advertisement? It is unlikely. This would be an innovative encroachment on the sovereignty of Parliament. This type of constitutional limitation would clearly stand apart from traditional fair warning requirements related to the promulgation of statutes. It is well known that publication of a statute in the books is the manner in which its content is usually made public. To declare unconstitutional all the laws that contain no link with the values of society, or to require that the government set up advertisement campaigns in relation to all these laws, would constitute an important limitation on State power. It is safer to read the Court's comments on the "substratum of values" issue in light of the following passage of Gonthier J.'s reasons, where he summarizes his view on fair warning: "Fair notice may not have been given *when enactments are in somewhat general terms,* in a way that does not readily permit citizens to be aware of their substance, when they do not relate to any element of the substratum of values held by society."[105]

The fact that Gonthier J. says "when enactments are in somewhat general terms" seems to imply that his views on the "substratum of values" are limited to the vagueness doctrine, especially considering that they were formulated in the context of a vagueness case. There might be one reservation to this, however. It might be considered, although this is debatable, that in criminal cases the "substratum of values" issue could invalidate laws independently. As already noted, Gonthier J. referred to Jeffries's article in the context of his explanation of the "substratum of values" issue. In fact, Gonthier J. even referred to the specific page of the article where Jeffries discusses in detail the *Lambert* case.[106] Although this seems to indicate that the Supreme Court of Canada approved the reasoning of that decision to assess fair notice, it is important to realize that *Lambert* was a criminal case. In the same line, when Jeffries was summarizing the "core concept of notice" in his article, he was concerned exclusively with penal statutes. Thus, while the *Lambert* reasoning may not be imported to all legislative schemes in Canada, its application to criminal provisions may be possible. As we have already seen, the concept of notice is most important as applied to penal law, and especially criminal law. Interestingly, it is these types of laws that usually contain values that citizens are aware of. It may therefore be speculated, following *Nova Scotia Pharmaceutical,* that a criminal provision not lacking in precision could be found unconstitutional for lack of notice if it is too remotely linked to the "substratum of values" of society, provided that the State does nothing to compensate for this defect through publicity or advertisement. It is difficult to apply the same reasoning to other types of laws, such as civil or administrative laws, for instance. The argument is more easily applicable to criminal laws because these laws are usually expected to reflect society's values. Thus, citizens are generally aware of their approximate content. They do not know all the details, but they usually have a sense of what might trigger criminal liability. Considering in addition the severe consequences of criminal convictions for individuals, it is conceivable that *Nova Scotia Pharmaceutical* could be read as requiring that criminal laws satisfy "substantive notice" even if they are not lacking in precision. Note that this would not impair the State's ability to reach its substantive aims because a law's weakness in relation to substantive notice could always be compensated for by publicity and advertisement. For example, several years ago drinking and driving was not criminal and was not perceived as criminal by the majority of citizens. When provisions were enacted in the *Criminal Code* to punish impaired driving,[107] large advertising campaigns were put forward to inform the public. Through this technique, adequate notice was given to citizens and these laws were gradually imported into the "substratum of values" of society.

My second inquiry on the "substratum of values" question pertains to its role in relation to the vagueness doctrine. How imperative is the issue of substantive notice in the analysis of vagueness in a given case? In other words, if a law does relate to the "substratum of values" of society, will it be upheld automatically no matter how vague it is? Here the question reaches another extreme. Whereas I was wondering in the preceding paragraphs whether the "substratum of values" issue can invalidate a law by itself, I am now asking whether it can be sufficient on its own to uphold a law. First of all, in answering this question it must not be forgotten that notice is not the only rationale underlying the vagueness doctrine. The concern of controlling law enforcement discretion, which I will examine later in greater detail, must also be considered in relation to vague laws. It therefore seems unlikely that the substantive notice issue would be sufficient to uphold a vague provision without even an examination of whether this provision represents a risk of arbitrary enforcement. Moreover, as will be seen later, the Supreme Court in *Nova Scotia Pharmaceutical* has developed a particular test for determining whether legislation is overly vague. The criterion is whether the enactment represents a "sufficient basis for legal debate."[108] It seems that if a law fails this test it will be unconstitutional, regardless of whether it satisfies the "substratum of values" question. Finally, we must not forget the importance of the classic conception of notice, which refers to the clarity of the actual text of the statute as it can be understood by citizens who read it. Note that the Court in *Nova Scotia Pharmaceutical* did not completely eliminate this aspect of notice as it maintained that legal enactment must "sufficiently delineate [an] area of risk"[109] in order to satisfy the constitutional norm. This idea obviously calls upon the precision of the command directed towards citizens and renders relevant the actual precision of the legislative text.

The classic conception of fair notice (i.e., clarity of the legal message sent to citizens) must remain as one of the two logical rationales of the vagueness doctrine, the other being the concern for controlling discretion. If this view is abandoned, it will be misleading to refer to a "vagueness doctrine." The analysis of laws under the vagueness doctrine must focus primarily on the clarity of the legal message, rather than on the values of society, which are relatively foreign to what the law contains and outside the control of the legislature.[110] Holding otherwise would negate the idea that citizens can and sometimes do consult the law, either directly or through legal counsel, to find out the extent of their legal rights and obligations. When citizens do consult the law, clarity of the legislative message does play an important role. It is this type of situation that the vagueness doctrine was originally designed to address through its first rationale of fair notice. It would be unduly patronizing to completely forget this idea in order to focus exclusively on the subjective understanding by citizens that certain conduct comes under law.

However, this does not mean the "substratum of values" question put forward by the Supreme Court is not useful. Its function is one of balancing. In other words, it can make the requirement of precision fluctuate from case to case. Thus, the constitutional standard should be heightened when the legislative enactment is so separated from the community's values that individuals have no reason to suspect that a particular conduct comes under law. Conversely, when the law is related to the "substratum of values" of society, the constitutional standard of precision should be relaxed. Let us note that the Court's approach to vagueness in concrete cases is not inconsistent with this view. Consider the case of *Canadian Pacific*, where a provision of the *Environmental Protection Act*[111] containing a general prohibition on pollution "of the natural environment for any use that can be made of it" was challenged under the vagueness doctrine. While upholding the law, Gonthier J. made the following comments in relation to fair warning:

> In 1988, when the pollution in the instant case took place, few citizens would have been aware of the actual terms of s. 13(1)(a) EPA. However, the average citizen in Ontario would have known that pollution was statutorily prohibited. It therefore would not have come as a surprise to citizens that the EPA prohibited the emission of contaminants into the environment that were likely to impair a use of the natural environment. In my view, the purpose and terms of s. 13(1)(a) are so closely related to the societal value of environmental protection that substantive notice of the prohibition in s. 13(1)(a) is easy to demonstrate.[112]

And further: "I therefore conclude that the purpose and subject matter of s. 13(1)(a) EPA, *the societal values underlying it,* and its nature as a regulatory offence, all *inform the analysis* of CP's s. 7 vagueness claim."[113]

In the latter passage, the Court is in fact using the "substratum of values" issue as a balancing factor rather than a strict and determining criterion, as it refers to it as an element that "inform[s] the analysis" of vagueness. Thus, influenced by the "substratum of values" issue, *inter alia,* the Court indicated that it was willing to be more tolerant towards the legislative assembly as to the precision of the language used in the provision.[114] The Court did not stop there with its analysis, however, as the mere presence of a modulating factor is not sufficient to conclude that the law is valid. Thus, after highlighting the influence of the values question, the Court indicated that "keeping this in mind, it is now necessary to consider the actual terms of s. 13(1)(a),"[115] which it did to finally conclude that the law was valid.

Therefore, the "subjective conscience" or "substratum of values" issue is not a strictly determining factor. It does not exempt courts from looking at the precision of the legal enactment itself. Such a task must still be undertaken to determine whether citizens who read the law would be able to understand it. The values of society, however, can have an impact in making the requirement of precision fluctuate. Thus, courts will be more permissive towards the legislature as far as precision is concerned if citizens are generally aware that a type of conduct comes under law. The requirement of precision will be heightened if the "substratum of values" factor is not satisfied, with the exception of criminal law where, as we have seen above, it could be sufficient to invalidate a law on its own.

To summarize the role of the notice and "substratum of values" issues, let us consider an illustration. Section 250 of the *Criminal Code* provides an interesting framework for our discussion. It states the following:

250.(1) *[Failure to keep watch on person towed]* Every one who operates a vessel while towing a person on any water skis, surf-board, water sled or other object, when there is not on board such vessel another responsible person keeping watch on the person being towed, is guilty of an offence punishable on summary conviction.

(2) *[Towing of person after dark]* Every one who operates a vessel while towing a person on any water skis, surf-board, water sled or other object during the period from one hour after sunset to sunrise is guilty of an offence punishable on summary conviction.

Concerning the second paragraph, it is obviously not vague since the statutory language clearly indicates what is prohibited. At first glance, it is therefore not constitutionally vulnerable. However, since this is a criminal provision, we have seen that the "substratum of values" issue can perhaps be sufficient to invalidate it on its own. Although the conduct targeted by this provision is inherently dangerous and one would probably expect it to be prohibited by boating statutes, the average citizen would most likely be quite surprised to know that such conduct is *criminally* punishable. Although this type of conduct may very well represent a high degree of danger, it is not generally perceived socially as so morally reprehensible as to deserve the stigma of criminal conviction. Morally reprehensible acts are usually public nuisances. Water skiing at night represents a danger only for the skier himself. In some cases, the danger may even be overstated. For example, if individuals were water skiing on a private lake on an evening when the moon shed sufficient light or where artificial lighting has been installed, they might be quite surprised if they were arrested and prosecuted under s. 250(2). Thus, it might be argued that this provision could be invalid under the authority of *Nova Scotia Pharmaceutical* as in the American case of *Lambert,* unless the government compensated for this weakness by attracting the attention of the public to this prohibition through publicity or advertisement.[116]

As far as the first paragraph is concerned, which criminalizes towing a person on water skis when there is not on the boat "another responsible person keeping watch on the person being towed," it is also remote from the "substratum of values" of society. Again, while safety obviously calls for the presence of an observer on the boat, one would not instinctively think that the stigma of *criminal* prosecution could follow a violation of this rule. In this case, an element of vagueness can be found in the "responsible person" element of the provision. What precisely determines whether a person is responsible? Is it a matter of age? If a fourteen-year-old person is keeping watch on the person being towed, for example, we do not know whether or not the provision is violated. Normally, an expression such as "responsible person" would probably not be so vague as to lead to the conclusion that the law is unconstitutional. Under the Supreme Court's *Nova Scotia Pharmaceutical* criterion, the "responsible person" element probably provides a sufficient "basis for legal debate." However, it could be considered that since the law is not linked to the "substratum of values" of society (unlike most other criminal offences), the constitutional standard of precision will be higher. Thus, the "responsible person" criterion could be unconstitutional through this reasoning.

This focus on the values of society to assess the validity of laws is somewhat similar to the tendency we observed in cases such as *Finta*,[117] *Dobbert*,[118] and the *Marital Rape Case*[119] to uphold breaches of legality more easily when highly reprehensible conduct is involved. As we saw in Chapter 1 when we examined the contours of the principle of legality, courts tend to close their eyes to the *ex post facto* operation of laws more easily when the act being prosecuted is highly repugnant to the moral values of society.[120] Thus, in *Finta*, the provisions of the *Criminal Code* targeting World War II criminals were upheld despite the fact that the accused's actions were not criminal at the time they were committed. Recall that the exceptions contained in s. 11(g) of the *Charter*, which allow prosecutions for criminal violations of "international law or ... the general principles of law recognized by the community of nations," could not be resorted to by the Crown in *Finta* according to the majority, because the acts were not criminal according to these norms in 1944. The acts could have involved collective responsibility at the time, but not individual criminal liability. The Court nevertheless upheld the provisions because of the nature of the acts involved. As Professor Kelsen stated in his article cited by the Court, "justice required the punishment of these men, in spite of the fact that under positive law they were not punishable at the time."[121] Therefore, the fair notice requirement – common to vagueness and the principle against *ex post facto* legislation – is more easily held to be satisfied by judges when the acts targeted offend society's values. However, it should be recalled that in all these cases (*Finta, Dobbert,* and the *Marital Rape Case*), legality had not been totally ignored. Although the courts were less demanding towards the government in the way it provided "notice," some kind of advance warning could still be found in the legislative schemes involved that would indicate that the conduct could be criminally punishable.[122] Similarly, in vagueness we have noted that the "substratum of values" issue cannot be sufficient by itself to uphold a law, as some reasonable degree of warning must still be found in the text of the legislative enactment. Thus, the moral values of society can "have an influence on the analysis of vagueness" (to use Gonthier J.'s words), but they cannot completely set aside the vagueness doctrine, just as these considerations could not completely set aside legality in *Finta, Dobbert,* and the *Marital Rape Case*.

The Rationale of Law Enforcement Discretion

The second rationale of the Canadian vagueness doctrine, as is the case in the United States, is the need to limit discretion in law enforcement. A vague law necessarily gives a greater discretionary power to the enforcing authority since the standard it contains leaves the decision open to a substantial range of possibilities. As this represents an element of arbitrariness in the administration of justice, it touches upon the chief concern identified earlier in relation to the principle of the rule of law: protecting citizens from arbitrary government.

This second rationale of the vagueness doctrine can be perceived to enjoy a certain form of primacy over the first one, insofar as it is more universally applicable than the question of fair notice. It must be realized that fair notice lends itself to a real analysis only in relation to laws that impose commands on citizens. They are most often laws creating penal offences. It is then relevant to ask whether the law has sufficiently delineated an area of risk so as to allow citizens to know what conduct is prohibited. But the vagueness doctrine can sometimes be applied to laws that purport to do something other than create penal offences. These laws do not necessarily involve a command to citizens in relation to which fair notice must be satisfied. Often, the law will not even speak to citizens, and will be oriented directly towards the executive or the judiciary. For example, in *Morales*,[123] s. 515(10)(b) of the *Criminal Code* was regulating in vague terms the bail conditions in the criminal process. This provision, like many other legislative enactments in Canada, was speaking directly to the judge, and it was therefore obviously futile to examine the fair notice rationale in that context. On the other hand, the law enforcement discretion rationale is always likely to receive some application in cases of vagueness. Since any law is likely to be eventually interpreted and applied by a court, the law enforcement discretion concern possesses a universal character that can confer upon it some kind of logical primacy.

We saw in Chapter 2 (on the rule of law) that the notion of "government by laws, not by individuals" is a very important constitutional ideal in Canada. In light especially of the preamble to the *Charter*, we saw that discretion in law should be limited to what is reasonably necessary without impinging on the legislative objectives. Thus, discretion created by vague laws will be legitimate when its presence is reasonably necessary in relation to the legislative scheme. By "reasonably necessary," it is not only the linguistic inability to articulate a rule that is being referred to. The notion must be understood in a broader sense that considers the need for the flexibility of discretion in instances where the State is attempting to reach complex legislative goals. Also, we have seen that coercive laws call for stricter limits to discretionary powers than other laws, such as those governing the administration of the State. Thus, we should be more tolerant than "reasonable necessity" when assessing the validity of laws that have a less direct impact on citizens' rights and obligations. In this regard, criminal laws require a more rigorous analysis of "reasonable necessity." Considering their serious repercussions on individuals, these laws are traditionally subject to greater scrutiny, although even in that field wide discretionary powers can also be legitimate when their allocation is required by the legislative objectives.[124]

The Court's Limited Understanding of the Discretion Rationale
in Nova Scotia Pharmaceutical
In a nutshell, we have seen thus far that the Constitution requires discretion to be limited to what is "reasonably necessary," especially in relation to coercive laws. The purpose is to ensure a level of certainty in our legal system without frustrating the need for flexibility. One would logically expect the vagueness doctrine to reflect this reality through its second rationale, that of law enforcement discretion. However, it must be noted that the Supreme Court of Canada in *Nova Scotia Pharmaceutical* did not voice the question of law enforcement discretion in this manner. Instead, Gonthier J. presented the second rationale of the vagueness doctrine as follows: "A law must not be so devoid of precision in its content that a conviction will automatically flow from the decision to prosecute. Such is the crux of the concern for limitation of enforcement discretion. When the power to decide whether a charge will lead to conviction or acquittal, normally the preserve of the judiciary, becomes fused with the power to prosecute because of the wording of the law, then a law will be unconstitutionally vague."[125]

Taken in isolation, this idea may be difficult to understand. The Court maintains that a law will be too vague if "a conviction will automatically flow from the decision to prosecute." Shortly after the case, one commentator wrote the following in relation to this standard: "[Translation] We can only note ... the extremely marginal character of this criterion: legislative texts which can trigger its application will inevitably be very rare, if existent at all. In addition, vagueness, leading to ambiguity, seems more likely to create a conflict on the interpretation to be given to the text than to lead to an automatic conviction as soon as the decision to prosecute has been taken. Paradoxically, it is absolute precision that, by eliminating any debate on the meaning of the text, can lead to a conviction as soon as prosecution occurs."[126]

A sensible understanding of the Supreme Court's "automatic conviction" assertion can be reached more easily when viewed in light of the American version of the law enforcement discretion rationale. In the United States, courts will find the rationale to be offended when a law has such a large breadth that it is, in fact, a catch-all that gives the police unfettered power to arrest "undesirables." The law is constitutionally problematic because it lends itself to selective and discriminatory enforcement.[127] The classic examples of these laws are "street-cleaning" statutes such as the ones involved in *Papachristou*[128] and *Lanzetta*,[129] which were discussed earlier. The general assumption surrounding these laws is that the legislature has more or less left it up to police officers and prosecutors to decide which individuals should be targeted, based more on their status than on their conduct. The net is cast very broadly so that it can cover a wide variety of situations. It is then left up to the enforcing authorities to decide which individuals will be arrested and prosecuted. The arrest is not based on the conduct of the accused, but rather on the fact that the person is perceived as an undesirable. When the citizen arrives in court, it is almost automatic that he will be convicted because the law covers such a broad range of situations. In other words, the law permits a "standardless sweep." That is what the Supreme Court of Canada is concerned with in relation to the automatic conviction criterion stated in *Nova Scotia Pharmaceutical*. The passage cited above thus refers to the American understanding of law enforcement discretion that we have discussed earlier at length. This other passage of Gonthier J.'s reasons in *Nova Scotia Pharmaceutical*, which purports to illustrate the automatic conviction criterion, confirms this reality as it expressly refers to the American case of *Papachristou*: "For instance, the wording of the vagrancy ordinance invalidated by the United States Supreme Court in *Papachristou* and quoted at length in the *Prostitution Reference*, at pp. 1152-53, was so general and so lacked precision in its content that a conviction would ensue every time the law enforcer decided to charge someone with the offence of vagrancy. The words of the ordinance had no substance to them, and they indicated no particular legislative purpose. They left the accused completely in the dark, with no possible way of defending himself before the court."[130]

Does all this mean that the protection of the law enforcement discretion concern in Canada is to be confined to the limited American version as described earlier? Again, similar to what was said in relation to the fair notice rationale, we should avoid a wholesale adoption of the American attitude. Thus, rather than being a *sine qua non* criterion of validity or invalidity, the catch-all character of a law should be seen as a factor that can make the requirement of precision fluctuate. In other words, the vagueness assessment should be more severe when prosecutions under the statute are likely to lead to automatic convictions. At the same time, an analysis of the discretion given to law-enforcing authorities should always be made separately in the broader perspective of protecting citizens from arbitrary government. Thus, the principle of the rule of law, which seeks to diminish the presence of unnecessary discretion, especially in relation to coercive laws, should govern the analysis of vagueness under the second rationale.

The analysis should not be limited to the automatic convictions issue derived from the United States and adopted in *Nova Scotia Pharmaceutical* essentially for two reasons. First, the Supreme Court described this notion of catch-all exclusively in terms of laws creating offences. Since we know that other types of laws can also render the vagueness doctrine applicable, we must necessarily consider that the law enforcement discretion rationale possesses a meaning outside the scope of what the Supreme Court has discussed. Thus, the criterion of automatic convictions does not preclude the application of the broader natural understanding of law enforcement discretion described earlier. Second, we must be guided by the principle of the rule of law, which even in its most limited version certainly prescribes the limitation of law enforcement discretion in a more complete manner than the criterion of automatic convictions. We have seen that the rule of law possesses a strong status in Canadian constitutional law. It is even expressly stated in the preamble to the *Charter,* which is not the case in the United States, where the constitutional text contains no mention of the rule of law. This reality may dictate a fuller recognition of the law enforcement discretion rationale in the Canadian version of the vagueness doctrine. Discretion will therefore be confined with greater care in Canada to better protect citizens against the drawbacks of arbitrariness, discussed in Chapter 2 in relation to the principle of the rule of law.

The Morales *Case: A More Complete Understanding of the Discretion Rationale*

My position on the second rationale of the vagueness doctrine is supported by the 1992 case of *Morales,*[131] which invalidated the only provision to this date found defective for vagueness by the Supreme Court of Canada.[132] Recall that *Morales* involved a challenge to s. 515(10)(b) of the *Criminal Code,* which allowed for a judge to deny bail to an accused when "necessary in the public interest." This criterion of public interest was struck down for vagueness under s. 11(e) of the *Charter.*[133] It is interesting to note that it was the broader (natural) meaning of the law enforcement discretion rationale that was determinative in this case. *Morales* did not involve a law that could lead to an automatic conviction as soon as prosecution occurred. First of all, it was not even a law creating an offence but rather a bail provision, which means that we cannot refer to it in terms of automatic *conviction.* In any event, the provision was not the kind that would automatically lead to a decision disfavouring every individual it was applied to. The law simply gave discretion to the judge to determine whether the public interest standard was satisfied. Therefore, it did not correspond to the "crux of the concern for limitation of enforcement discretion" identified by Gonthier J. in *Nova Scotia Pharmaceutical*. Although the law was certainly vague and broad, it did not give discretionary power to the police or prosecutors to target so-called undesirables. Nothing suggests that the public interest criterion would be enforced more often against the poor or against racial minorities, for example. Still, the standard was incompatible with the notion of government by law, as the accused's right to bail was subject to the arbitrary whim of the judge. This was the reason why it was invalidated. It was not the narrow idea of automatic conviction, nor was it the question of fair warning, since the law was directed towards the judge of bail hearings and did not prescribe anything to be followed by individuals.

Morales therefore confirms the view that the catch-all character of a law that allows an automatic conviction as soon as prosecution occurs is merely a factor that can make the requirement of precision fluctuate in some cases. This decision maintains the relevance of the classic understanding of the law enforcement discretion rationale to assess the constitutional validity of uncertain legislation. In that sense, *Morales* is similar to the American case of *Giacco*.[134] Recall that in this decision the Supreme Court of the United States invalidated a law that gave juries the power to assess costs against defendants acquitted of misdemeanours if they had committed "some misconduct." The law was not of the "street-cleaning" type allowing automatic convictions, and therefore did not fall within the scope of what the law enforcement discretion rationale usually protects in the United States. It was nevertheless invalidated because it was incompatible with the rule of law ideal of protecting citizens from arbitrary government. We have seen that the *Giacco* decision is rather isolated in American jurisprudence. In Canada, given that *Morales* was rendered less than five months after *Nova Scotia Pharmaceutical,* and considering the other reasons I have mentioned that justified giving the law enforcement discretion rationale full scope, I believe this decision should not be seen as isolated like *Giacco* in the United States. Rather, *Morales* confirms the view that the catch-all character of the law giving rise to a likelihood of selective enforcement and automatic convictions is merely a criterion that can make the requirement of precision fluctuate in some cases.

Moving on to other considerations, note that the *Morales* case is interesting in relation to the study of the second rationale of the vagueness doctrine in at least one other regard. It reveals that an expression can be considered precise enough when used in a certain context and become overly vague in another context. Thus, in *Morales* the majority of the Court believed that the expression "public interest" used in the context of s. 515(10)(b) of the *Criminal Code* was insufficient to guide judicial discretion.

It is important to realize that nothing in the interpretative context of the provision clarified the meaning of this expression. But *Morales* does not suggest that the use of the words "public interest" in any legislation is now constitutionally prohibited. Otherwise, this would have an unfortunate impact on a large number of laws, which sometimes use the words "public interest" within a reasonable interpretative setting. Consider the following inventory referred to by Cory and Iacobucci JJ. in a case decided a few months before *Morales:* "A survey of federal statutes alone reveals that the term 'public interest' is mentioned 224 times in 84 federal statutes. The term appears in comparable numbers in provincial statutes. The term does not and cannot have a uniform meaning in each statute. It must be interpreted in light of the legislative history of the particular provision in which it appears and the legislative and social context in which it is used."[135]

Thus, in 1993 (one year after *Morales*) the Ontario Court of Appeal held in the case of *R. v. Farinacci*[136] that the same expression of "public interest" was not unconstitutionally vague when used in the context of s. 679(3) of the *Criminal Code*. This provision, permitting the preventive detention of an accused pending appeal in the public interest, was surrounded by a richer interpretative context than the public interest criterion invalidated in *Morales,* therefore allowing the Court to distinguish the two cases. Unlike the situation that prevailed in *Morales,* the purpose of the provision involved in *Farinacci* allowed courts to derive a meaning from the words "public interest" as used in s. 673(3) of the *Criminal Code*. As Arbour J.A. (then at the Ontario Court of Appeal) wrote: "I can find nothing suggesting that 'public interest' will be unconstitutionally vague every time it appears in a statute conferring discretion, nor can I find anything to suggest that 'public interest' has no workable meaning in the constitutional context governing s. 679 of the *Criminal Code*."[137]

Further, Arbour J.A. was able to summarize in a fairly sound manner how the criterion of public interest should be interpreted in the context of this provision:

> Section 679(3)(c) of the *Criminal Code* provides, in my opinion, a clear standard against which the correctness of any decision granting or denying bail pending appeal can be reviewed. The concerns reflecting public interest, as expressed in the case-law, relate both to the protection and safety of the public and to the need to maintain a balance between the competing dictates of enforceability and reviewability. [It] ... requires a judicial assessment of the need to review the conviction leading to imprisonment, in which case execution of the sentence may have to be temporarily suspended, and the need to respect the general rule of immediate enforceability of judgments.[138]

In *Morales*, the public interest criterion did not lend itself to such an interpretation. It left the accused's right to bail at the complete discretion of the judge. The underlying purpose behind the legislative standard could not be discovered, and therefore could not shed light on judicial interpretation. But in *Farinacci*, although the wording of the criterion was identical, it could be given a reasonable content by referring to the apparent purpose of the provision that had previously been articulated in the case law. Another example of a case that could be distinguished from *Morales* was *Protection de la jeunesse – 618*,[139] where the Quebec Youth Court held that the expression "interest of society" was sufficiently precise when used in s. 16 of the *Young Offenders Act* (R.S.C. 1985, c. Y-1). This provision makes it possible for a young offender's trial to be referred to the adult jurisdiction by taking into consideration the "interest of society." This expression is obviously similar to the public interest criterion invalidated in *Morales*, but as Mr. Justice Dubois rightfully noted, the interpretive context of each provision must be taken into consideration to assess whether discretion is adequately limited. In this case, the Court noted that s. 16(2) lists a series of factors to be considered in evaluating the "interest of society" (in cl. [a] to [e]). Moreover, the purposes of the Act set out in s. 3 (cl. [a] to [h]) helped to clarify the meaning of the "interest of society" in the circumstances. Thus, as Mr. Justice Dubois wrote, "[translation] the Court is not situated in a vacuum or in an arbitrary setting."[140]

As the cases of *Farinacci* and *Protection de la jeunesse* suggest, when contrasted with *Morales*, the interpretive context of each legislative provision is very important in assessing the extent to which the law enforcement discretion rationale is satisfied. The procedural safeguards that can vary from one legislative scheme to another can have the same effect of making the same language acceptable in one provision and unacceptable in another.[141] These factors can make the difference between the validity or invalidity of laws that at first glance are very similar.

All the elements of statutory interpretation are relevant for the purpose of controlling law enforcement discretion since they have the potential to clarify the meaning of an apparently vague provision. For example, to compensate for the uncertainty of certain legislative provisions, the Supreme Court of Canada has resorted, among other things, to indications derived from the rest of the provision containing the uncertain expression,[142] to pragmatic considerations,[143] or to interpretations already given to the words under scrutiny by external authorities[144] or by prior judicial decisions.[145]

The most widely used method is the one relying on prior judicial interpretations of the actual provision or other provisions containing a similar expression. This technique has the obvious effect of granting older provisions a better chance of being upheld, as they are more likely to have been subjected to interpretation over the years in the case law. For instance, the

Criminal Code provisions on possession and sale of obscene material have been held sufficiently precise considering, *inter alia*, that courts have managed over the years to elaborate definitions of obscenity (although these definitions are still very general).[146]

This emphasis on prior judicial interpretations has been criticized by some commentators[147] because it forces citizens to consult a large number of legal decisions in addition to the legislative text in order to regulate their conduct. Also, when a judicial decision injects meaning into a provision in order to avoid declaring it void for vagueness, the newly created standard becomes an *ex post facto* law if it is applied in the case at bar to facts that took place in the past. This problem will be examined later in greater detail.[148]

The Assessment of Legislative Precision in Canada

Having considered the two rationales of the vagueness doctrine, I will now examine the appropriate threshold of constitutional validity against which vague laws will be measured. Since legislative uncertainty can lead to judicial declarations of invalidity, it is important to know which degrees of vagueness will be tolerated and which will not. The Supreme Court of Canada has stated a rather permissive threshold under which vague laws will be assessed. This very low standard affords poor protection to the rationales of fair notice and law enforcement discretion. Let us examine the Supreme Court's standard before considering how it can be improved to ensure greater compliance with the principles of legality and the rule of law.

The Supreme Court's "Legal Debate" Test

Speaking for a unanimous Court in *Nova Scotia Pharmaceutical*, Gonthier J. set out a general test for determining whether legislation is unconstitutionally vague. After mentioning that "the threshold for finding a law vague is relatively high,"[149] Gonthier J. stated the standard of constitutional validity as follows: "A vague provision does not provide an adequate basis for legal debate, that is for reaching a conclusion as to its meaning by reasoned analysis applying legal criteria. It does not sufficiently delineate any area of risk, and thus can provide neither fair notice to the citizen, nor a limitation of enforcement discretion. Such a provision is not intelligible, to use the terminology of previous decisions of this Court, and therefore it fails to give sufficient indications that could fuel a legal debate. It offers no grasp to the judiciary."[150]

Under this standard, a law will be upheld as soon as it possesses some element, minimal though it might be, to fuel a legal debate. This test is obviously very permissive. As Peter Hogg points out, "almost any provision, no matter how vague, could provide a basis for legal debate."[151] All that is required is simply that the law be "intelligible." If some element can be found in the law that provides a "grasp to the judiciary"[152] and allows speculation on its meaning, the law is deemed sufficiently precise.

The Court insisted on the importance of this test of legal debate a number of times in the *Nova Scotia Pharmaceutical* decision itself,[153] and has since then confirmed it in several other decisions.[154] An interesting case is *Ontario v. Canadian Pacific*,[155] which confirmed the relevance of the "legal debate" test and purported to further clarify its meaning. In *Canadian Pacific*, the permissive character of that constitutional standard was reaffirmed by Lamer C.J., who maintained that "the fact that there is some identifiable 'core' of activity prohibited by the law will often be a strong indicator that the terms of the law provide sufficient guidance for legal debate."[156] Similarly, Gonthier J. held in separate reasons that "where a court has interpreted a legislative provision, and then has determined that the challenging party's own fact situation falls squarely within the scope of the provision, then that provision is obviously not vague ... it is clear that the law provides the basis for legal debate."[157] These comments, as well as Lamer C.J.'s comments, were formulated for the purpose of ruling that an accused to whom a law clearly applies has little to gain by asserting that the law would be vague as applied to others. As the vagueness doctrine requires only that the law furnish a basis for "legal debate," the fact that an accused is clearly within the scope of the law is sufficient to indicate that the constitutional standard is satisfied, and references to other hypothetical situations become moot. It is easy to see how the legal debate test is very permissive, especially when viewed from this angle. As Mr. Justice Hugessen from the Federal Court of Appeal rightfully noted in one of Canada's earliest vagueness decisions: "Even the most defective provision is unlikely to be so vague as not to permit the placing of some cases on one side of the line or the other. What is significant is the size and importance of the gray area between the two extremes."[158]

The legal debate test as a general criterion for determining the validity of statutes under the vagueness doctrine is overly deferential to legislative assemblies. The insufficient character of this test becomes apparent especially when considered in light of the principles of legality and the rule of law, both of which require that great care be devoted to the drafting of legislation. As seen in Chapters 1 and 2, these principles, which enjoy a high status in Canadian constitutional law, imply that laws must provide adequate notice to citizens to adjust their conduct (principle of legality) and that the influence of discretion in the enforcement of these laws be limited (rule of law). These concerns, which constitute the two basic rationales of the vagueness doctrine, are thus far given poor protection with the unique criterion of legal debate. As will be explained below, an adequate protection of these important constitutional considerations is to be attained through a more elaborate and, in some cases, more demanding standard of review while at the same time preserving flexibility and efficiency in legislative action.

A Balanced Approach towards the Assessment of Legislative Precision
The mere fact that a law provides a basis for legal debate should not be sufficient to automatically declare it constitutionally valid. This minimal standard may be appropriate in some cases, but in other cases the threshold clearly should be higher. In this study, we have come across several elements somewhat derived from the traditional fair notice and limitation of discretion concerns, which have the capacity to make the requirement of precision fluctuate depending on the circumstances of each legislative scheme. Let us recall these elements before illustrating how they are to be used for the assessment of vague legislation.

1   *The presence of a "substratum of values":* As we have seen, substantive notice requires that citizens be generally aware of a law's potential for triggering legal liability before such a law can legitimately operate. In this sense, a law that touches upon some conduct that is not related to society's values (or has not been the object of advertisement or publicity) will be more vulnerable under the vagueness doctrine.[159]

2   *The likelihood of selective enforcement:* This involves the question of whether the law is designed to be a catch-all, allowing a "standardless sweep" on citizens' liberty. A law that has the capacity to cover a wide range of different situations can, depending on the circumstances, have the effect of giving the police dictatorial power to arrest so-called undesirables. In such a framework, vagueness will be less tolerable because discretion is more likely to be exercised in a selective and discriminatory manner.[160]

3   *The issue of "reasonable necessity":* The need for greater flexibility regarding certain subject matters must be taken into consideration. If it would have been reasonably possible for the legislature to draft more precisely, greater precision should be required. By the same token, the difficulty of resorting to more definite standards due to the unforeseeable nature of the situations involved should relax the constitutional requirement. As we have seen earlier, the philosophy behind s. 1 of the *Charter* can be useful when manipulating this criterion of reasonable necessity.[161]

4   *The type of law involved:* The requirement of precision will be more stringent in relation to laws that have a coercive aspect, mostly penal laws. This phenomenon will be even stronger in the area of criminal law, considering the possibility of severe repercussions on an individual's liberty, as well as the stigma associated with convictions. Other types of laws, such as civil, tax, or immigration laws, will be subject to

a lesser constitutional standard insofar as their aim is not to punish individuals for past acts, and also considering the fact that their effect is often less severe. These distinctions, however, are not clear-cut, and nonpenal provisions will sometimes call for a higher degree of scrutiny if their effect is to punish individuals or if their repercussions are very severe. Within this same philosophy, deference will be appropriate in relation to laws that simply seek to administer the State or to achieve some objective of social policy.[162]

This short list of criteria is not exhaustive. Although these four factors are probably the most important, they are not the only ones that can be taken into consideration in making the requirement of precision fluctuate. Other relevant factors can be envisioned.[163] Of course, none of the elements is absolutely determinative on its own. Rather, an overall analysis of the different criteria must be undertaken in every case to determine the appropriate constitutional standard in relation to which a law's validity will be assessed.

What is the appropriate function of the elements just outlined in the context of the vagueness doctrine in Canada? In other words, what role do they play in relation to the legal debate test put forward in *Nova Scotia Pharmaceutical?* As seen earlier, the "substratum of values" issue (first factor) and the question of the likelihood of selective enforcement (second factor) were recognized in *Nova Scotia Pharmaceutical,* but their role and meaning remained somewhat unclear. I attempted earlier to clarify their possible impact as modulating criteria.[164] Thus, these concerns should be used to make the requirement of precision more or less demanding, depending on the circumstances. What about the other two factors I have outlined? The question of reasonable necessity (third factor) and the type of law involved (fourth factor) should also enable Canadian courts to depart from the criterion of legal debate and impose a stricter constitutional standard in some cases.

Note that the importance of these elements has never been negated by the Supreme Court of Canada. In fact, their relevance in relation to vagueness has been pointed out on a few occasions,[165] but the Court does not seem willing to allow these criteria to be used to depart from the low threshold of the legal debate test. In other words, the Court seems to use the modulation criteria only to *lower* the constitutional standard – a standard that is already so low to begin with under the authority of *Nova Scotia Pharmaceutical.* The modulating criteria are used to support a deferential attitude towards the legislature, but never to argue that the constitutional threshold should be higher than legal debate.[166]

For example, we may recall the *Canadian Pacific* case, which involved a challenge to a law prohibiting pollution in relatively general terms.[167] The

Court first noted that "the social importance of environmental protection is obvious, yet the nature of the environment does not lend itself to precise codification."[168] The Court then insisted on the "substratum of values," stating that "citizens have become acutely aware of the importance of environmental protection, and of the fact that penal consequences may flow from conduct which harms the environment."[169] The Court also noted that greater deference was appropriate since the law was of a regulatory nature and was aimed at achieving social objectives.[170] These factors are appropriate, but we see that they are used simply to argue for greater deference towards the legislator. Thus, in *Canadian Pacific,* note that the Court did not even point out, for instance, the need for greater precision when penal laws are involved.[171] Neither was this factor considered in *Nova Scotia Pharmaceutical,* where the Court even expressly denied that a law's criminal character should have importance in the analysis of vagueness. Consider the following comments by Gonthier J.: "In the criminal field, it may be thought that the terms of the legal debate should be outlined with special care by the State. In my opinion, however, once the minimal general standard has been met, any further arguments as to the precision of the enactment should be considered at the 'minimal impairment' stage of s. 1 analysis."[172]

The Court therefore refuses to recognize the impact of the nature of the law on the general constitutional requirement of precision. According to Gonthier J., under the vagueness doctrine, we should apply the same test for all enactments regardless of their nature. An enactment creating a criminal offence that can send someone to prison for life will be subject to the same standard of precision as a statute governing the restructuring of school boards.[173] This reasoning runs afoul of the traditional conceptions underlying legality and the rule of law, which were recognized two years before *Nova Scotia Pharmaceutical* by Lamer J. in the *Prostitution Reference:* "It is essential in a free and democratic society that citizens are able, as far as possible, to foresee the consequences of their conduct in order that persons be given fair notice of what to avoid, and that the discretion of those entrusted with law enforcement is limited by clear and explicit legislative standards. *This is especially important in the criminal law, where citizens are potentially liable to a deprivation of liberty if their conduct is in conflict with the law.*"[174]

In the passage quoted prior to the above, Gonthier J. maintained that the nature of the law may be taken into consideration under "minimal impairment." However, this is insufficient because the analysis will often not reach the stage of s. 1. If a law has no other defect besides vagueness, and the legal debate test is held to be satisfied under s. 7, the *Oakes* test will never be applied and the accused will not have the opportunity to raise the importance of precise legislative drafting dictated by some areas of law, such as criminal law. As previously outlined in earlier chapters, the principles

of legality and the rule of law are applicable with greater strength to enactments that attempt to coerce individuals, most often by imposing penal
sanctions on them.[175] The area in which this reality is the most stringent
is the field of criminal law. The severity of the vagueness doctrine should
therefore vary accordingly.

Another very important criterion involves the content of the law (i.e.,
the possibility of being more precise). As seen in Chapter 2, it is essential
when assessing the legitimacy of grants of discretion to ask whether it
would have been reasonably possible for the legislature to reach the policy
objective of its statute while granting less discretion. Thus, if the law
grants unnecessary discretion to law-enforcing authorities, it becomes
constitutionally suspect. In the same line of thinking, in relation to the
vagueness doctrine, the degree of precision allowed by the subject matter
involved should allow the vagueness test to fluctuate. If greater precision
is reasonably possible, the constitutional requirement should be stricter,
and vice versa. The relevance of this criterion has been recognized by the
Court on a few occasions.[176] For example, while upholding s. 163 of the
Criminal Code, which deals with obscenity, Sopinka J. made the following
observations in the case of *R. v. Butler:*

> The attempt to provide exhaustive instances of obscenity has been shown
> to be destined to fail (Bill C-54, 2nd Sess., 33rd Parl.). It seems that the
> only practicable alternative is to strive towards a more abstract definition
> of obscenity which is contextually sensitive and responsive to progress
> in the knowledge and understanding of the phenomenon to which the
> legislation is directed. In my view, the standard of "undue exploitation"
> is therefore appropriate. The intractable nature of the problem and the
> impossibility of precisely defining a notion which is inherently elusive
> makes the possibility of a more explicit provision remote. In this light, it
> is appropriate to question whether, and at what cost, greater legislative
> precision can be demanded.[177]

However, this type of reasoning is rarely used the other way around to
require more precision than legal debate from enactments that could reasonably be more precise.[178] Considering the importance of protecting
legality and the rule of law, we should not hesitate to adopt a stricter constitutional requirement than legal debate in cases where it is apparent that
the legislature could have drafted the law with greater precision without
compromising the results. Let us consider a hypothetical situation to illustrate this point.

Imagine a statutory provision stating that *"it is forbidden to circulate too
rapidly on a highway."* The expression "too rapidly" creates an obvious problem of fair notice, in addition to creating a basis for arbitrary enforcement.

However, it certainly provides a basis for legal debate. It is indeed possible to debate in court on what can constitute an excessive speed on a highway. There is no doubt that this provision does create a certain "area of risk" and therefore satisfies the criterion set out in *Nova Scotia Pharmaceutical*. Moreover, by using the reasoning dictated by the recent *Canadian Pacific* case, it is easy to see how the provision satisfies the legal debate test, as it would be clearly applicable to a certain core of situations. For example, if someone was driving at 220 kilometres per hour, he would clearly be violating the law. Should this be sufficient to declare that this type of provision is constitutionally valid? Even if the law does satisfy legal debate, it is obvious that the legislator could have been more precise by specifying the speed allowed in kilometres per hour. This would have the advantage of affording better protection to legality and the rule of law. It would provide better notice to citizens as to what the law prescribes, in addition to reducing the influence of arbitrary considerations and discretion in the enforcement of the law.

Of course, police officers still have a certain discretionary power even when the law specifies a settled limit (100 kilometres per hour, for example) because they have the option of not charging certain drivers who may be slightly over the limit. This is, in fact, the case with any law: no matter how specific the rule is, the police can always choose not to arrest and the prosecutor can always choose not to lay charges. When the law is specific, however, even if the citizen does not know when he will be charged if he goes over the limit, he at least knows that if he *does* respect the limit, he will not be arbitrarily charged. Thus, when the law sets a 100 kilometre per hour limit, the individual is at least assured that he will not be the victim of unfair surprise if he stays within that limit, and he will not be at the mercy of a police officer's whim.

The hypothetical legislative provision just discussed is somewhat of a caricature, but it is nonetheless interesting as it demonstrates the manifestly insufficient character of the legal debate test as a unique standard for evaluation of vague laws. In order to avoid such results, it is appropriate to consider an approach that takes into account the possibility of drafting more precisely, *inter alia,* when determining the appropriate threshold of constitutional validity in every case. In this regard, it is revealing to recall the reasons put forward by the Supreme Court to support its deferential approach. In *Nova Scotia Pharmaceutical,* Gonthier J. notes that "semantic arguments based on a perception of language as an unequivocal medium, are unrealistic. Language is not the exact tool some may think it is."[179] Similarly, he points out in the *Canadian Pacific* case that "the mediating role of the judiciary is of particular importance in those situations where practical difficulties prevent legislators from framing legislation in precise terms."[180] In other words, Gonthier J. outlines the difficulties of articulating rules in advance to effectively reach certain policy objectives. Often, the different applications of a law are quite unforeseeable, and it is necessary to resort to a substantial amount of law enforcement discretion. Those concerns are in fact very legitimate. It is true that the vagueness doctrine should not be used to impinge on the State's capacity to reach its policy objectives, and in that sense discretion is often needed. But this does not mean that discretion must *always* be allowed, regardless of how necessary it may be in the circumstances. If it is true that some laws cannot operate effectively without resorting to general terms, it is also true that other laws can reasonably be more precise without having their efficiency compromised. It would be naive to think that vagueness is always present in statutes for legitimate reasons. In fact, the legislature will sometimes draft in vague terms simply for political reasons or by sheer carelessness. In such cases, not to require greater precision would mean denying the importance of legality and the rule of law as constitutional ideals.

Unfortunately (and perhaps ironically), we cannot precisely determine ahead of time which categories of subject matters will lend themselves to precise legislation and which ones will require more discretion. Indeed, this varies and cannot be determined in advance in terms of particular types of laws. One must therefore look at each particular provision and see whether it is drafted with sufficient care to warn citizens and to limit law enforcement discretion as much as reasonably practicable. Of course, the type of law involved (penal, tax, civil, etc.) does have an impact on the level of precision required by the Constitution because, as we have seen, the importance of protecting fair notice and the rule of law *from the citizen's point of view* varies with the type of law involved. Thus, for example, it is considered more important to give adequate notice to citizens and to control discretion in the field of criminal law. This does not mean, however, that criminal laws are easier to draft than other laws. Despite the importance, from the individual's point of view, of precise drafting in criminal law, the State may still face practical difficulties that make vague provisions unavoidable. Thus, in the previously mentioned case of *Butler,* the *Criminal Code*'s vague standard of obscenity was upheld despite its vagueness because it was highly impracticable for the legislative assembly to reach greater precision.

How to Improve Legislative Precision

I have explained throughout this book the appropriate method for assessing the compatibility of vague laws with the Constitution. Depending on the circumstances, it may constitute a more demanding approach than the standard that has thus far been suggested by the Supreme Court of

Canada. While the Court since the *Nova Scotia Pharmaceutical* case requires only for the law to provide a basis for legal debate, the refined approach I have presented will, at least in some cases, be less tolerant towards the legislator. A series of factors is to be taken into consideration to ensure a more appropriate protection of fair notice to citizens and a limitation of arbitrariness in the operation of laws. Of course, this approach requires more effort on the government's part, since some laws will have to be made more precise in order to be sustained. How can this be done? It will be useful here to make a few comments on the possible avenues towards greater certainty in laws.

The Questionable Technique of Specification through Case Law
To this day, courts have taken upon themselves the task of remedying laws they believe are too vague. This is done through a process of interpretation, with the obvious purpose of preserving the immediate validity of legislation. Although it can sometimes diminish the disadvantages associated with vague laws, this method is to be approached with caution. As will be demonstrated below, the judicial redrafting of laws answers in only an incomplete manner the concerns of fair notice and law enforcement discretion. In order to promote legality and the rule of law, it is more appropriate that statutes be made more precise not by judges but by legislators (or their subordinates). Before examining the appropriate approach and how legislators themselves can make laws more precise, it will be useful to examine why the technique of creating specification through case law is less appropriate.

First, when the specification of statutes is found in judicial decisions, the fair notice provided to citizens is unsatisfactory. Although notice is given in theory, it is very difficult in practice for individuals not accustomed to legal research to access these decisions and analyze them. In the *Canadian Pacific* case, Gonthier J. indicated that in the area of pollution law, excessive specification through the use of technical terms would not be appropriate because it might confuse citizens even more: "In my view, in the field of environmental protection, detail is not necessarily the best means of notifying citizens of prohibited conduct. If a citizen requires a chemistry degree to figure out whether an activity releases a particular contaminant in sufficient quantities to trigger a statutory prohibition, then that prohibition provides no better fair notice than a more general enactment ... If specialized knowledge is required to understand a legislative provision, then citizens may be baffled."[181]

In the same line of thinking, should we not consider it preferable that the content of laws be accessible to the average citizen without it being necessary for him to consult a lawyer or to possess knowledge in legal research? As Jeffries points out in the American context:

The "fair warning" that the law regards as the "first essential of due process" may be discoverable only by a search of the precedents. As every first-year law student knows (and has not had time to forget), this process of research and interpretation is anything but easy. For the trained professional, the task is time-consuming and tricky; for the average citizen, it is next to impossible. Where there is a lawyer at hand, this kind of notice may be meaningful. But in the ordinary case, the notice given must be recovered from sources so various and inaccessible as to render the concept distinctly unrealistic.[182]

In addition to this problem of notice, specification through case law has the disadvantage of making legislators less concerned with the need to draft laws with precision. If legislators know that a provision lacking in precision can always be specified judicially afterwards and therefore declared constitutionally valid, the incentive for precise legislative rule making is diminished and more vague laws are enacted.

Moreover, the judicial specification of vague laws that eventually occurs does not address the problem in a timely fashion. In fact, until these laws are given meaning by an authoritative court (the Supreme Court of Canada or at least a Court of Appeal), the uncertainty remains. During the period between the enactment of the law and its authoritative specification through case law, the principles of legality and the rule of law are betrayed. Citizens are not given fair notice and the enforcement of the vague law can be overly arbitrary. When the Supreme Court finally injects meaning into the law, it says, "From now on, it is clear." But what about the accused in the case at bar, to whom the new standard is being applied retroactively? And what about all the other citizens to whom the law was applied in an overly arbitrary manner and without adequate notice before this authoritative specification of the law?

If a court is able to inject meaning into the law, it was obviously not impossible for the legislator to do the same several years before, when the law was enacted. This would have had the advantage of protecting more adequately notice and the rule of law in the meantime, not to mention the fact that even when the law is judicially specified, notice is still unsatisfactory because, as we have seen, it remains fairly inaccessible to the average citizen.

For example, in the case of *Nova Scotia Pharmaceutical*, the provision challenged for vagueness was s. 32(1)(c) of the *Combines Investigation Act*,[183] which punishes "every one who conspires, agrees or arranges with another person ... to prevent, or lessen, unduly, competition." The element of uncertainty came from the word "unduly." The requirement that the restriction on competition be "undue" does not say what factors must be taken into consideration. In its general sense, "undue" would mean something like "improper," "illegitimate," or "unjustifiable." It would mean that there is something "wrong" in the way competition is being limited. This would suppose that there is a frame of reference with which to assess which restrictions are right and which are wrong. However, the provision provides no such frame of reference. The legislator seems to have entrusted to the courts the task of determining which restrictions on competition should be prohibited by law. As Professor K.C. Davis would put it, the legislator seems to be saying to the courts, "Here is the problem: deal with it."[184]

Conscious of the fact that this attitude could be constitutionally questionable under the vagueness doctrine, Gonthier J. defined "unduly" quite differently from its usual meaning to hold that "it expresses a notion of seriousness or significance."[185] We realize that the law's meaning is being bent here to avoid uncertainty. To the ordinary citizen, something that is "undue" may often be different from something that is "serious." It is obvious that something may be serious without being undue, and vice versa. A federal or provincial election is inherently important and serious, but can it be said by the same token that it is undue? If a group of friends are playing golf and one of them cheats on his score, it is certainly undue, but can it also be considered serious or important? Unlike in the game of golf, where there are established rules to determine what is undue, the legislator did not provide guidelines to circumscribe the meaning of what may be undue when limiting competition in s. 32(1)(c) of the *Combines Investigation Act*. As drafted, the provision does not give potential offenders notice as to what agreements will be covered. It is therefore left more or less to the appreciation of prosecutors and judges. In the case at bar *(Nova Scotia Pharmaceutical)*, the Court decided to inject a tangible meaning into the provision. First, "unduly" was held to mean "seriously." Then the Court described the factors that are to be taken into consideration in assessing whether the criterion of seriousness is satisfied.[186]

What is the result of this approach? Of course, once the decision has been rendered henceforth, the scope of the provision is clear, at least as clear as the subject matter reasonably allows. From this day forward, fair notice is given to some extent to citizens[187] and discretion in law enforcement is limited. The law concerning conspiracies to lessen competition is now reasonably clear.

There are several disadvantages to this approach, however. The accused in the case at bar is convicted under a newly created standard, and is therefore the victim of an *ex post facto* application of the law. This offends the principle of legality studied in Chapter 1 because it criminalizes a conduct where fair notice had not previously been given. Moreover, and perhaps even more importantly, it sends an unhealthy message to the legislature. If legislative assemblies feel free to draft laws in general terms knowing that courts will eventually give them meaning, betrayals of legality and the rule of law may become more and more common. Therefore, the price to pay for not striking down the law in the case at bar and sending it back to the legislature for specification is that more laws will be drafted vaguely. Fair notice and the desire to minimize discretion will be ignored in the interval between the enactment of vague laws and their judicial specification. At the same time, the interpretative burden of the courts is amplified, which causes delays in the administration of justice. We see that by trying to find a quick solution to the vagueness of a law through judicial redrafting, we only "patch a hole," while several other problems are maintained and even created.

Another illustration of this type of approach can be seen in the case of *R. v. Zundel*. This case involved a challenge to s. 181 of the *Criminal Code*, which prohibited the willful publication of false news likely to "cause injury or mischief to a public interest." The majority in this case found that the provision was invalid as it breached s. 2(b) of the *Charter*. The justification failed under s. 1 because the prohibition was overly vague. Most interesting for the sake of our discussion is the dissenting opinion by Cory and Iacobucci JJ. in this case. These dissenting judges, with whom Gonthier J. concurred, would have held that the provision was not so vague as to be unjustifiable under s. 1. Although they agreed that until that day the provision did not provide a basis for legal debate, they purported in the case at bar to inject meaning into the expression "public interest" as used in s. 181. Thus, in order to avoid the fatal uncertainty, the following reasoning is adopted: "The term 'public interest' as it appears in s. 181 refers to the protection and preservation of those rights and freedoms set out in the *Charter* as fundamental to Canadian society. It is only if the deliberate false statements are likely to seriously injure the rights and freedoms contained in the *Charter* that s. 181 is infringed. This section, therefore, provides sufficient guidance as to the legal consequences of a given course of conduct. It follows that the section cannot be said to be so vague that it is void."[188]

The problems with this approach are similar to those pointed out earlier. The clarification of the law is made *ex post facto* and legislators are invited to neglect the virtues of advance rule making. As McLachlin J. (writing for the majority) rightfully noted while commenting on the dissenting judges' opinion: "My colleagues have arguably created a new offence, an offence hitherto unknown to the criminal law."[189]

I am not attempting here to deny the role of the judiciary in interpreting and actualizing legislation. As Lamer J. had already noted before *Nova Scotia Pharmaceutical* in the *Prostitution Reference*, "the vagueness doctrine does not require that laws be absolutely certain"[190] and "the role of courts in giving meaning to legislative terms should not be overlooked when discussing the issue of vagueness."[191] Of course, legislation cannot be applied clearly to all situations and judges have an important interpretative role to play. I am referring here not only to factual determinations. The role of the courts goes beyond the appreciation of factual evidence and its application to legal standards. No matter how much effort legislators put into legislative drafting, there will always be a multitude of situations where the proper standard governing a set of facts will be unclear. In order to determine the proper solution in particular cases, judges may use the canons of interpretation as guides, but some level of discretion will always remain. Even with the help of these principles of interpretation, therefore, the operation of legislation is far from being mechanical. This reality and the interplay between the different principles of interpretation have been described by several eminent legal scholars who have helped us understand the complex task of actualizing legislation.[192] As already mentioned, this reality is not what I am condemning. These uncertainties in interpretation are inherent in the law. No legal system is perfect. There will always be gaps that need to be resolved by some authority, namely, the judiciary or other decision makers.[193] However, the fact that courts will inevitably have a rule-making role does not discharge us from attempting to control this phenomenon. In other words, an attempt must be made to limit arbitrariness in the administration of justice, even if we know that it cannot (nor should it) be completely eliminated.

Gonthier J. stated in *Nova Scotia Pharmaceutical* that "the judiciary always has a mediating role in the actualization of law, although the extent of this role may vary."[194] This is true but, as has been argued, it does not logically justify the overly deferential approach towards vague laws advocated in *Nova Scotia Pharmaceutical,* nor does it render acceptable the judicial clarification of vague laws to avoid constitutional invalidity. While the uncertainties inherent in the law often cannot be foreseen by the drafters, vagueness can be foreseen as it appears on the face of the law. From the moment the law is drafted, the legislator ought to know that there will be problems in understanding the meaning of a particular expression. When this vagueness is excessive if considered in light of the principles outlined earlier, the legislator has the constitutional duty to resolve the problem before enacting such a law. For instance, in relation to *Nova Scotia Pharmaceutical,* it could very easily have been foreseen that the word "unduly" as used in the *Combines Investigation Act* would create uncertainty. Especially when the criminal character of the *Act* is considered, this uncertainty should have been reduced before the law was enacted.

Other Approaches towards Legislative Precision
If precision through case law is not the appropriate solution, how should laws be made more precise so as to satisfy the constitutional imperatives of

the vagueness doctrine? Of course, the first option is simply for the legislative assembly to make the rules more specific by articulating in greater detail the conditions to which they apply. It is true that this requires greater effort on the part of the legislator. It demands more time and expertise, and consequently more money at the stage of legislative drafting, but this investment will yield substantial long-term benefits, not only from a practical perspective (because more precise laws will be cheaper and quicker to enforce) but also from a constitutional perspective, since legality and the rule of law will be better protected.

If a law cannot be made more precise in the traditional way (by spelling out the rule with accuracy), it can at least be made more certain by providing nonexhaustive illustrations of its applicability. A better understanding of the law's meaning is thus ensured since the rule can be interpreted in light of the illustrations. This technique of interpretation is commonly known as *ejusdem generis*.[195] Let us consider, for example, s. 515(10) of the *Criminal Code,* which outlines the situations where a judge may deny bail to an accused pending trial. Besides the situations where detention of the accused in custody is justified by the need to ensure his or her attendance in court or the safety of the public, the provision contains a residual ground for denying bail. Until 1992, this residuary ground was simply described as "the public interest." This criterion was invalidated by the Supreme Court of Canada in the *Morales* case.[196] As a result of that decision, Parliament amended the provision as follows: "515(10) For the purposes of this section, the detention of an accused in custody is justified only on one or more of the following grounds: ... *(c)* on any other just cause being shown and, without limiting the generality of the foregoing, where the detention is necessary in order to maintain confidence in the administration of justice, having regard to all the circumstances, including the apparent strength of the prosecution's case, the gravity of the nature of the offence, the circumstances surrounding its commission and the potential for a lengthy term of imprisonment."

The constitutional validity of this new provision was again challenged in *Hall.* The Supreme Court of Canada saw in s. 515(10)(c) two distinct grounds that could justify detention. The first ground of "just cause" was invalidated as being equivalent to the previously struck down "public interest" notion of *Morales.* However, the second ground, stating "where the detention is necessary in order to maintain confidence in the administration of justice," was held to be valid, as it was complemented by a series of nonexhaustive illustrations. Thus, through this technique, Parliament was able to render the law more precise, although it remains flexible.[197]

Another technique that may be valuable in meeting the constitutional standard of the vagueness doctrine may be to resort to delegated legislation. If a statute lays down a general standard and provides for the details to be spelled out through regulation, it may constitute a very useful way of balancing certainty and flexibility. A similar idea was put forward in the United States by Kenneth C. Davis in a book addressing the need to confine discretion in the field of administrative law.[198] Davis emphasized the elimination of unnecessary discretion so as to limit the injustice associated with arbitrariness. According to him, a key element in such a framework is to resort more extensively to administrative rule making.[199] Often, when a statute contains vague standards, it would be possible for the enforcing agency to confine its own discretion by spelling out the standards in greater detail through regulation, provided, of course, that a regulation-making power exists in the statute. When such is the case, Davis urges the agency to take the initiative and exercise its rule-making power as soon as it is able to articulate standards more definite than the ones contained in the statute. As he points out, "legislators and their staffs know they are ill-equipped to plan detailed programs," but this should not be considered as a legitimate excuse to preserve overly vague standards in the law. As Davis adds, legislators also "know that administrators and their staffs are better equipped because they can work continuously for long periods in limited areas."[200] It follows that administrators should make the effort to use their regulation-making powers as soon as possible to render vague standards more specific.

It is interesting to note that the practical reasons that usually lead legislative assemblies to delegate their power to regulatory agencies very closely resemble the motivations behind the use of vague statutory formulas. In the *Third Report of the Special Committee on Statutory Instruments*,[201] presented before the Canadian House of Commons in 1968, the following was noted in relation to the growing phenomenon of delegated legislation: "The reasons usually given to justify the delegation by Parliament of the power to make laws are: lack of parliamentary time; lack of parliamentary knowledge on technical matters; the necessity of rapid decisions in cases of emergency; the need to experiment with legislation, especially in a new field; the need for flexibility in the application of laws; and unforeseen contingencies which may arise during the introduction of new complex pieces of legislation."[202]

In light of these comments, the appropriateness of resorting to regulations to render vague laws more specific becomes obvious. Similar to what Davis suggested in the context of American administrative law, the technique of precision through regulation can help us solve the constitutional problem of vagueness in statutes. When legislators feel unable to draft precise standards because of limited resources and expertise regarding a certain subject, they can state a general standard and provide for the details to be spelled out through regulation. The regulation-making power in that regard could be given to any entity that legislators feel is suited to carry out the task of specifying the legislation. A difference between Davis's theory and mine is that while he directly urges administrators to take the initiative and use their general rule-making powers to confine their own discretion as a matter of administrative law, I am advising legislators from a constitutional perspective to indicate in the statute itself that a particular vague provision will have to be made more specific through regulation. Ideally, the regulation would have to be enacted by the appropriate authority before the relevant statutory provision could come into force.

The resulting scheme would have several advantages, both for the State and for individuals. It would represent a very satisfactory way of balancing certainty and flexibility. Let us examine the advantages of this approach. First, the regulatory power will be delegated to agencies possessing expertise in the subject matter involved. It will therefore be easier for them to spell out detailed provisions than it would be for legislators or the courts. Second, since the process for the adoption of regulation is less burdensome than the legislative process, the time required before the rule can come into force will be reduced. Third, and related, regulations are more easily modifiable than statutes because the process for their adoption and amendment is often less burdensome. We want legal standards to be flexible, to be able to evolve easily with the changing needs of practicality. If the details concerning the application of a law are contained in regulation, they can be more easily and rapidly modified. The fear of having a rule that is unable to evolve and adapt to new situations is one of the main reasons why legislators sometimes choose to draft in general terms. This problem is greatly reduced if the rule can be easily modified through regulation. This has the advantage of discretion since this technique is flexible, but it still respects the principles of legality and the rule of law because the rule is expressed *a priori* and can be discovered by citizens before they act. Thus, the standard has no *ex post facto* application. The problems of unfair surprise and arbitrary enforcement are reduced, while the element of flexibility is maintained.

Finally, this tandem statute/regulation can sometimes have the advantage of making the law even clearer than if the detailed provisions were contained directly in the statute. An argument sometimes resorted to by supporters of vague laws is that a more detailed standard would be too complicated for citizens to understand, and therefore provide less efficient notice.[203] In some cases, numerous detailed provisions can indeed constitute an obstacle to the understanding of the law, while a more general standard would be more intelligible for the average citizen. The technique of precision through regulation would answer this concern by preserving the vague standard in the law, and spelling out the specifications in the regulation. One could therefore refer only to the law in order to get a general idea of one's rights and obligations, and refer to the regulations in order to know more. Note that the use of informatics could be very help-ful in ensuring the link between the statutes and their regulations, there-fore facilitating the task of the reader.

A final note on the issue of specification through regulation: it would be appropriate for a hearing to take place to allow for public participation in the process leading to the adoption of these regulations. In the United States, a minimal hearing requirement for the adoption of most regula-tions is dictated by a statutory provision of general application, the opera-tion of which is described as follows by Davis: "The usual procedure is that prescribed by the Administrative Procedure Act, the central feature of which is publishing proposed rules and inviting interested parties to make written comments. Anyone and everyone is allowed to express himself and to call attention to the impact of various possible policies on his busi-ness, activity or interest. The agency's staff sifts and summarizes the pre-sentations and prepares its own studies. The procedure is both fair and efficient. Much experience proves that it usually works beautifully."[204]

The requirement of a hearing makes regulations an even more appropri-ate tool to balance the advantages of rules and discretion. It enables inter-ested parties to comment, at least in writing, on proposed regulations before they can be adopted. This increases the democratic legitimacy of the whole process, while at the same time providing some feedback to the rule-making authority, thus enabling it to assess even more fully the mat-ter being regulated. In Canada, there is no general statutory requirement that all proposed regulations be subject to some form of hearing prior to their adoption.[205] In recent years, however, there has been a growing ten-dency to consult the public prior to adoption of regulations at the federal level, as well as in several provincial jurisdictions.[206] I do not intend to state here the details of how this need for public participation should be addressed or how the hearings should be carried out in practice. It may be asked, for example, whether it would be more appropriate to have a gen-eral statutory requirement commanding hearings. It may also be asked whether written submissions can be an acceptable alternative to oral hear-ings, or what would be the appropriate stage at which these hearings should occur prior to the adoption of the regulations. The answers to these questions are still the subject of debates in Canada and even in the United States. They are obviously beyond the scope of this study. Leaving these details aside, however, I am satisfied with noting that some form of prior public consultation would certainly enhance the legitimacy of resorting to regulations as a middle-ground solution to the problem of vagueness. If no statutory requirement to that effect is enacted in the future, it is to be hoped that there will at least be a generalized practice favouring public participation. This will make regulations an even more satisfactory tool for balancing the needs for flexibility and certainty in the legal system.

An Illustration: *The Canadian Bar Assn.* Cases

The appropriateness of this approach for dealing with vagueness is illustrated by two related cases from the Supreme Court of British Columbia, rendered in 1993 and 1994. In both cases, new provisions amending the *Social Service Tax Act* were challenged on grounds of vagueness.[207] In *Canadian Bar Assn. No. 1,* the legislation that imposed a tax on the purchase of legal services unless they had "no connection to British Columbia" was declared invalid as that standard was held to be too vague. Rather than appealing the decision, the government decided to redraft the law to make it more precise. This new law was again challenged on grounds of vagueness in *Canadian Bar Assn. No. 2,* and this time it was upheld.

Let us examine more closely the influence the vagueness doctrine had on the legislative rules involved in these two judicial decisions. The *Social Service Tax Amendment Act, 1993* (the "old act"),[208] challenged in *Canadian Bar Assn. No. 1,* provided under s. 2.01(1) for the creation of a tax on legal services: "2.01(1) Unless subsection (2) applies, if a purchaser or recipient of legal services resides, ordinarily resides or carries on business in British Columbia, the purchaser shall pay to Her Majesty in right of the Province a tax at the rate of 6% of the purchase price of the legal services, whether those services are provided inside or outside British Columbia."[209]

A restriction to this taxation was provided under s. 2.01(2): "(2) No tax is payable under subsection (1) if the legal services have no *connection to British Columbia,* other than the mere fact that the purchaser or recipient resides, ordinarily resides or carries on business in British Columbia, or that the legal services are provided in British Columbia, or both."[210]

Thus, in order for the tax to be payable, the legal services had to have a "connection to British Columbia" other than the "mere fact" that one of the parties was located in the province, or that the legal services were provided within the province. Nowhere in the *Act* was the notion of "connection" defined, and Lysyk J. concluded that it was unconstitutionally vague:

> Counsel for the Attorney-General does not suggest that the term "connection" has been given a constant or settled meaning by the courts in the context of other legislation or elsewhere. Nor does he say that any connection whatsoever will satisfy the statutory requirement. In his submission, some connections will suffice while others will not, and this will be a matter for the courts to determine when the issue comes before them on a case-by-case basis. But according to what criteria? As discussed earlier, the enactment as a whole provides no reliable guidance ...
>
> I conclude that the term "connection" as employed in conjunction with the general charging provision is too vague to meet *Charter* requirements. To borrow the language employed in the *Pharmaceutical Society* and

Morales decisions, the term so lacks in precision as not to give sufficient guidance for legal debate. It does not supply an intelligible standard and it offers no grasp to the judiciary.[211]

Was the law really so vague in *Canadian Bar Assn. No. 1* as not to provide a "basis of legal debate"? It is doubtful. Even if the standard was rather vague, it was probably still capable of fuelling a legal debate. The criterion of "connection to British Columbia" was not totally unintelligible, and it may therefore be strongly speculated that it would have been upheld by the Supreme Court of Canada under the permissive threshold of legal debate. The element of "connection to British Columbia" would have been clearly applicable in at least *some* circumstances and, as we have seen earlier, the fact that a standard clearly applies to "an identifiable 'core' of activity"[212] constitutes a strong indicator that the legal debate test is satisfied. For example, if legal services were provided in the genesis of court proceedings that were later to take place in British Columbia concerning a property located in the province, there is little doubt that the standard of "connection to British Columbia" would apply. Thus, despite the substantial uncertainty created by the provision challenged in *Canadian Bar Assn. No. 1*, it would probably have been held sufficiently precise to meet the minimal standard of precision of legal debate put forward by the Supreme Court of Canada.

Although Lysyk J.'s approach was, in my view, incompatible with *Nova Scotia Pharmaceutical*, I nonetheless believe that his decision was the most appropriate on the merits. In fact, the *Canadian Bar Assn. No. 1* case applied a threshold higher than the one of legal debate, which is what I have been proposing throughout this book. Even if the "connection to British Columbia" standard was arguably precise enough to meet the legal debate test, the rule was still poorly articulated by the legislature. Many uncertainties were created as to the application of this rule that, if not complied with, could lead to the imposition of penal sanctions. In that sense, the ideal of fair notice to citizens was betrayed. By the same token, the rule of law was given short shrift through this vague standard, which delegated to judges the discretionary power of determining the scope of the law. This is not a case where more precision in drafting would have been difficult to attain, as was clearly demonstrated by the events that followed the invalidation of the law by Lysyk J. Following the decision in *Canadian Bar Assn. No. 1*, the British Columbia legislature enacted the *Social Service Tax Amendment Act, 1993*[213] to replace the legislation that had been struck down. In s. 2.012 of this new act, the legislature wanted to express the notion of connection to British Columbia to tax legal services provided in British Columbia when neither the purchaser nor the recipient are located in the province. Instead of using the standard of "connection to British Columbia" alone, which had led to the invalidation of the previous legislation, the new law stated:

> 2.012(3) If neither the purchaser nor the recipient of legal services provided in British Columbia resides, ordinarily resides or carries on business in British Columbia, a tax on the provision of the legal services shall be paid to Her Majesty in right of the Province by the purchaser at the rate of 7% of the purchase price if the legal services are in relation to one or more of the following:
> (a) real property situated in British Columbia;
> (b) tangible personal property, within the meaning of paragraph (a) of the definition of tangible personal property, that is ordinarily situated within British Columbia or that is to be delivered in British Columbia, or the contemplation of either of these;
> (c) the ownership, possession or use in British Columbia of property other than that referred to in paragraphs (a) and (b), or the right to use such property in British Columbia, or in contemplation of any of these;
> (d) a court of administrative proceeding in British Columbia or a possible such proceeding;
> (e) the incorporation or contemplated incorporation of a corporation under the Company Act or the Society Act, or the registration or contemplated registration of a corporation as an extraprovincial company under the Company Act or as an extraprovincial society under the Society Act;
> (f) *other matter that relates to British Columbia and is prescribed as being included for the purposes of this section.*[214]

We see here that the legislature was able to express with greater precision the idea of "connection to British Columbia." Thus, several of the provision's possible applications are spelled out in paragraphs (a) to (e). To allow for flexibility, paragraph (f) adds that "any other matter that relates to British Columbia and is prescribed as being included for the purposes of this section" also makes the tax applicable. This paragraph was challenged for vagueness before the Supreme Court of British Columbia in *Canadian Bar Assn. No. 2.* In upholding the new law, Humphries J. wrote: "In the old act, Lysyk J. was concerned that there was no definition of 'connection to British Columbia' ... Here, the Lieutenant Governor In Council has a regulation making power that is limited by the qualification that it must relate to B.C. If the regulation does not, it can be struck down on individual consideration. As well, the general clause will necessarily be interpreted in light of the preceding matters and will be subject to the principle ejusdem generis."[215]

Thus, we see that the standard of "connection to British Columbia" was indeed capable of being stated with greater precision. Even if it might have been difficult to provide a strict *definition* of the notion of "connection to British Columbia" (which corresponds to the traditional approach), the legislature used imaginative yet simple techniques to comply with the constitutional requirement of certainty. The legislator resorted to the tools discussed earlier to make the law more compatible with fairness and the rule of law. Thus, illustrations of "connection to British Columbia" were given (in paragraphs [a] to [e]) to activate the principle *ejusdem generis* and therefore better circumscribe the scope of the law. In addition, the government was given a regulation-making power to make other specific matters come within the definition.

It is interesting to note that the two techniques may be even more appropriate when, as in the case at bar, they are used in conjunction. On the one hand, when the law uses only a nonexhaustive list of illustrations but no regulation-making power, there obviously still remains an appreciable amount of uncertainty because the list is nonexhaustive. On the other hand, when the law contains only a regulation-making power but no illustrations to guide its exercise, arbitrary considerations are again substantially present as the delegation to the executive can be broad and unfettered. Moreover, we must wait until the regulation is passed before the statutory provision can come into force. But when both techniques are used together, as in s. 2.012(3) of the *Act*, these problems are greatly diminished. Thus, even before regulations are enacted, the government can begin collecting taxes through paragraphs (a) to (e). Since the section is not open-ended, the uncertainty is adequately contained. Meanwhile, there is still flexibility because the government can easily enlarge the scope of the provision by adding additional elements to be taxed under the authority of paragraph (f). Finally, the regulation-making body's power is contained since, as Humphries J. noted in the extract cited above, the regulation can be declared *ultra vires* on individual consideration if it ignores the guidelines provided by the rest of the provision.

We can see how well the *Canadian Bar Assn. No. 1* and *No. 2* cases illustrate the appropriateness of the approach I have explained for applying the vagueness doctrine. The first tax legislation presented substantial uncertainties. This was detrimental to the principles of legality and the rule of law. Instead of upholding the law under the weak standard of legal debate, Lysyk J. thought that the legislator could and should do better. This had a beneficial effect. As demonstrated by the new law upheld in *Canadian Bar Assn. No. 2,* a more precise articulation of the standard of "connection to British Columbia" was in fact reasonably possible. This new standard is more likely to give adequate notice to citizens and to control the discretion involved in enforcement. Such an approach to vagueness is preferable to the overly deferential view currently favoured by the Supreme Court of Canada in *Nova Scotia Pharmaceutical*. It ensures greater protection for the important constitutional concerns of legality and the rule of law, derived mainly from ss. 7 and 11(g) as well as the preamble to the *Charter*. As a long-term effect of this more demanding approach, it is foreseeable that legislators will tend to use greater care in drafting laws, which will improve the overall certainty of the legal system.

Conclusion

In this chapter, we have assessed the content of the vagueness doctrine in American and Canadian constitutional law. A preliminary inquiry into the American situation has shown the rather narrow protection afforded to concerns of fair notice and law enforcement discretion in the United States. Doctrinal accounts of the void-for-vagueness doctrine in that country, as well as our conclusions drawn from cases such as *Papachristou*, *Lanzetta*, *Roth*, and *Rose*, have revealed the reluctance of American courts to consider statutory precision as a significant constitutional concern. Apart from cases driven by other substantive interests such as free speech, for example, we have seen that the Supreme Court of the United States is willing to invalidate vague laws only in limited circumstances. Fair notice will be seen as offended only if citizens are not conscious of their conduct's possible legal repercussions, as in the *Lambert* case. The second rationale of the vagueness doctrine will be seen as offended only if the law lends itself to selective enforcement against so-called undesirables. Apart from these limited situations, encroachments upon the principles of legality and the rule of law will usually remain unchallenged.

The Canadian version of the vagueness doctrine has been the main object of our attention. We examined at length the decision of the Supreme Court of Canada in the *Nova Scotia Pharmaceutical* case, and concluded that the approach it has sketched out to deal with the constitutional problem of vagueness needed to be further developed. We saw that the Court's description of the doctrine's two rationales, which was derived from the United States, needed to be expanded in order to protect the principles of legality and the rule of law in a satisfactory manner. To describe the first rationale of vagueness exclusively in terms of a "substratum of values" ignores the importance of precise legislative drafting to promote certainty in the legal system and avoid unfair surprise to citizens. Similarly, an understanding of law enforcement discretion exclusively in terms of "catch-all laws leading to automatic convictions" fails to limit the influence of arbitrary power in the legal system as dictated by the rule of law. We noted, however, that the factors identified by the Supreme Court in describing the rationales of the vagueness doctrine are far from useless. In fact, we saw that they can be used quite legitimately as elements that can make the requirement of precision fluctuate in particular cases.

The central point of the *Nova Scotia Pharmaceutical* case was the creation of the legal debate test to assess the constitutional validity of statutes challenged for vagueness. As we realized, this standard is very easy for legislative assemblies to satisfy. Consequently, it does little to promote certainty in the legal system. It does not ensure that citizens are given fair notice, nor does it allow for law enforcement discretion to be adequately controlled. To solve the inadequacies of this low threshold of constitutional validity, we have suggested a balanced approach that takes into account the competing interests of individuals and the State. Specifically, we showed that the standard of review's severity should fluctuate according to a variety of factors, most importantly: (1) the presence of a "substratum of values," (2) the likelihood of selective enforcement, (3) the issue of reasonable necessity, and (4) the type of law involved. This scheme of analysis leads to a threshold of validity that can be higher than legal debate, depending on the circumstances.

As illustrated by the *Canadian Bar Assn.* cases, a higher threshold of legislative precision can be more appropriate than legal debate to protect fair notice and control law enforcement discretion. Techniques such as nonexhaustive enumerations to activate the principle of *ejusdem generis* or the use of specifications through regulation can help legislative assemblies comply with this more elaborate and demanding version of the doctrine. Meanwhile, we have seen that the need for flexibility in the legal system is never forgotten. Far from attempting to eliminate it, the doctrine of vagueness that I have explained merely seeks to reconcile this concern with the competing imperatives of legality and the rule of law. This will impose a more demanding administrative burden on the State, but it will not deprive it of the flexibility it needs to reach its legislative objectives efficiently.

4
The Place of the Vagueness Doctrine in the *Charter*

The purpose of this chapter is to examine the appropriate place of the vagueness doctrine in the *Canadian Charter of Rights and Freedoms*, and to analyze and assess the impact of the different ways pursuant to which requirements of legislative precision can be derived from this constitutional document.[1] It is important to note at the outset that there is no particular provision in the *Charter* or in the *Constitution Act, 1867* that expressly requires precision in legislation. Canadian courts have, however, derived such an implicit requirement from certain provisions of the *Charter*. Some of its provisions can render the vagueness doctrine applicable in individual cases, depending on the circumstances. These provisions are essentially ss. 1 and 7, as well as other provisions that, much like s. 7, contain an "internal limitation."[2] From this fragmented recognition of the vagueness doctrine can arise certain procedural and substantive problems, which will be addressed in this chapter. A study of the constitutional bases of the doctrine is important in determining its applicability in particular cases and in understanding the influence the bases can have on the nature of the vagueness analysis on the merits.

Under s. 1 of the *Charter*, vagueness can become relevant in two ways. First, it can be raised in connection with the requirement that limitations on *Charter* rights be "prescribed by law." In this regard, an overly vague law is considered not to be a law, and the Crown is thus denied access to justification under s. 1. Second, vagueness can acquire importance under the "minimal impairment" branch of the *Oakes* test. A vague law, since it possesses the potential for being interpreted in an overly broad manner, is problematic with regard to minimal impairment. In this sense, the concepts of vagueness and overbreadth are similar in some respects, but also exhibit some differences. I will analyze the relationship between these first two bases of the vagueness doctrine under s. 1, the "prescribed by law" and minimal impairment requirements. Courts usually consider "prescribed by law" to be useless, and prefer most of the time to devote their attention to minimal impairment. I will examine the reasons for this and point out the potential, though limited, usefulness of the "prescribed by law" requirement.

I will then examine the bases that have been recognized in substantive provisions of the *Charter.* Vagueness is normally applicable every time a provision of the *Charter* contains an "internal limitation." For example, it is considered to be a "principle of fundamental justice" under s. 7. I will examine some problems surrounding the applicability of the doctrine in the framework of s. 7, as well as in other provisions of the *Charter* containing an "internal limitation."

Next, I will examine the doctrine's degree of autonomy pursuant to current jurisprudence. To this day, the vagueness doctrine does not have autonomous status. This means that there must always be some other *Charter* interest at stake in order for the precision of legislation to become relevant. As the case law is not particularly clear on this issue, it lends itself to divergent interpretations. Some jurists might even be led to believe that the vagueness doctrine is in fact autonomous. This controversy will be addressed. Then, departing from this current state of the jurisprudence, I will explore the possibilities of a broader applicability of the doctrine in the future. The strong interpretative influence of the principles of legality and the rule of law, studied in Chapters 1 and 2, will be helpful in this regard. In particular, we will see that ss. 7 and 11(g) can reasonably be interpreted in light of these principles as permitting an autonomous recognition of the vagueness doctrine in the future, or at least allowing its applicability in all penal matters. Finally, I will attempt to address the impact of constitutional bases on the severity of vagueness analysis. I will show that, especially because of the interplay between the concepts of overbreadth and vagueness, the requirement of precision can vary depending on the constitutional basis under which it is being analyzed.

The "Prescribed by Law" Requirement in Section 1 of the *Charter*
Vagueness is relevant first under s. 1 of the *Charter.* We know that whenever the breach of any specific guarantee under the *Charter* has been established, the Crown must meet a preliminary requirement before it can proceed to demonstrate that the limitation is justified in a free and democratic society. This preliminary requirement, also called "s. 1 *in limine,*" is that the limitation be prescribed by law. Section 1 reads as follows: "1. The *Canadian Charter of Rights and Freedoms* guarantees the rights and freedoms set out in it subject only to such reasonable limits *prescribed by law* as can be demonstrably justified in a free and democratic society" [emphasis added].

The fact that the limitations must be prescribed by law means, in the first place, that they must originate from a legal source in a formal (material) sense.[3] For example, if a police officer decides to deprive someone of a

Charter right without any legal authorization, it is obvious that the Crown will not be allowed to invoke s. 1 to justify the restriction. The reason is that the said restriction was not prescribed by law, but rather prescribed by the police force. What is interesting for us is that the "prescribed by law" requirement also has a substantive (qualitative) meaning. This is where vagueness can become relevant. It is considered that a law severely lacking in precision is not a law, and a *Charter* right limitation cannot therefore be "prescribed by law" in the qualitative sense.[4] Thus, if a statute restricts a *Charter* guarantee in overly vague terms, the government will not be given the opportunity to demonstrate under the *Oakes* test that the restriction is justified. In other words, the court will deny the Crown access to the *Oakes* test if the statute is so vague that it is considered not to be law.

For the sake of comparison, let us note that the same type of preliminary requirement can be found with regard to the several limitation provisions contained in the *European Convention for the Protection of Human Rights and Fundamental Freedoms.*[5] This document does not contain a general limitation provision like s. 1 of the *Charter,* but rather several specific provisions, namely paragraphs 8(2), 9(2), 10(2), and 11(2), and article 2(3) of Protocol No. 4 to the *Convention.* In a way similar to s. 1, these provisions require that the limitations be "in accordance with the law or prescribed by law." The European Court of Human Rights has given a broad interpretation to this wording so as to require that the law reach a certain level of precision. Thus, in the *Sunday Times* case,[6] the concern of providing citizens with fair warning with regard to form as well as content was considered to be an integral part of the "prescribed by law" requirement. Later, in the *Malone* case,[7] the European Court added the concern of limiting the discretionary power of law-enforcing authorities as a reason for requiring that limitations to rights and freedoms be determined by precise laws.

The Supreme Court of Canada ruled in the same direction as the European Court in its interpretation of the "prescribed by law" element in s. 1 of the *Charter.* The Court extracted from it the same two concerns of providing fair warning to citizens and limiting the discretionary power of law-enforcing authorities. In their joint opinion in the *Irwin Toy* case,[8] Dickson C.J. and Lamer and Wilson JJ. stated with regard to s. 1 that "where there is no intelligible standard and where the legislature has given a plenary discretion to do whatever seems best in a wide set of circumstances, there is no limit 'prescribed by law.'"[9]

Only a few cases have led to the invalidation of statutes under the "prescribed by law" test. Among them is the *Board of Censors* case[10] from the Ontario Court of Appeal. The statute in question gave wide discretionary powers to an administrative commission to censor movies in the province. The Court concluded that the unlimited discretion given to the commission permitted restrictions on freedom of expression that were not prescribed by law. Similarly, in *Commonwealth of Canada*,[11] L'Heureux-Dubé J. decided that a piece of legislation giving unlimited discretionary power to the Minister of Transport to grant authorizations related to expressive activities in airports[12] did not meet the "prescribed by law" requirement.[13]

These two cases were related to grants of unfettered discretionary powers to executive bodies. Even though the question was analyzed within the framework of the vagueness doctrine, it is interesting to note that the challenged pieces of legislation were not vague in the strict sense. It cannot be said that the prescribed norms for administrative decisions were vague: there were simply no norms at all.[14] Although these laws were clear in theory, the courts dealt with the problems within the confines of the vagueness doctrine because they raised problems similar to those triggered by vague laws. In both cases, there was no legal obstacle to prevent the authority from giving pre-eminence to its personal preferences in restricting certain types of expression.

The "prescribed by law" element is thus a basis for invoking the vagueness doctrine. Interestingly, this is not the only way the vagueness of a law can acquire importance under s. 1. The precision of legislation can also become a key factor in the context of the "minimal impairment" branch of the *Oakes* analysis mandated by s. 1, which we will now examine.

The "Minimal Impairment" Branch of the *Oakes* Test

The Notion of Overbreadth
When the State attempts to justify the breach of a *Charter* guarantee, it must satisfy the criteria set out in the *Oakes* case.[15] In particular, under the "minimal impairment" branch, it must demonstrate that the challenged legislation uses the least drastic means to fulfill its objectives.[16] If the means used by the State are disproportionate in relation to the objectives, the law will be invalid. The law is then said to be "overbroad." In fact, as Gonthier J. noted in the *Nova Scotia Pharmaceutical* case, "overbreadth is subsumed under the 'minimal impairment branch' of the *Oakes* test, under s. 1 of the *Charter*."[17]

Vagueness is relevant in this regard because a law that does not sufficiently limit the judges' or the administration's discretion can potentially be interpreted in an overbroad manner. In other words, it is not so much the lack of precision *per se* that is considered problematic in the circumstances but rather the fact that the law, because of its vagueness, can be interpreted in a way that restricts constitutional guarantees in an excessive manner. This overbreadth created by statutory interpretation is unacceptable, to the same extent that laws that are overbroad by their express terms are inconsistent with the requirement of minimal impairment.

Notions of vagueness and overbreadth are distinct in the sense that a law can suffer from only one or both of the two defects. In *R. v. Heywood*, Cory J. described the relationship between vagueness and overbreadth as follows:

> Overbreadth and vagueness are different concepts, but are sometimes related in particular cases. As the Ontario Court of Appeal observed in *R. v. Zundel* (1987), 58 O.R. (2d) 129, at pp. 157-58, cited with approval by Gonthier J. in *R. v. Nova Scotia Pharmaceutical Society, supra,* the meaning of a law may be unambiguous and thus the law will not be vague; however, it may still be overly broad. Where a law is vague, it may also be overly broad, to the extent that the ambit of its application is difficult to define. Overbreadth and vagueness are related in that both are the result of a lack of sufficient precision by a legislature in the means used to accomplish an objective. In the case of vagueness, the means are not clearly defined. In the case of overbreadth the means are too sweeping in relation to the objective.[18]

Thus, in some contexts the two concepts can be totally distinct. They are, however, inevitably linked under the "minimal impairment" branch since vagueness is then relevant only to the extent that it can lead to overbreadth. As the Supreme Court recognized in the *Nova Scotia Pharmaceutical* case, "vagueness as it relates to the 'minimal impairment' branch of s. 1 merges with the related concept of overbreadth."[19]

We realize that the analysis of legislative precision in the framework of the "minimal impairment" branch does not relate to the vagueness doctrine in the strict sense. In fact, in this particular context, vagueness becomes relevant only through its potential for triggering overbreadth. The Court's concerns at this stage are not related to the two related rationales of providing fair notice to citizens and limiting law enforcement discretion, as is usually the case within the framework of the vagueness doctrine. In other words, it is not so much the *manner* in which a right is being restricted that matters anymore, but rather the *degree* of restriction it suffers.[20]

The Notion of "Chilling Effect"

The phenomenon of "chilling effect" is a particular type of overbreadth that can occur because of the vagueness of a law. Normally, the overbreadth triggered by statutory indefiniteness occurs when the judge or the other deciding authority exploits the vagueness of a law to restrict a *Charter* guarantee in a disproportionate manner. In this framework, note that the law acquires the defect only at the moment it is being applied by the deciding authority, usually the judiciary. Indeed, before being applied by that authority, the law does not yet have an overbroad effect. In some circumstances, however, the vagueness of a law can trigger a different kind of overbreadth, known as "chilling effect." This notion is derived from a belief that some of the rights and freedoms guaranteed by the Constitution must be given "breathing space." When citizens are uncertain of their rights, they will often indulge in auto-censorship in order to avoid the risk of punishment. In the *Commonwealth of Canada* case, L'Heureux-Dubé J. described the problem as follows: "Right and freedoms must be nurtured, not inhibited. Vague laws intruding on fundamental freedoms create paths of uncertainty onto which citizens fear to tread, fearing legal sanction. Vagueness serves only to cause confusion and most people will shy from exercising their freedoms rather than facing potential punishment."[21]

Thus, there will be a "chilling effect" if citizens, because of the vagueness of a law, fear to exercise a constitutionally protected conduct. It is possible that this fear is not justified, in that the law as interpreted might not end up covering the particular conduct at stake. The vagueness is nonetheless unacceptable because of the auto-censorship it leads to. In practice, the guaranteed freedom in question ends up being restricted to a greater degree than is allowed under the *Charter*. In that sense, chilling effect is another form of overbreadth.

Note that concerns related to legality and the rule of law (i.e., classic vagueness) are not the reason why the defective warning given by the law is considered problematic in this framework. Rather, it is considered problematic because it leads to chilling effect, and therefore to overbreadth. It must also be realized that a vague law will not necessarily trigger chilling effect. In fact, the concept will come into play only when a vague command is directed to citizens concerning the exercise of a constitutional right taking the form of a conduct.[22] Thus, for example, rights protected by ss. 2 and 6 of the *Charter* lend themselves easily to concerns of chilling effect because they involve the protection of conduct, as opposed to most rights contained in ss. 7 to 15, which merely constitute guarantees against State interference. It is most often with regard to freedom of expression that chilling effect is invoked in Canada under s. 2(b)[23] as well as in the United States under the First Amendment.[24]

An interesting fact about chilling effect is that it can sometimes occur in relation to a law that has been the object of "reading down." We know that when courts consider a law that excessively restricts a *Charter* guarantee, they have at least two remedial options. They can either declare the statute invalid or bend its interpretation to cure the overbreadth and preserve the validity of the legislation. In the latter case, the process is called "reading down." At least two types of concerns must guide the courts in their choice of an appropriate remedy. First, the courts must take care not to assume the legislature's role when attempting to reconcile statutes with the Constitution.[25] Thus, if the forced interpretation does not simply and naturally flow from the constitutional requirements, reading down must be avoided because it would constitute judicial redrafting of the law. Second – and that is what concerns us here – the courts must avoid a reading down that would create uncertainty as to the scope of the law in a manner leading to chilling effect. Otherwise, overbreadth would reappear in an extra-judicial manner through this chilling effect. Laurence H. Tribe states the problem as follows in the American context:

> The risk of introducing vagueness when attempting to reconstruct statutes reveals a structural relationship of general importance in the interplay of overbreadth and vagueness. This relationship is most sharply focused in a hypothetical statute: *"It shall be a crime to say anything in public unless the speech is protected by the first and fourteenth amendments."* This statute is guaranteed not to be overbroad since, by its terms, it literally forbids nothing that the constitution protects. The statute is nonetheless patently vague, although it is identical with the gloss Chief Justice Rehnquist would apparently put on every law to "save" it from an overbreadth challenge ... The problem with that solution is that it simply exchanges overbreadth for vagueness.[26]

This type of concern can be illustrated in the Canadian context in light of the decision of the Supreme Court of Canada in *Osborne*.[27] This case involved a challenge to s. 33 of the *(Federal) Public Service Employment Act*,[28] which, apart from a few exceptions, prohibited public servants from working for or against a candidate or a political party, or to be candidate in an election. As drafted, this provision was seen to be in violation of s. 2(b) of the *Charter,* and was unjustifiable under s. 1 because of its overbreadth. The means resorted to by Parliament to ensure the impartiality of the civil service were seen as excessive with regard to the scope of the activities and the persons targeted. Inevitably, the question of remedy arose. Should the Court attempt to preserve the valid applications of the statutory provision or simply invalidate it?

In the Federal Court, trial division level,[29] Walsh J. had chosen the first option. He decided to interpret the law as prohibiting only activities that could validly be restricted by the State under the *Charter*. In other words, he read the law as though it included the requirements of s. 1. This approach resembles the classic American remedy of "as applied" declaration of invalidity. In the United States, the "as applied" remedial approach means that courts will use case-by-case invalidations in response to overly broad statutes impinging on constitutional rights instead of striking them down "on their face."[30] This American approach and the one adopted by Walsh J. are fairly similar in that they both purport to measure the particular factual situation in the case at bar against the requirements of the Constitution.

This type of approach has the immediate advantage of preserving the validity of the law, but it has the inconvenient consequence of creating the problem of vagueness. Indeed, it is very difficult for the average citizen to know whether particular expressive conduct can validly be restricted "in a free and democratic society." Therefore, the citizen will be very careful about the activities (protected by the *Charter*) that he or she chooses to engage in, raising the problem of chilling effect. It is interesting to note that the only cases where American courts accept or rely on the "on its face" approach rather than the "as applied" remedy are cases where a chilling effect arises, mainly in the context of the First Amendment's freedom of speech.[31] Thus, the threat of chilling effect has the potential, in the United States, to broaden the remedial approach. *A fortiori*, in Canada, where the remedial approach in constitutional cases is traditionally more liberal, the threat of a chilling effect should certainly be a strong deterrent towards the abuse of the reading down remedy.

In *Osborne*, the Supreme Court of Canada did not share the views of Walsh J. concerning the remedial approach. The statutory provision was indeed invalidated on its face. Surprisingly, however, note that the Court did not rely expressly on the chilling effect argument to support its choice of remedy. Instead, the Court merely invoked concerns related to avoiding a judicial redrafting of the law. This relates to the deference towards the legislative role that I mentioned earlier. It would certainly have been appropriate for the Court to invoke, in addition, the concept of chilling effect in support of the chosen remedy. A reading down could have introduced vagueness in the law, and civil servants would therefore have been "chilled" in the future from exercising the constitutional rights at stake. This is especially true considering that the statutory provision at stake in *Osborne* was directed towards a specific group of individuals (civil servants), and therefore possessed perhaps an even greater potential for chilling effect than a law of general application would have. As Carol Rogerson notes: "The idea of chilling effect rests upon an assumption that citizens know the law and govern their behaviour in accordance with it. The truth of the assumption will obviously vary and might be stronger, for example, in circumstances where the law is directed at regulating the behaviour of a specific group of individuals, such as civil servants or lawyers, and weaker in circumstances where the law is a general trespass statute."[32]

The case of *Rocket v. Royal College of Dental Surgeons of Ontario*[33] offers another illustration of chilling effect arising at the stage of remedy in a *Charter* case. *Rocket* involved a challenge to restrictions on advertising imposed by the College of Dental Surgeons on its members. The regulatory provision at stake, which contained very limited exceptions to this prohibition, constituted a breach of s. 2(b) of the *Charter* and was struck down as over-broad. The Supreme Court refused to "read down" the law and preserve its valid applications "because of the adverse effect it might have on legitimate speech."[34] In addition to chilling effect, the Court's choice of remedy was motivated by a desire to avoid a judicial redrafting of the law. A reading down would have required the Court to supply further exceptions to the prohibition, which would impinge on the legislator's role.[35] With regard to chilling effect, note that the Court's approach constitutes a departure from the conservative view of American courts, which refuse to apply the doctrine in cases where "commercial" speech is at stake.[36] McLachlin J., writing for the Court in *Rocket,* justified this departure by invoking the argument that "professionals are typically very concerned with their standing in the profession and few would be inclined to set themselves against the governing bodies."[37] This view reflected concerns similar to that in the Rogerson passage quoted above, indicating that chilling effect is a serious concern, even, and perhaps more importantly, when a law restricting expression is directed towards a specific group of individuals.

With these concerns in mind, I will make a few comments in relation to another decision of the Supreme Court of Canada: the case of *Ruffo v. Conseil de la Magistrature.*[38] This case involved a challenge based on s. 2(b) and the vagueness theory to s. 8 of the *Judicial Code of Ethics,*[39] which states that "in public, the judge should act in a reserved, serene and courteous manner." Considering the particular concerns mentioned above surrounding laws directed towards a specific group of individuals, the concept of chilling effect should have been of primary importance in this case. However, the Court neglected to take into consideration the adverse effect that such a vague statutory formula could have on the exercise of judges' freedom of speech. The Court relied on the following passage from Yves Ouellette: "[Translation] Breaches of discipline do not have to be defined as precisely as penal offences. Codes of ethics and discipline may thus be considered an exception to the rule that regulations must be certain or precise. Indeed, an examination of some codes of professional ethics reveal a number of provisions that, while vague, *set out fundamental principles that by their very nature are general yet probably perfectly intelligible to those in the profession"* [emphasis added by Gonthier J.].[40]

In the case at bar, the regulation was being challenged against the *constitutional* vagueness doctrine.[41] As the Court noted,[42] however, Ouellette's comments had been expressed in the context of the *administrative law* vice of vagueness. This should have had the effect of diminishing the importance of Ouellette's comments when imported in the constitutional context of the *Ruffo* case, but this was not acknowledged by the Court. In administrative law, vagueness can be grounds for declaring invalid a piece of regulation independently from the *Charter.* The analysis is to focus mainly on the capacity for the addressees of the law to ascertain its meaning.[43] Thus, requiring less precision from professional codes of ethics is justified, since those in the profession possess a certain expertise allowing them to understand vague regulatory formulas that would probably be unintelligible to the average citizen.

In the context of a *constitutional* analysis of vagueness, however, additional concerns, such as chilling effect on protected freedoms, can intervene to require more precision from professional codes of ethics than is required in administrative law. In *Ruffo,* it must not be forgotten that besides being vague, the provision touched upon freedom of expression, protected by s. 2(b) of the *Charter.* The Court decided not to rule on the s. 2(b) issue since the guidance by lower courts was insufficient for the moment.[44] Given Canadian jurisprudence regarding s. 2(b), however, there does not seem to be any doubt that this guarantee is breached by s. 8 of the *Code,* subject to s. 1 analysis.[45] Note that in *Ruffo,* the Court did not specify the constitutional basis or provision pursuant to which the vagueness analysis was performed. However, it is only in the context of s. 1 that vagueness could have acquired importance in this case, in relation to a hypothetical breach of s. 2(b).[46] In the context of s. 1, we know that concerns of overbreadth and chilling effect can become relevant, given the need to impinge as little as possible on freedom of expression. Note that s. 8 of the *Code* is a very broad prohibition on the public expression of judges. It apparently encompasses speech concerning all subject matters, performed anywhere, with any means of communication. Given the fact that the *Code* is aimed at specific individuals and carries embarrassing career repercussions upon conviction, we have already seen that the threat of chilling effect can be particularly important. Instead of taking this fact into consideration to require greater precision from the legislation, Gonthier J. writing for a majority of the Court seemed to approve the chilling effect created by the *Code:*

> Ethical rules are meant to aim for perfection. They call for better conduct not through the imposition of various sanctions but through compliance with personally imposed constraints. A definition, on the other hand, sets out fixed rules and thus tends to become an upper limit, an implicit authorization to do whatever is not prohibited. There is no doubt that these two concepts are difficult to reconcile, and this explains the general rule of the duty to act in a reserved manner: as an ethical standard, it is more concerned with providing general guidance about conduct than with illustrating specifics and the type of conduct allowed.[47]

It is striking to see how Gonthier J. describes what is in essence a deliberate creation of chilling effect only to approve the whole process. What seems to be forgotten is that, contrary to vagueness analysis in administrative law, concerns of overbreadth and chilling effect must always be assessed in conjunction with constitutional vagueness challenges, especially in areas involving speech. These are essential components of assessments of the precision of legislation under s. 1.

The Relationship between "Prescribed by Law" and "Minimal Impairment"

A reference to vagueness theory usually has little impact when invoked in the context of the "prescribed by law" requirement. Indeed, considering that vagueness is also relevant, at least indirectly, under the "minimal impairment" branch of the *Oakes* test, the Supreme Court will usually refuse to conclude that the law is so vague as not to constitute a limit "prescribed by law," which would put an end to the analysis under s. 1.[48]

Although the problems created by vagueness are of different natures under these two constitutional bases, in practice a law that fails the first test will usually fail the second one as well. It is generally considered that if a law does not provide an "intelligible standard" and therefore fails the "prescribed by law" requirement, it also has the potential to be interpreted in an overbroad manner. The contrary is not always true, however, and a law can be too vague to prevent overbreadth but at the same time precise enough with regard to the "prescribed by law" requirement. The fact that the second test usually asks for greater precision in practice has prompted the Court to declare that "it is preferable in the vast majority of cases to deal with vagueness in the context of a s. 1 analysis rather than disqualifying the law *in limine*."[49]

Despite this reality, there still might be circumstances in which vagueness under the "prescribed by law" test could acquire a real and tangible importance. This would be due to the difference of nature between the two requirements under s. 1. Recall that under the "prescribed by law" requirement, the analysis is concerned essentially with legality and the rule of law (i.e., classic vagueness). We want to avoid seeing constitutional guarantees restricted in a way that is unpredictable and arbitrary. In contrast, with regard to the "minimal impairment" branch, it is not so much classic vagueness that prompts courts to fight uncertainty but rather the fear of overbreadth. What is to be avoided is situations where the law-enforcing authority will use its wide discretion in a manner that limits constitutional guarantees more than necessary.

As we have seen, these two interrelated but distinct objectives merge most of the time in practice, and that is why courts prefer to analyze directly the most demanding test, which is the one of minimal impairment. I believe, however, that there might occur situations in which the two tests will retain mutually exclusive importance. As an illustration, let us consider the case of *Slaight Communications v. Davidson.*[50] Our particular problem was not raised *per se* in the *Slaight* case, but the case is of interest because it provides a useful framework for illustrating the point.

Slaight contained a challenge to s. 61.5(9)(c) of the *Canadian Labour Code,*[51] which provides that an arbitrator may order an employer to do any "thing that is equitable" to remedy an unjust dismissal. In the case at bar, the arbitrator had ordered the employer to write a letter of recommendation in which he would recognize that the dismissal was unjust. In addition, the employer was prohibited from responding to any request for information otherwise than by sending this letter. The Court decided that this constituted a breach of s. 2(b) of the *Charter,* which protects freedom of expression. At the stage of justification under s. 1, the "prescribed by law" requirement in the formal sense[52] was controversial because it was the order from the arbitrator (and not the statute) that was in actual fact subjected to the *Oakes* test. The Supreme Court nonetheless decided that the formal "prescribed by law" requirement was satisfied because the arbitrator had exercised his power under the law. The breach was then put to the test under s. 1 and was judged reasonable, therefore valid. The "minimal impairment" branch was satisfied as the law and the order were both found not to be overbroad. The statute itself respects minimal impairment through a reading down done by the Court: the legislation shall be interpreted as not allowing the arbitrator to order anything that would impinge on s. 2(b) in a way that is unjustifiable under s. 1.

Thus, note that in *Slaight* the law is considered precise enough to satisfy the "minimal impairment" branch. This is due to the reading down that shields the law from overbreadth. However – and that is where it becomes interesting – it may be asked whether the law satisfies the "prescribed by law" requirement in the qualitative sense (i.e., vagueness). The legislation gives a very wide discretionary power to the arbitrator with regard to the appropriate remedy to be applied in cases of unjust dismissal. In that sense, the law may be too vague to meet the standard set out by Dickson C.J. and Lamer and Wilson JJ. in *Irwin Toy* that "where there is no intelligible standard and when the legislature has given a plenary discretion to do whatever seems best in a wide set of circumstances, there is no 'limit prescribed by law.'"[53]

The granting of such a wide discretionary power in *Slaight* bears some similarity to the pieces of legislation invalidated in *Board of Censors*[54] and *Commonwealth of Canada* (concurring opinion by L'Heureux-Dubé J.)[55] on the grounds that they permitted limits on expression that could not be said to be prescribed by law. It is true that with regard to *Slaight,* the discretionary power is not absolute in the sense that it must be exercised within the limits of minimal impairment now included in the law through the process of reading down. It should be noted, however, that these measures immunizing the law from overbreadth only manage to create a maximum above which arbitrators do not have the power to rule. Even if arbitrators must act within these prescriptions, they nonetheless possesses a wide discretionary power to decide in what way freedom of expression will be limited. This may be incompatible with the concern of protecting the rule of law in the context of restrictions to fundamental *Charter* rights. In this way, the legislation from which the arbitrator's order originated might be incompatible with the "prescribed by law" requirement in the qualitative sense, despite the fact that the law is not overbroad with regard to the "minimal impairment" branch.

Thus, we see that there are some circumstances that could give a significant importance to the "prescribed by law" vagueness element. It is therefore not to be perceived as a totally empty aspect of the vagueness doctrine. However, the realm of circumstances under which the "prescribed by law" vagueness analysis loses its mootness is rather narrow. Indeed, there must be a legal scheme similar to the one that was prevalent in *Slaight*: a vague law repugnant to a *Charter* guarantee, such as s. 2(b), that is read down to comply with the requirement of minimal impairment. Such a situation is rather uncommon because of the phenomenon of chilling effect described earlier. Due to the chilling effect concern, courts will usually refuse to apply the remedy of reading down to a vague law breaching a *Charter* guarantee such as s. 2(b). For example, in the *Osborne* case analyzed earlier, the law restricting expressive activities in vague terms could not be read down under minimal impairment because a chilling effect would have been triggered. If the law had been read as restricting only the political activities deemed not to be protected by the *Charter,* civil servants would have been "chilled" in the exercise of their s. 2(b) rights because it is obviously not clear what restrictions can "be demonstrably justified in a free and democratic society."

In contrast, *Slaight* represents perhaps the uncommon case of a vague statute repugnant to s. 2(b) that can be read down under minimal impairment without creating the problem of chilling effect. The reason is that in *Slaight,* the law does not contain a standard against which the legality of expressive activities will be assessed. Rather, it constitutes an enactment allowing an arbitrator to make certain orders restricting future expressive activities. The vagueness of the standard on which the order is based obviously does not create a risk of chilling effect, and therefore the remedy of reading down becomes possible. Thus, in this type of situation, it can be relevant to examine the "prescribed by law" element, as it will not completely merge with the "minimal impairment" branch. Minimal impairment might be remedied with reading down, while "prescribed by law" could at the same time remain problematic.

Having examined the different possibilities involving vagueness under

s. 1, let us now focus on some of the other constitutional bases of the doctrine as recognized by the Supreme Court of Canada.

Recognition in Substantive Provisions of the Charter

In the *Nova Scotia Pharmaceutical* case, Gonthier J. noted that "vagueness can be raised under the substantive sections of the *Charter* whenever these sections comprise some internal limitation."[56] Section 7 is one of those provisions, as Lamer J. had already stated in the *Prostitution Reference*.[57] To that extent, legislative precision is a "principle of fundamental justice." In addition to s. 7, other provisions of the *Charter* may be considered as having an internal limitation rendering the vagueness theory applicable. For example, the Supreme Court of Canada stated in the *Morales* case[58] that the vagueness of a piece of legislation restricting the right to bail in criminal proceedings breached s. 11(e) of the *Charter*, which guarantees any accused person the right "not to be denied reasonable bail without just cause."[59] The balancing raised by the notion of "just cause" is, in fact, an internal limitation allowing concerns of vagueness to become relevant in the same manner as the "principles of fundamental justice" in s. 7.

Section 7 of the *Charter*

With regard to substantive provisions of the *Charter*, it is most often in the context of s. 7 that the vagueness issue is raised.[60] Recall that the scheme of analysis dictated by this provision consists of two steps. To invoke it, a party must first demonstrate a breach of either life, liberty, or security of the person. Then it must be shown that this deprivation is not "in accordance with the principles of fundamental justice." A statute restricting life, liberty, or security of the person in vague terms is therefore constitutionally vulnerable.

In the context of s. 7, it would seem that vagueness is relevant in relation to classic vagueness concerns (i.e., legality and the rule of law) as well as to overbreadth concerns. This is a mixture of the concerns relevant under the "prescribed by law" and "minimal impairment" elements of s. 1. On the one hand, s. 7 borrows the same rationales that are relevant under the "prescribed by law" requirement (i.e., fair notice and limitation of law enforcement discretion). On the other hand, as with minimal impairment, overbreadth is relevant within the framework of a s. 7 vagueness analysis. Overbreadth has been recognized to be contrary to the principles of fundamental justice in *Heywood*.[61] As we saw earlier, vagueness usually represents potential overbreadth. It must be mentioned, however, that overbreadth, whether or not resulting from the vagueness of a law, must be assessed with less severity in s. 7 than in minimal impairment, as it does not presuppose the violation of a substantive *Charter* guarantee. As greater deference will be afforded to the legislator, it will not be necessary

under s. 7 for the law to use the least drastic means, a reasonable proportionality being sufficient.[62]

Let us now consider a difficulty that might occur in the future with
regard to the applicability of vagueness in relation to s. 7. Recall that to
establish a breach of this provision, two elements must be demonstrated:
the limitation of life, liberty, or security of the person, and the noncompliance with the principles of fundamental justice. Moreover – and this
is what is worthy of our interest at this moment – the text of s. 7 seems
to require a link between these two elements. The provision states: "7.
Everyone has the right to life, liberty and security of the person and the
right not to be deprived thereof *except in accordance with* the principles of
fundamental justice" [emphasis added].

Most of the time, the existence of a link between the two elements is not
problematic. For example, in the case of a statute defining a crime in vague
terms, it is clear that the injustice created by the lack of clarity has a direct
impact on the possibility of imprisonment. The lack of fair notice and the
broad discretionary power given to law enforcement authorities are then
elements having an immediate link to the deprivation of liberty. In other
cases, however, the link between the vagueness of the law (breaching the
principles of fundamental justice) and the suppression of one of the rights
mentioned in s. 7 is far from obvious. This raises the question of whether
s. 7 would be applicable.

As an illustration of the problem, take the example of the factual situation that gave rise to the case of *Canada (Human Rights Commission) v. Taylor*.[63] Section 13(1) of the *Canadian Human Rights Act*[64] prohibits telephone
messages that might expose "persons to hatred or contempt by reason of
the fact that ... those persons are identifiable on the basis of a prohibited
ground of discrimination." On the basis of this provision, a tribunal had
ordered the accused to cease communicating certain anti-Semitic messages When he refused to comply with the order, the accused was sanctioned to imprisonment for contempt of court. In the Supreme Court of
Canada, the provision was challenged under s. 2(b) of the *Charter,* which
protects freedom of expression, and the argument of vagueness was raised
in the context of s. 1. For the purpose of the illustration, let us put aside
s. 2(b) to ascertain whether s. 7 could have been applicable and whether
vagueness could have been invoked in this framework.

There appears to be no link between the deprivation of liberty (imprisonment for contempt of court) and the alleged vagueness of the law (the
words "expose ... to hatred or contempt"). Indeed, even admitting that the
statutory language is unacceptably vague,[65] the order given on the basis of
this statute was not in itself lacking in precision. The accused knew he was
violating the order. We are confronted here with a clear order based on a
hypothetically vague law. It is the deliberate violation of the order (and

not vagueness) that leads to the deprivation of liberty. The link between the two branches of s. 7 is lacking in this kind of situation, and this could compromise the applicability of the vagueness theory.

Recognizing the applicability of s. 7 in this type of situation could have the effect of giving a broad reach to the vagueness doctrine. This is true to the extent that it could be invoked not only when a breach of life, liberty, or security of the person results directly from the statute but also when imprisonment may follow the disobedience of a legal order made under that statute. This broadening of the concept of liberty might force the respect of principles of fundamental justice every time a penal or civil order can potentially result in imprisonment for contempt of court if it is disobeyed. This hypothesis was lightly touched upon in the *Motor Vehicle Reference*.[66] In this case, an absolute liability offence leading to imprisonment was declared to be a violation of s. 7. Without ruling on the dilemma I have raised, which was not relevant in the case at bar, Lamer J. left open this possible indirect applicability of the principles of fundamental justice: "As no one has addressed imprisonment as an alternative to the non-payment of a fine, I prefer not to express any views in relation to s. 7 as regards that eventuality as a result of a conviction for an absolute liability offence."[67]

In order to reach an answer regarding the problem I have raised, it is useful to recall the double function that vagueness has under s. 7. In essence, legislative precision is relevant under s. 7 for reasons related to classic vagueness (fair notice and control of law enforcement discretion). In addition, it can acquire importance to the extent that it has the potential to trigger the problem of overbreadth.[68]

From the angle of classic vagueness, s. 7 would probably be inapplicable in the kind of situation presented above. This can be explained by referring to the reasons why vagueness in its classical dimension is recognized as a principle of fundamental justice. The concern under s. 7 is obviously to avoid a situation where unfair surprise or arbitrary considerations are the cause of a deprivation of liberty.[69] In the situation I have outlined with regard to the *Taylor* case, however, the accused knew what to expect as a result of his refusal to comply with the court order. It cannot be said that he did not receive fair notice that what he did was punishable, or that law-enforcing authorities had discretionary power to convict him for contempt of court.

To help us better understand the question, let us examine another Supreme Court of Canada decision that could have given rise to a similar problem: the 1988 case of *Morgentaler*.[70] At the time, s. 251 of the *Criminal Code* prohibited abortions unless continuation of pregnancy would "be likely to endanger [the] health" of the mother. The evaluation of the "danger for health" criterion was done by committees of physicians that could grant authorizations through complex and long procedures. Among other grievances, the vagueness of the "danger for health" criterion was raised. Beetz J. and Dickson C.J. concluded, in separate reasons, that the procedure breached the pregnant woman's security of the person. In this framework, there is no problem regarding the applicability of the vagueness doctrine, given the direct link for the woman between the allegedly vague norm and the breach of her security. As for the physician (Dr. Henry Morgentaler), he could invoke in his own defence a violation of s. 7 on behalf of the pregnant woman.[71]

However, in the framework of McIntyre J.'s reasons, the applicability of the vagueness argument was more controversial. According to him, s. 251 did not breach the woman's security. He therefore had to call upon the right to liberty to render s. 7 applicable. This liberty is jeopardized by the imprisonment that may result from the disrespect of a (clear) decision by the committee of physicians. In this context, there is no link between the alleged vagueness of the "danger for health" criterion under the principles of fundamental justice, and the breach of the right to liberty. As long as the decision by the committee of physicians is obeyed, no deprivation of liberty occurs. Thus, vagueness cannot be the direct cause of the deprivation of liberty. It is interesting to note that McIntyre J. did not even examine whether the health standard was sufficiently precise, being satisfied to merely cite a passage from the decision of the Court of Appeal, according to which "there is no doubt the respondents knew that the acts they proposed and carried out were in breach of the section ... they could not have doubted that the procuring of a miscarriage which they proposed ... could only be carried out in an accredited or approved hospital after the securing of the required certificate."[72] This type of approach supports the thesis according to which s. 7 is not violated in the absence of a direct link between vagueness on the one hand and life, liberty, or security of the person on the other.

This does not, however, mean that vagueness will be inapplicable every time such a direct link is missing. Here, the second function of vagueness in the framework of s. 7, which was discussed earlier, comes into play. It is the concern to avoid problems of overbreadth. Indeed, even if the vagueness problems related to legality and the rule of law disappear once a clear order is made pursuant to the statute, overbreadth may remain because of the vagueness of the standard on which the said order is based. If the legislative provision is so vague that it allows the authority to make an arbitrary and disproportionate order, there may be an overbreadth problem if a citizen is sent to prison for refusing to comply with it. Thus, in certain cases, vagueness may have a link with liberty through the overbreadth it triggers. This argument would not apply in every situation, however. For example, in the *Morgentaler* case, it is not very likely that the "danger

for health" criterion could have had the effect of triggering overbroad results. The leeway given to therapeutic committees was probably not large
enough to raise the problem of overbreadth.[73] With regard to the *Taylor*
case, still ignoring s. 2(b) for our purposes, the risks of overbreadth might
have been greater, although the Court ruled otherwise in the context of
s. 1 analysis.[74]

This demonstration shows the possibility of invoking s. 7 despite the
lack of a direct link between the vague standard and the breach of either
life, liberty, or security of the person. This may be the case if the law grants
a wide discretion to the authority and simultaneously raises the risk of
overbreadth.

Other Provisions of the *Charter* Containing an Internal Limitation
Besides s. 7, the Supreme Court of Canada recognized the possibility of
invoking the vagueness doctrine in the context of other provisions of the
Charter containing an internal limitation: "Vagueness may be raised under
the substantive sections of the *Charter* whenever these sections comprise
some internal limitation."[75]

For example, as we saw earlier, s. 11(e), through its internal limitation of
just cause, was interpreted in the *Morales* case as rendering the vagueness
theory applicable. By reading the several provisions of the *Charter,* it may
be noted that there are two types of internal limitations.

First, when a provision of the *Charter* provides that a guarantee is subject
to legal (i.e., legislative) restrictions, vagueness in its classic aspect can
become relevant. Vagueness is then analyzed objectively, as is the case
within the "prescribed by law" requirement of s. 1. For example, ss. 6(3)
and 6(4) of the *Charter* provide that the mobility rights guaranteed in ss.
6(1) and 6(2) are subject to some legislative limitations.[76] Thus, the vagueness doctrine can require that these limitations be specified by relatively
clear laws. Imagine a statute that states that "a judge can issue an order
forbidding any person to cross any interprovincial lines if he believes it is
in the public interest." An order made under this law could breach the
right of a Canadian citizen under s. 6(2)(a) to "move to and take up residence in any province." Would the fact that the order is made pursuant to
a "law of general application" be sufficient to render the breach acceptable
under s. 6(3)(a)? It could be argued that, as it constitutes an internal limitation of a *Charter* guarantee, s. 6(3)(a) could be prevented from applying
because of the vagueness of the "public interest" standard contained in
the statute.

Note that this type of basis renders the doctrine applicable in a relatively
narrow fashion. Section 6 is a rather technical provision and its reach is
restricted to a relatively limited number of situations. In addition, recall that
vagueness in that framework represents only an objective requirement of

precision linked to legality and the rule of law. Thus, vagueness will not come into play to assess any proportionality concern under s. 6, with the possible exception of s. 6(3)(b), which provides that residency requirements provided by law must be "reasonable." Apart from the latter provision, where vagueness could acquire a "subjective" relevance related to overbreadth, arguments of vagueness would be relevant under s. 6 strictly for reasons related to classic vagueness, as under the "prescribed by law" requirement of s. 1.

Quite differently, some provisions of the *Charter* include concerns of proportionality within the definition of the guarantee itself. This raises the question of overbreadth in a manner similar to the "minimal impairment" branch of the *Oakes* test. Vagueness can then be said to have a subjective impact. We have seen that s. 7 includes both types of concerns (overbreadth and classic vagueness) to render the vagueness doctrine applicable. Let us examine some other provisions that follow similar guidelines.

Section 8 of the *Charter* states that "everyone has the right to be secure against unreasonable search or seizure." Within the framework of this provision, it may be considered that the "unreasonable" character that must be associated with the search or seizure is an internal limitation that can make arguments of legislative precision relevant. In order for a search or seizure to be considered reasonable, the power to execute it must be provided by law.[77] This is derived from the principle of the rule of law.[78] In this framework, it can be considered that if a law authorizes an intrusion in overly vague terms, the requirement of a law will not be satisfied. Vagueness will thus be relevant for reasons related to the rule of law. The precision of legislation can also become a concern under s. 8 in an overbreadth perspective, since the word "unreasonable" triggers concerns of proportionality of the breach. Similarly, s. 9 of the *Charter*, which provides that "everyone has the right not to be arbitrarily detained or imprisoned," can also make vagueness applicable. The comments expressed with regard to s. 8 are equally applicable to s. 9. Thus, the arbitrary character that must be linked to a detention can render concerns of vagueness applicable. The *Charter* jurisprudence already recognizes that an overly broad discretionary power given by law can make a detention arbitrary.[79] There must be sufficient legal criteria to orient the discretion of the administrative or judicial authority.[80] Even though case law has not yet analyzed the vagueness question in the framework of ss. 8 and 9 of the *Charter*, it seems obvious to us that these two provisions can make vagueness applicable through the internal limitations they contain.[81]

Finally, let us consider the case of s. 12 of the *Charter*, which might allow the application of the vagueness doctrine since it contains an internal limitation. It provides that "everyone has the right not to be subjected to any cruel and unusual treatment or punishment." The inclusion of the vagueness doctrine within the scope of s. 12 would be interesting since the Canadian sentencing process often lacks appropriately defined standards to guide judges and juries in the imposition of punishments.[82]

Can the "cruel and unusual" elements render concerns related to the rule of law, including vagueness, relevant under s. 12? Lamer J. suggested in *R. v. Smith* that the question of whether a punishment was imposed through an arbitrary process had little relevance in the context of s. 12.[83] The analysis should focus on the punishment itself rather than on the process leading to it. Note, however, that Lamer J. was then writing only for himself and for Dickson C.J. Other members of the Court in *Smith* expressed a different view of this question. In separate opinions, Wilson,[84] McIntyre (dissenting),[85] and LeDain[86] JJ. were willing to accept the relevance of the criterion of arbitrariness in the analysis of s. 12. This position follows American jurisprudence related to the Eighth Amendment.[87] This provision of the American Bill of Rights provides, quite like s. 12, that "cruel and unusual punishments [shall not be] inflicted." It is recognized as a constitutional basis for the void-for-vagueness doctrine in the United States.[88] Although the question is still unanswered in Canada, s. 12 could constitute a basis for requiring precision in legislative provisions relating to punishments, especially considering the interpretative impact of the principle of the rule of law discussed in Chapter 2.[89]

Non-Autonomous Character of the Theory

In looking at the different constitutional bases of the doctrine, it can be noted that vagueness does not, to this day, have an autonomous existence as a means to invalidate legislation. Indeed, the Supreme Court of Canada has recognized the legitimacy of arguments related to vagueness only in relation to constitutional provisions containing limits to an identifiable *Charter* interest. These are s. 1 (under the "prescribed by law" requirement or under minimal impairment) and provisions containing an internal limitation, such as s. 7. None of these constitutional provisions allows pleadings to be based solely on the alleged vagueness of a statute. There must be a breach of a specific *Charter* interest in order for vagueness to acquire constitutional importance. In the framework of s. 1 *in limine* (prescribed by law), as well as under minimal impairment, it is obvious that there must be a breach of a specific *Charter* provision in order to render vagueness relevant. With regard to s. 7, vagueness is not autonomous either, but constitutes instead a principle of fundamental justice. As the Court noted in the *Motor Vehicle Act Reference:* "It is clear to me that the interests which are meant to be protected by the words 'and the right not to be deprived thereof except in accordance with the principles of fundamental justice' of s. 7 are the life, liberty and security of the person. The principles of fundamental justice, on the other hand, are not a protected interest, but rather a qualifier of the right not to be deprived of life, liberty and security of the person."[90]

Since the protection against vagueness in legislation is recognized under s. 7 as a principle of fundamental justice, it should logically abide by the same rule. Thus, according to current jurisprudence, it seems difficult to argue that vagueness is, to this day, an autonomous ground for rendering legislation invalid under s. 7. However, the following statement by Gonthier J. in *Nova Scotia Pharmaceutical* can potentially be interpreted as rendering the vagueness doctrine autonomous: "I wish to point out that the standard I have outlined applies to all enactments, irrespective of whether they are civil, criminal, administrative or other. The citizen is entitled to have the State abide by constitutional standards of precision whenever it enacts legal dispositions."[91]

In fact, this statement has led lower courts to consider on at least one occasion that the vagueness doctrine possesses an autonomous status. In the case of the *Canadian Bar Assn. No. 1*,[92] a vagueness challenge was brought against a provision of the *Social Service Tax Act*[93] that imposed a tax on the purchase of legal services unless they had "no connection to British Columbia." Under this statute, a lawyer who failed to collect the tax was subject to a fine but not to imprisonment. In order to bypass this apparent obstacle to the applicability of s. 7, Lysyk J. relied on the passage by Gonthier J. quoted above to render the vagueness doctrine applicable,[94] which led to the invalidation of the provision. This way of reading the *Nova Scotia Pharmaceutical* case is questionable. It must be noted that a few pages before the passage quoted above, Gonthier J. discussed at length the appropriate constitutional bases of the vagueness doctrine in a section of his reasons entitled "The Proper Place of the Doctrine of Vagueness in *Charter* Adjudication."[95] After explaining the different ways in which vagueness can be invoked under ss. 1 and 7, as we have studied thus far, he concluded that "the 'doctrine of vagueness' ... is a principle of fundamental justice under s.7 and is also part of s.1 *in limine* ('prescribed by law')."[96] Why would Gonthier J. have gone through such an analysis if he were to announce later in the same judgment that the doctrine was autonomous? How useful would it be to recognize the applicability of vagueness in s. 1, as well as in the principles of fundamental justice, if the same decision were to proclaim the autonomous character of the vagueness theory? In fact, it is probably more appropriate to read the passage by Gonthier J. as meaning simply that the nature of a law, whether it involves the definition of crimes or other matters such as civil matters, will not constitute *per se* an obstacle to a litigant who wishes to invoke the vagueness doctrine, as long as the other criteria of applicability are satisfied.

For example, the case of *R. v. Morales*[97] involved a vagueness challenge to s. 515(10)(b) of the *Criminal Code,* which allows a judge to deny bail to an accused when "necessary in the public interest." In this type of situation, ss. 7 and 11(e) apply *prima facie* since the provision purports to deny bail (s. 11[e]), thereby unquestionably affecting the liberty interest (s. 7). However, one of the interveners in the case had argued before the Court that the vagueness doctrine should not apply because the provision at stake "does not define an offence or prohibit conduct, but rather provides grounds on which pre-trial detention is authorized."[98] Lamer C.J., speaking for a majority of the Court, rejected this argument and held the vagueness doctrine applicable, which led to the invalidation of the public interest criterion as inconsistent with s. 11(e).[99] To secure the applicability of the doctrine despite the fact that the provision at stake did not involve the definition of an offence, Lamer C.J. relied on the passage by Gonthier J. in *Nova Scotia Pharmaceutical* according to which the doctrine "applies to all enactments," to conclude himself that "all dispositions are subject to the doctrine regardless of their form."[100] This, however, does not mean that the applicability conditions of ss. 11(e) and 7 can be bypassed. It simply means that the vagueness doctrine can be applied to any type of enactment, provided, of course, that there is a sufficient constitutional basis.

In a similar vein, the passage by Gonthier J. could be used, for example, to reject American jurisprudence from the early part of the twentieth century that had disputed the applicability of the vagueness doctrine in civil cases. In *Levy Leasing Co. v. Siegel,*[101] the Supreme Court of the United States had held that the doctrine of vagueness did not apply to a rent control statute that made it a partial defence to a rent action that "such rent is unjust and unreasonable and that the agreement under which the same is sought to be recovered is oppressive." It did not matter whether the statute represented a potential breach of liberty or property interests protected by the due process clause of the Fourteenth Amendment. The vagueness doctrine was held inapplicable because the statute did not involve the definition of a crime.[102] In Canada, the possibility of this type of reasoning is avoided as a result of the comments by Gonthier J. in *Nova Scotia Pharmaceutical.* However, the passage in question does not stand for the proposition that the vagueness doctrine has acquired an autonomous status in the jurisprudence of the Court.

Note that other Supreme Court of Canada decisions may create confusion as to the non-autonomous character of the vagueness doctrine in that they include discussions on the validity of legislation in relation to vagueness despite a lack of constitutional basis for doing so. For example, the case of *Young v. Young*[103] involved a challenge to ss. 16(8) and 17(5) of the *Divorce Act,*[104] which state that judicial decisions related to child custody and parents' access rights must take into consideration the "best interests of the child." Relying on these provisions, a British Columbia judge had issued an order restricting Mr. Young's possibilities of teaching the religion of Jehovah's Witnesses to his children. The father challenged both the statute and the order, based on ss. 2(a) (freedom of religion), 2(b) (freedom of expression), 2(d) (freedom of association), and 15(1) (equality rights), besides arguing that the "best interests of the child" standard was vague. As we saw earlier, arguments related to vagueness in this case should normally be examined only after a breach of a substantive *Charter* right has been demonstrated. It is interesting to note, however, that L'Heureux-Dubé J. examined the vagueness argument in her reasons without acknowledging any prior violation of such substantive right.[105]

The case of *P.(D.) v. S.(C.)*[106] contains the same type of problem. This case involved a challenge to s. 30 of the *Civil Code of Lower Canada (C.C.L.C.)*,[107] which affirms the "child's interest" standard with regard to decisions on child custody for parents separated under the provincial regime. Section 30 had been used as a basis for issuing an order similar to the one at stake in the *Young* case, and the same constitutional grievances were raised by the father. L'Heureux-Dubé J., writing this time for a majority of the Court, again analyzed the vagueness question without any conclusion that another protected right had been breached.[108] There were no consequences since the vagueness argument was rejected on the merits. However, the fact that the reasons show no obstacle to the applicability of vagueness due to a lack of constitutional basis is regrettable because it leads to confusion. We would have expected that before a statement was made that the "the criterion of the child's best interest, set out in art. 30 *C.C.L.C.* ... could not be vague within the meaning of s. 1 of the *Charter*,"[109] some violation of a substantive *Charter* guarantee would have been demonstrated, which was not done. Moreover, it would have been appropriate that before a statement was made that "art. 30 *C.C.L.C.* ... could not be vague within the meaning of s. 7 of the *Charter*,"[110] the question of a possible breach to either life, liberty, or security of the person would have at least been addressed, which was not done either.

The third Supreme Court case in which vagueness was analyzed despite the lack of sufficient constitutional basis is the case of *Ruffo v. Conseil de la Magistrature*.[111] This case involved, *inter alia*, a challenge based on s. 2(b) and the vagueness theory to s. 8 of the *Judicial Code of Ethics*,[112] which states that "in public, the judge should act in a reserved, serene and courteous manner." After stating that it did not wish to rule on the speech issue in the context of this appeal, the Court analyzed the vagueness question without relying on any constitutional basis for doing so.[113] We can only speculate as to the basis pursuant to which the vagueness theory was applied. We realize that *Ruffo*, as well as the two other cases mentioned above, have the potential for creating confusion concerning the non-autonomous character of the vagueness theory. Are we in the presence of *obiter dicta* to the effect that the law would not have been too vague with regard to s. 1 in the event of a proven violation of a substantive *Charter* guarantee? Probably so, but the Court should have stated this fact more explicitly to ensure consistency with its prior jurisprudence. I do not believe that these cases can be read as expressing a willingness to grant the vagueness doctrine an autonomous status since the question of the applicability of the theory is not even discussed or mentioned in these decisions. Given prior jurisprudence governing the question of applicability, we must consider that the Court would have done so expressly had it wished to grant the doctrine of vagueness the power to invalidate legislation independently.[114]

Broadening the Applicability of Vagueness

Thus far the constitutional bases that can render the vagueness doctrine applicable under current jurisprudence have been presented. These are the bases that are relatively secure in law at this time. Let us now consider whether it would be possible under our Constitution to broaden the applicability of the doctrine in the future to a larger number of circumstances. I will examine how the requirement of precision could be made applicable to penal laws in general, and even possibly to all laws, regardless of their nature. Sections 7 and 11(g) of the *Charter,* as considered in light of the principles of legality and the rule of law, will be helpful in this regard.

Broader Recognition through Section 7

Under s. 7, current jurisprudence recognizes the vagueness doctrine as a "principle of fundamental justice." It is therefore applicable as long as a breach of either life, liberty, or security of the person has been demonstrated. The right to liberty certainly includes protection against imprisonment.[115] Thus, penal laws that include the possibility of this kind of punishment trigger the applicability of the vagueness doctrine without question. Subject to a few exceptions,[116] however, it is rather uncertain in current jurisprudence whether the right to liberty goes any further than protection against imprisonment.[117] In fact, Canadian courts are reluctant to extend the scope of liberty beyond actual physical restraint.[118] Note, however, that Lamer J., writing in separate reasons in the *Prostitution Reference,* expressed the view that liberty would put at stake essentially every law involving punitive measures: "There are ... situations in which the state restricts other privileges or, broadly termed, 'liberties' in the guise of regulation, but uses punitive measures in cases of non-compliance. In such situations the state is in effect punishing individuals, in the classic sense of the word, for non-compliance with a law or regulation. In all these cases, in my view, the liberty and security of the person interests protected by s. 7 would be restricted, and one would have to determine if the restriction was in accordance with the principles of fundamental justice."[119]

Pursuant to this reasoning, virtually all penal laws would have to comply with the principles of fundamental justice to the extent that they inevitably impinge on citizens' liberties at large and use punitive measure in cases of noncompliance. The future will tell whether a majority of the Supreme Court will come to share the view expressed by Lamer J. It is not necessary for our purposes to speculate on this issue, which depends in large part on the degree of activism judges are willing to engage in. As the American experience has demonstrated for more than half a century, the scope of the right to liberty is at the core of constitutional debates that involve political concerns to a great degree.[120] This complex question regarding the appropriate meaning of the concept of liberty is beyond the scope of this study. Note, however, that it is at least uncertain whether penal laws providing for punishments other than physical restraint, such as fines, are within the scope of s. 7.

In the particular case of the vagueness doctrine, however, our constitutional structure and jurisprudence would militate for a recognition of its applicability to at least all penal laws in the framework of s. 7. In this regard, the impact of the principle of the rule of law, studied in Chapter 2, becomes relevant. As we saw earlier, vagueness and the rule of law are closely related.[121] We have seen that the rule of law is a fundamental principle of the Canadian Constitution that enjoys express recognition in the preamble to the *Charter*. Pursuant to recent jurisprudence, it possesses a strong status[122] allowing it to "fill out the gaps" in the provisions of the Constitution.[123] Moreover, the rule of law is a principle that is considered to be mostly applicable to coercive,[124] hence penal, matters. Therefore, the rule of law could be used to "fill out the gaps" in s. 7 of the *Charter*. If "liberty" does not cover all penal laws pursuant to normal interpretation, the rule of law can be used to argue that, at least when the vagueness doctrine is involved as a principle of fundamental justice, the liberty interest should cover all penal laws.

It could also be argued through the use of the rule of law's gap-filling potential that the concept of liberty *itself* could require compliance with the vagueness doctrine in general. Thus, the *first* branch of the s. 7 analysis would require precision in legislation. Vagueness would therefore be autonomous under s. 7, due to the interpretative influence of the rule of law. However, given the fact that the rule of law is best, if not exclusively, applicable in the context of coercive laws, the degree of required legislative precision would fluctuate depending on the type of law involved. For example, if the rule of law were to render the vagueness doctrine applicable to literally every law, noncoercive statutes, such as the one involved in the *Ontario School Boards* decision discussed in Chapter 2,[125] would certainly deserve greater deference from the courts.

Recognition through Section 11(g)

A provision of the *Charter* that has been overlooked so far in the context of the vagueness doctrine is s. 11(g). This provision sanctions the principle of legality *(nullum crimen nulla poena sine lege)* in the following terms: "11. Any person charged with an offence has the right ... (g) not to be found guilty on account of any act or omission unless, at the time of the act or omission, it constituted an offence under Canadian or international law or was criminal according to the general principles of law recognized by the community of nations."

The relevance of this provision in rendering the vagueness doctrine applicable has not yet been addressed by Canadian courts. It is appropriate, however, to consider s. 11(g) as a potential basis for requiring precision of legislation, at least for penal laws creating offences. As we saw in Chapter 1 when we examined the principle of legality, the essential aim of s. 11(g) is to ensure that citizens will not be punished for offences regarding which they did not receive fair warning. In that context, the link between s. 11(g) and the vagueness doctrine becomes obvious. This provision is designed primarily for *ex post facto* statutes, but vague laws have a similar effect. An overly vague statute that allows in reality for the decision maker to decide, after the alleged behaviour of the accused, whether or not a certain prohibition exists, resembles *ex post facto* legislation achieved through the judicial process. Although vague laws of this type have, strictly speaking, only a prospective reach, the underlying purpose of s. 11(g) will be satisfied only if we acknowledge that the effects of such vague laws are similar to the effects of *ex post facto* laws. As vague penal laws and *ex post facto* penal laws both create "unfair surprise" for citizens in a similar manner, they should both be prohibited under s. 11(g).[126]

As further support for this interpretation of s. 11(g), recall that under s. 1, a restriction to a *Charter* right must emanate from a relatively precise statute in order to be considered "prescribed by law."[127] Can we not consider that if a vague law is not a law within the meaning of s. 1, it is neither a law that can create "an offence under Canadian ... law" in the context of s. 11(g)?

Moreover, s. 11(g) could also be viewed as being one of these provisions containing an internal limitation. As we saw earlier, "vagueness may be raised under the substantive sections of the *Charter* whenever these sections comprise some internal limitation."[128] Thus, s. 11(g) could be seen as guaranteeing the substantive right "not to be found guilty on account of any act or omission," the only limitation to this being if the act or omission "constituted an offence under Canadian ... law." Thus, similar to s. 6 of the *Charter* referred to earlier, it could be considered that this "law," in order to create this "limitation" (the offence), would have to be sufficiently precise.

It is interesting to note that s. 11(g) is drafted in terms very similar to Article 7 of the *European Convention for the Protection of Human Rights and Fundamental Freedoms,*[129] which has long been interpreted as prohibiting vague legislation.[130] The text of this provision is as follows:

Article 7
1. No one shall be held guilty of any criminal offence on account of any act or omission which did not constitute a criminal offence under national or international law at the time it was committed. Nor shall a heavier penalty be imposed than the one that was applicable at the time the criminal offence was committed.
2. This Article shall not prejudice the trial and punishment of any person for any act or omission which, at the time it was committed, was criminal according to the general principles of law recognized by civilized nations.

It is useful to recall the following comments expressed by Dickson C.J. on the use of international instruments to interpret the *Charter:* "In particular, the similarity between the policies and provisions of the *Charter* and those of international human rights documents attaches considerable relevance to interpretations of those documents by adjudicative bodies, in much the same way that decisions of the United States courts under the Bill of Rights, or decisions of the courts in other jurisdictions are relevant and may be persuasive."[131]

Thus, s. 11(g) could logically receive an interpretation similar to that given by European instances to Article 7, requiring that penal laws creating offences be sufficiently precise. The concerns mentioned earlier concerning the underlying purposes of s. 11(g), as well as the light shed by the *European Convention,* are in my view plainly sufficient for us to consider that this provision renders the vagueness theory applicable to all laws creating offences. Such an interpretation would also be compatible with the philosophy defended by the Supreme Court according to which the interpretation of *Charter* rights and freedoms must be a "generous rather than a legalistic one, aimed at fulfilling the purpose of the guarantee and securing for individuals the full benefit of the *Charter's* protection."[132]

In my view, such an understanding of s. 11(g) rendering the theory of vagueness applicable can easily be reached through conventional principles of constitutional interpretation. If the influence of the principle of the rule of law is added to this scheme, it becomes even more obvious that s. 11(g) ought to be interpreted as prohibiting vague penal legislation. By resorting to the rule of law, the reach of s. 11(g) could go even further, to render the doctrine applicable to all laws, regardless of whether they create penal offences. As we saw earlier, the rule of law can have a strong impact to "fill out the gaps" in the provisions of the Constitution, thus expanding the reach of these provisions further than what the text seems to suggest. For example, in the *Judges Remuneration Reference*,[133] s. 11(d) of the *Charter* was interpreted as protecting the independence of judges hearing cases in *all matters*, despite the fact that the text of that provision seemed to protect only courts with jurisdiction on penal matters. In a strikingly similar fashion, s. 11(g), which by virtue of its express terms receives application only in penal matters, could be interpreted through the rule of law as applying also in nonpenal matters.[134]

The Impact of Constitutional Bases on Substantive Vagueness Analysis

Having presented the different constitutional bases that can permit the applicability of the vagueness doctrine, I will now say a few words on the impact this reality can have on the substantive assessment of the validity of legislation. In fact, the degree of precision required to uphold the validity of statutes can vary, depending on the constitutional basis that rendered the theory applicable in a particular case. This can appear to contradict a statement made by the Supreme Court in *Nova Scotia Pharmaceutical,* according to which the vagueness doctrine is "a single concept."[135] In order to better understand why the vagueness assessment can vary depending on the constitutional basis invoked, it will be useful to recall the distinction between classic vagueness (i.e., legality and the rule of law) and overbreadth.

As we already saw, vagueness is not yet an autonomous ground upon which to render legislation invalid.[136] Instead, it is a way of rendering unreasonable a restriction to a substantive *Charter* interest. In relation to vague laws, two types of concerns can be relevant. First are the elements related to classic vagueness, namely, fair notice and limitation of law enforcement discretion. In this framework, what is analyzed is the *manner* in which constitutional rights are being restricted. The vagueness of the law allows the process that leads to restrictions on constitutional rights to be governed by arbitrary considerations. The vagueness doctrine in its classic version purports to address this problem. Second, the vagueness of a law can cause problems related to overbreadth. Vague statutory formulas possess the potential for being interpreted in a way that restricts *Charter* rights more than the State can legitimately do. Lack of statutory precision can therefore constitute an obstacle to the proportionality we wish to preserve in the context of restrictions of constitutional rights. It is not so much the *manner* in which rights and freedoms are restricted that matters here but rather the *degree* of restriction they suffer.

Recall that in the *Nova Scotia Pharmaceutical* case, Gonthier J. preferred to use the expression "vagueness doctrine" only to designate the classic version of vagueness (i.e., legality and the rule of law).[137] Since overbreadth is seen as an independent problem in the abstract, it is dissociated from vagueness. However, it will be interesting to say a few words here on the interplay between overbreadth and vagueness, as it can allow us to better understand how a legislative provision can be seen as sufficiently precise under one provision of the *Charter* and at the same time too imprecise under another constitutional basis.

To illustrate the latter proposition, let us consider the decision of the Supreme Court in the *Morales* case.[138] The public interest criterion in s. 515(10)(b) of the *Criminal Code* was held to be too imprecise in the context of s. 11(e) of the *Charter*.[139] It was then suggested that it might be sufficiently precise to pass the "prescribed by law" requirement,[140] but was finally invalidated under minimal impairment.[141] As one commentator has noted,[142] this kind of reasoning is incompatible with the statement in the *Nova Scotia Pharmaceutical* case according to which the doctrine of vagueness is "a single concept."[143] In fact, the concept of vagueness can vary depending on the constitutional basis it is being related to. This is due to the interaction between the concepts of overbreadth and classic vagueness. Thus, in the *Morales* case, it was suggested that the provision could be precise enough under "prescribed by law" because this requirement triggers only concerns related to classic vagueness. It was, however, held to be too imprecise under s. 11(e), as well as under minimal impairment, because overbreadth became a relevant concern in the framework of these two constitutional bases.

Since statutory precision can acquire constitutional importance for reasons related to classic vagueness or overbreadth, different provisions of the *Charter* can require more or less precision, depending on the degree to which they include these two concerns. Some provisions of the *Charter* include only one of the two concerns, or render one of them relevant to a different degree, which can have an impact on the level of precision required. Thus, some *Charter* provisions explicitly or implicitly provide that constitutional rights can be limited only in a nonarbitrary fashion (preferably by the legislator). These provisions can be said to include only concerns related to classic vagueness.[144] Other *Charter* provisions render relevant concerns of proportionality in relation to breaches of specific *Charter* interests. In this regard, vagueness in its overbreadth aspect acquires importance.[145] Finally, some provisions render both types of concerns relevant at the same time,[146] which inevitably has the effect of increasing the level of precision required.

In the context of the "prescribed by law" requirement of s. 1, therefore, the test applied by the Supreme Court of Canada is more permissive towards the legislator because only concerns related to classic vagueness are relevant in that framework. In contrast, under minimal impairment, we are no longer concerned with classic vagueness but rather with over-breadth. This concern is of great importance since the law must impair constitutional rights as little as possible. In this framework, courts will be less tolerant towards the legislator's enactment of vague statutory formulas. The idea is to avoid a situation in which the adjudicator can take advantage of vague legislative drafting to restrict constitutional rights more than the State can legitimately do.

The degree of precision required in the framework of s. 7 and other provisions of the *Charter* containing an internal limitation will therefore vary depending on the manner and fashion in which they can render concepts of overbreadth and classic vagueness relevant. In the context of s. 7, for example, classic vagueness is important, as is overbreadth (although to a lesser degree than in minimal impairment).[147] It is considered that the principles of fundamental justice require respect for legality and the rule of law, and at the same time require a certain proportionality in restrictions of either life, liberty, or security of the person. Thus, the degree of precision required under s. 7 will be more demanding than under "prescribed by law," and arguably less demanding than under minimal impairment.[148]

Conclusion

As we have seen in this chapter, the applicability of the vagueness doctrine to legislative enactments is far from simple. Since no particular provision of the Constitution expressly prohibits vague legislation, the bases of the doctrine are implicit. Many factors have to be taken into consideration in determining under what heading litigants can be permitted to argue the vagueness of a law to trigger a declaration of constitutional invalidity. Essentially, to this day the vagueness doctrine can be invoked in the context of s. 1 (under "prescribed by law" or minimal impairment) or in relation to provisions containing an internal limitation, such as s. 7. The interplay as well as the differences between vagueness in its classic dimension and overbreadth must be taken into account under these different constitutional bases. In addition, whenever protected freedoms such as freedom of expression are at stake, the question of chilling effect can further influence the assessment of legislative precision.

Most importantly, it must be remembered that vagueness does not have an autonomous status in the current state of jurisprudence. There must always be a threat to some other element contained in a substantive provision of the *Charter* to render the vagueness doctrine applicable. In this sense, the vagueness doctrine remains merely an "insulating buffer zone"[149] designed to ensure added protection to substantive *Charter* interests. However, this reality is only what has been recognized to this day. Possible judicial developments may lead to an expanded applicability of the doctrine. It will be especially interesting to see how ss. 7 and 11(g) will be interpreted in the future in light of the principles of legality and the rule of law. As I have shown, these provisions have the potential for providing a broader scope of applicability for the vagueness doctrine, even to the extent of rendering it autonomous.

Conclusion

In Chapter 1, we saw that the principle of legality requires at least two things: (1) that penal offences be created by the legislature rather than the courts, and (2) that these laws be prospective in reach. These requirements serve the purpose of providing "fair warning" to citizens regarding the possibility of legal punishment in a manner very similar to the first rationale of the vagueness doctrine. Concerning the creation of new offences by courts, we saw that such power has vanished over the years in the common law, partly because of the expanded activity of legislatures and partly because of a wish by courts and academics to promote legal certainty. Influenced by the civil law tradition that forms part of our country's legal heritage, we saw that our legal history has been dominated by the values affiliated with legality, particularly in the area of penal law. Canadian authorities have generally realized that breaches to the principle of legality, as innocuous as they might sometimes appear in particular cases, may lead to long-term uncertainty in the legal system and to the proliferation of situations where citizens are victims of "unfair surprise." A similar reasoning has led to the adoption of s. 11(g) of the *Canadian Charter of Rights and Freedoms,* which forces legislatures to respect the principle of legality in enacting penal legislation. We have seen that although this provision is designed primarily for laws creating penal offences, the principle of the rule of law might be used to expand the scope of s. 11(g) by making it applicable to a wider variety of legislation. However, the underlying motivation of the principle of legality, which is to avoid unfair surprise, should be kept in mind to limit its application to laws that have the effect of negatively affecting citizens for past actions in a manner similar to penal law.

In Chapter 2, we examined the principle of the rule of law. In a manner quite similar to the second rationale of the vagueness doctrine, we saw that the rule of law requires that the influence of arbitrary power be limited. In this regard, rules will be favoured over discretion. Of course, this does not mean that the use of discretion will be plainly illegitimate. As mentioned on several occasions, certainty in law must always be balanced against the need for flexibility. The rule of law is wary of this usefulness of discretion to promote efficiency and justice in the legal system. It merely seeks to balance this need against the competing concern of certainty. In recent years, we saw that the rule of law's status has grown considerably. Being expressly included in the preamble to the *Charter*, the principle has been given considerable importance either directly or as an unwritten constitutional principle by the Supreme Court of Canada. We have seen that it can be used to "fill out the gaps" in the express provisions of the Constitution, and might even be interpreted as having an autonomous status that enables it to invalidate legislation on its own. Regarding the content of the rule of law, it is safer to limit its ambit to formal limitations on State power, as conveyed by the expression "government by laws, not by men." This restrictive version of the rule of law merely standing as a repugnance towards excessive arbitrary powers is the one that attracts the greatest consensus among judicial and academic authorities. In that sense, the rule of law is useful in the context of our study of vagueness (and especially of its second rationale), as it requires that discretion be limited to what is reasonably necessary to achieve State objectives. We have seen that this requirement is most applicable in the context of coercive statutes that have a direct impact on citizens' rights and obligations.

In Chapter 3, we examined the content of the vagueness doctrine *per se*. A survey of the American void-for-vagueness theory has shed some light on specific understandings of the two rationales of fair notice and law enforcement discretion. As American courts are reluctant to invalidate vague legislation, we have seen that they will find fair notice to be offended essentially if citizens are not conscious that a certain type of conduct could trigger legal liability. In relation to the second rationale of vagueness, we saw that it is viewed as offended in the American context only if the law lends itself to selective enforcement against so-called undesirables. Outside of these situations, breaches of legality and the rule of law will rarely trigger declarations of invalidity.

In the study of the content of vagueness in Canada, still in Chapter 3, we examined at length the views of the Supreme Court of Canada on this emerging topic. As the Court derived its understanding of the two rationales of the vagueness doctrine from the American experience, we saw that the principles of legality and the rule of law are being protected in a limited manner. Thus, the Court's description of fair warning only in terms of a "substratum of values" is not fully protective of the principle of legality. Similarly, a description of the law enforcement discretion rationale only in terms of "catch-all laws leading to automatic convictions" does little to promote the constitutional theory of the rule of law outlined in Chapter 2. This does not mean, however, that these understandings of the two rationales of the vagueness doctrine are useless. As we saw, they can be used to make requirements of precision more or less demanding whenever they come into play in a given legislative scheme.

After these preliminary remarks, I examined and questioned the sufficiency of the general standard enunciated by the Supreme Court of Canada for determining whether legislation is unconstitutionally vague. Under the Court's low standard, any law will be upheld if it provides a "basis for legal debate." As I explained throughout this book, an appropriate assessment of legislative precision requires balancing a series of interests in order to reach an ideal equilibrium between certainty and flexibility in our constitutional structure. The assessment of precision should therefore vary according to a variety of factors, which I have pointed out, instead of being governed only by the invariable and permissive threshold of legal debate. Among these factors, the presence of a "substratum of values," the likelihood of selective enforcement, the reasonable possibility of more precise drafting, and the type of law involved will have a paramount effect on the approach that must be taken to apply the vagueness doctrine. As we saw, techniques such as nonexhaustive enumerations to activate the principle *ejusdem generis* or the use of specifications through regulation may be very useful in helping legislatures comply with this more demanding understanding of the doctrine. We saw that these techniques to improve legislative precision through the legislative and executive branches of government are more appropriate than case-by-case specifications achieved through the judicial process.

Chapter 4 studied the appropriate place of the vagueness doctrine in the context of the *Charter*. There is no particular provision that expressly prohibits vague legislation. Implicit requirements of precision in statutes have been derived from ss. 1 and 7 of the *Charter*, as well as other provisions that comprise some "internal limitation." We studied the different possible applications of the doctrine under these constitutional headings and examined the manner in which the related doctrine of overbreadth can play a role in that context. The essential conclusion that may be drawn from Chapter 4 is that the vagueness doctrine does not have an autonomous status, in the sense that it must always be invoked in conjunction with another *Charter* interest to become relevant. However, we saw that it may be possible in the future to render the doctrine applicable to a greater number of situations and perhaps even to render it autonomous through ss. 7 and 11(g), under the interpretative influence of legality and the rule of law. Of course, any conclusion that the vagueness doctrine could be autonomous would not mean that requirements of precision would apply with the same strength to all laws, but merely that the lack of a constitutional basis would not constitute a preliminary obstacle to the applicability of the doctrine.

In sum, the main object of this book was to examine the operation of the vagueness doctrine in Canadian constitutional litigation. The short-term effect of this study may be to shed light on the possibility for individuals and their legal counsel to use the vagueness doctrine to frame challenges to legislation. It can also be hoped that it might eventually lead the judges and legislators of Canada to ensure a more adequate equilibrium between certainty and flexibility in the legal system by taking a more balanced approach towards the vagueness doctrine.

One other issue that would be interesting to discuss in the future in relation to the problem of vagueness is the concept of separation of powers. This well-known theory was presented as follows by Dickson C.J. in *Fraser v. Public Service Staff Relations Board:* "There is in Canada a separation of powers among the three branches of government – the legislature, the executive and the judiciary. In broad terms, the role of the judiciary is, of course, to interpret and apply the law; the role of the legislature is to decide upon and enunciate policy; the role of the executive is to administer and implement that policy."[1]

This separation can be blurred when the legislature, by resorting to vague statutory formulas, transfers its power to "decide upon and enunciate policy," as Dickson C.J. describes it, to the judiciary. Thus, in addition to the concerns of legality and the rule of law already identified, overly vague laws can be perceived as creating institutional concerns as they arguably have the effect of granting powers of a legislative nature to unelected decision makers.

In this study, we saw that legality and the rule of law were concerned mainly with the impact of vague laws on legal certainty. The separation of powers, however, focuses more on the institutional identity of the decision maker. It would be interesting in a further study to explore in greater detail the scope of this principle, especially regarding the separation between the legislative and judicial branches of government. Of course, as has been acknowledged in this book, judges have a role to play that reaches far beyond the mechanical interpretation and application of legislation. The separation of powers should never be perceived as something so rigid as to negate the creative role of judges.[2] Under a modern and flexible version of the separation of powers, however, some form of separation must remain. It would be interesting to examine to what extent the vagueness of a law could have the effect of blurring the roles of legislators and judges so as to render the doctrine of the separation of powers relevant in the analysis.

Although the status of the separation of powers still needs to be clarified in the context of our Constitution, we may note that it has been referred to on some occasions by the Supreme Court of Canada as a fundamental principle.[3] It could therefore arguably have an influence similar to the one enjoyed by the rule of law on the analysis of the vagueness doctrine. It could increase the strength of the arguments requiring greater precision in laws, besides perhaps expanding the applicability of the doctrine.

While the question of including the separation of powers as a rationale of the vagueness doctrine remains to be examined in another study, we have seen in this book that legality and the rule of law are two compelling concerns that invite the legislator to aim for a reasonable degree of precision in legislation. To this day, the Supreme Court of Canada has seemed to be concerned mostly with the imperative of flexibility through the general criterion of legal debate. This study has attempted to show that the need for certainty is also a pressing concern under the Constitution, thus mandating an analysis of vagueness that can be more demanding for the State in certain cases while not overly impinging on legislative efficiency and flexibility.

It may appear contradictory for this book to defend a constitutional norm favouring greater certainty in the law while at the same time advocating standards of review that are themselves more uncertain than the test currently favoured by the Supreme Court of Canada. In other words, the legal debate test said to be applicable in an invariable manner to all laws in *Nova Scotia Pharmaceutical* has the paradoxical merit of being clearer and more certain than the flexible set of standards that I have spelled out.

It is, however, the nature of constitutional standards to be flexible. The guarantees entrenched in the *Charter* inevitably have an uncertain scope, and the extent to which these rights can be limited under s. 1 is even more unclear. The fact that constitutional standards can be vague does not mean that it is illegitimate for courts to require certainty in legislation through the vagueness doctrine. Constitutional documents and their interpretations are even more difficult to modify than legislative standards. Still, they need to have the capacity to evolve. Just as statutes need a degree of flexibility because they are to be applied to unforeseeable circumstances, constitutional standards also, and perhaps even more so, are likely to be confronted with a wide variety of circumstances. A constitutional standard of statutory definiteness that is overly strict cannot efficiently attain its purpose of protecting legality and the rule of law, just as many legal standards would not reach their purpose if they were drafted in overly precise terms.

Although the standards I have presented in this book do make the task of legislatures somewhat more difficult and add an element of uncertainty related to the possible invalidity of laws for vagueness, this is still preferable to citizens having to suffer the unnecessary consequences of defective warning and arbitrary decision making when they are confronted with the State. This is especially true for laws that are penal or otherwise significantly coercive in nature, in relation to which the individual's personal sphere stands alone against the power of the State. The idea behind a constitutional document such as the *Charter* is the protection of individuals against abusive State power. In such a framework, it is inevitable that the State will have to cope with some uncertainty in the determination of what it can or cannot do. Just as the individual has to face uncertainties that are inevitable in a legal system, the State must bear the burden of uncertainties that are inevitable in a constitutional democracy.

Notes

Foreword

1 *R. v. Nova Scotia Pharmaceutical Society*, [1992] 2 S.C.R. 606.
2 P.W. Hogg, *Constitutional Law of Canada*, 4th ed. (Scarborough, ON: Carswell, 1996) at 867.
3 D. Stuart, *Canadian Criminal Law: A Treatise*, 3d ed. (Scarborough, ON: Carswell, 1995) at 26.
4 A. Jodouin, "La Charte canadienne et la nouvelle légalité" in G.A. Beaudoin and E. Mendes, eds., *The Canadian Charter of Rights and Freedoms*, 3d ed. (Scarborough, ON: Carswell, 1996) ch. 13.
5 L. Huppé, "La fonction des lois et la théorie de l'imprécision" (1992) 52 R. du B. 831.
6 *R. v. Morales*, [1992] 3 S.C.R. 711.
7 *R. v. Farinacci* (1993), 86 C.C.C. (3d) 32 (Ont. C.A.).

Introduction

1 *Canadian Charter of Rights and Freedoms*, Part I of the *Constitution Act, 1982*, being Schedule B to the *Canada Act 1982* (U.K.), 1982, c. 11 *[Charter]*.
2 *Winters v. New York*, 333 U.S. 507 at 524 (1948) (dissenting opinion) *[Winters]*.
3 L. Fuller, *The Morality of Law*, 2d ed. (New Haven, CT: Yale University Press, 1969) at 43.
4 *R. v. Morgentaler*, [1988] 1 S.C.R. 30 at 68-69 (per Dickson C.J.) *[Morgentaler]*. Along with other factors, vagueness contributed in that case to the invalidity of s. 251 of the *Criminal Code*, which prohibited abortions unless "the continuation of the pregnancy of the female person ... would be likely to endanger her ... health."
5 *Reference re ss. 193 and 195.1(1)(c) of the Criminal Code (Man.)*, [1990] 1 S.C.R. 1123 at 1151-52 *[Prostitution Reference]*. Note that the vagueness doctrine is most often invoked in the context of s. 7 of the *Charter* in relation to penal laws. Although this book focuses in large part on such illustrations, it is intended to cover the operation of the doctrine beyond the scope of penal law.
6 *Committee for the Commonwealth of Canada v. Canada*, [1991] 1 S.C.R. 139 at 209-10 *[Commonwealth of Canada]*.
7 *R. v. Nova Scotia Pharmaceutical Society*, [1992] 2 S.C.R. 606 *[Nova Scotia Pharmaceutical]*.
8 R.S.C. 1970, c. C-23.
9 *Nova Scotia Pharmaceutical*, *supra* note 7 at 626.
10 *Ibid.*
11 *Ibid.*
12 *R. v. Oakes*, [1986] 1 S.C.R. 103 *[Oakes]*.
13 *Nova Scotia Pharmaceutical*, *supra* note 7 at 626.
14 *Ibid.* at 630, citing *R. v. Zundel* (1987), 58 O.R. (2d) 129 (Ont. C.A.) at 157-58.
15 *Ibid.* at 630-31.
16 *Nova Scotia Pharmaceutical*, *supra* note 7 at 631-32.

17 *Ibid.* at 633-34.

18 *Ibid.* at 636.

19 As we shall see in Chapter 3, the Unites States Supreme Court also uses the two rationales of fair notice and law enforcement discretion to assess the validity of legislation under the vagueness doctrine. However, it has never purported to set a fixed threshold seeking to encompass both these rationales in order to assess the validity of vague legislation.

20 *Nova Scotia Pharmaceutical, supra* note 7 at 632.

21 *Ibid.* at 639-40.

22 Only one statutory provision has thus far been declared invalid by the Supreme Court of Canada on grounds of vagueness under this criterion of legal debate; see *R. v. Morales,* [1992] 3 S.C.R. 711 *[Morales],* and *R. v. Hall,* 2002 S.C.C. 64, file no. 28223 *[Hall].* In both these cases, s. 515(10)(c) of the *Criminal Code,* which provides for grounds to deny bail to an accused pending trial was found to be defective. See Chapter 3, notes 196 and 197 and accompanying text.

23 P.W. Hogg, *Constitutional Law of Canada,* 4th ed. (Scarborough, ON: Carswell, 1996) at 867.

24 *Nova Scotia Pharmaceutical, supra* note 7 at 640.

25 *Constitution Act, 1867* (U.K.) 30 & 31 Vict., c. 3.

26 These provisions are essentially ss. 1 and 7 of the *Charter,* as well as other provisions that, much like s. 7, comprise some "internal limitation." See *Nova Scotia Pharmaceutical, supra* note 7 at 631. The conditions under which vagueness may be invoked in relation to the *Charter's* provisions will be discussed extensively in Chapter 4.

27 For instance, it is interesting to note that when Lamer J. linked the principle of legality to the vagueness doctrine in the *Prostitution Reference* (*supra* note 5), he related it to both rationales of the doctrine, and not only to the fair notice rationale. Similarly, when L'Heureux-Dubé J. established a link between vagueness and the principle of the rule of law in *Commonwealth of Canada* (*supra* note 6), she did so without distinguishing between the two rationales of vagueness.

28 See, *e.g.,* F.A. Hayek, *The Constitution of Liberty* (Chicago: University of Chicago Press, 1960) at 206; I. Jennings, *The Law and the Constitution,* 5th ed. (London: University of London Press, 1959) at 51; E. Colvin, "Criminal Law and the Rule of Law" in P. Fitzgerald, ed., *Crime, Justice and Codification* (Toronto: Carswell, 1986) ch. 9 at 141.

29 As mentioned earlier, Gonthier J. in *Nova Scotia Pharmaceutical* held that overbreadth is not a component of the vagueness doctrine *per se,* even though vague laws can incidentally trigger problems of overbreadth. While the analysis in the first three chapters will respect this method of reasoning for the purpose of defining the content of the vagueness doctrine, Gonthier J.'s distinction will be somewhat overlooked in Chapter 4 in order to reach an understanding of when and how the concepts of overbreadth and vagueness can interact in practice in the context of the different provisions of the *Charter.*

Chapter 1: The Principle of Legality

1 E.A. Goerner, ed., *The Constitutions of Europe* (Chicago: H. Regnery, 1967) at 38 [translation]. For the original version, see G. Conac, M. Debene, & G. Teboul, eds., *La déclaration des droits de l'homme et du citoyen de 1789* (Paris: Economica, 1993) at 363: "nul ne peut être puni qu'en vertu d'une loi établie et promulguée antérieurment au délit et légalement appliquée."

2 Reproduced in C. Debbasch & J.-M. Pontier, *Les Constitutions de la France* (Paris: Dalloz, 1989) at 9.

3 Reproduced in Goerner, *supra* note 1 at 122: "An act can be punishable only if the penalty was fixed by law before the act was committed" [translation].

4 P. Feuerbach, *Lehrbuch des peinlichen Rechts* (Goldbach: Keip Verlag, 1997) para. 20 (1st ed. by P. Feuerbach: 1801).

5 It is interesting to note that this personal safeguard was one of very few "civil rights" included in the original United States Constitution of 1787, and the only one applicable to both the federal Congress and the individual state legislatures. For an account of the protection of individual rights in the United States Constitution prior to the 1791

Amendments, see G. Gunther and K.M. Sullivan, *Constitutional Law,* 13th ed. (Westbury, NY: Foundation Press, 1997) at 418.

6 See documents referred to in J.W. Bridge, "Retrospective Legislation and the Rule of Law in Britain" (1967) 35 UMKC L. Rev. 132 at 132.

7 *Universal Declaration of Human Rights,* GA Res. 217(III), UN GAOR, 3d Sess., Supp. No. 13, UN Doc. A/810 (1948).

8 *European Convention for the Protection of Human Rights and Fundamental Freedoms,* 4 November 1950, 213 U.N.T.S. 222 *[European Convention].*

9 *International Covenant on Civil and Political Rights,* 19 December 1966, 999 U.N.T.S. 171.

10 E. Edinger, "Retrospectivity in Law" (1995) 29 U.B.C. L. Rev. 5 at 12.

11 See E.E. Smead, "The Rule against Retroactive Legislation: A Basic Principle of Jurisdiction," (1936) 20 Minn. L. Rev. 775 at 775.

12 *Ibid.* at 776.

13 See D.E. Troy, *Retroactive Legislation* (Washington, DC: A.E.I. Press, 1998) at 26; Smead, *supra* note 11 at 777; H. Broom, *A Selection of Legal Maxims,* 10th ed. (London: Sweet & Maxwell, 1939) at 352-58.

14 See S.G.G. Edgar, ed., *Craies on Statute Law,* 7th ed. (London: Sweet & Maxwell, 1971) at 389; *Taylor v. The Queen,* [1877] 1 S.C.R. 65 at 109: "The rule against retroactivity of statutes ... is the same in English and French law because it has the same origin, Roman law" (Fournier J.); translated from French in P.A. Côté, *The Interpretation of Legislation in Canada,* 3d ed. (Toronto: Carswell, 2000) at 115.

15 W. Molesworth, ed., *The English Works of Thomas Hobbes,* vol. 6 (London: J. Bohn, 1840) at 227.

16 See J.E. Cooke, ed., *The Federalist,* No. 44 (Cleveland: World Publishing, 1961) at 301.

17 See T. Maslowski, *De Domo Sua* (Leipzig: B.G. Teubner, 1981), XVIII.

18 Bridge, *supra* note 6 at 137.

19 F.A.R. Bennion, *Statutory Interpretation* (London: Butterworths, 1984) at 314.

20 L. Fuller, *The Morality of Law,* 2d ed. (New Haven, CT: Yale University Press, 1969) at 53.

21 See, *e.g.,* the concurring opinion of Lamer J. (as he was at the time) in *Reference re ss. 193 and 195.1(1)(c) of the Criminal Code (Man.),* [1990] 1 S.C.R. 1123 at 1151-52 *[Prostitution Reference],* expressly linking the *nullum crimen* principle with the requirement of clarity in laws.

22 O.W. Holmes, *The Common Law,* 42d printing (Boston: Little, Brown and Company, 1948).

23 See s. 19 of the *Criminal Code.*

24 See J.C. Jeffries Jr., "Legality, Vagueness, and the Construction of Penal Statutes" (1985) 71 Va. L. Rev. 189 at 208-10.

25 See similarly G. Williams, *Criminal Law: The General Part,* 2d ed. (London: Stevens & Sons, 1961) at 602-3; Troy, *supra* note 13 at 24.

26 *R. v. Jacobson* (1988), 46 C.C.C. (3d) 50 (Sask. C.A.) *[Jacobson].*

27 See, *e.g., R. v. Silveira,* [1995] 2 S.C.R. 297.

28 *R. v. Edwards,* [1996] 1 S.C.R. 128 at 149-50.

29 *Ibid.* at 153.

30 This account of the history of judicial creation of offences in Great Britain, the United States, and Canada will be drawn principally from the following sources: Jeffries, *supra* note 24; P.W. Low, J.C. Jeffries Jr., & R.J. Bonnie, *Criminal Law: Cases and Materials* (Mineola, NY: Foundation Press, 1982); E.G. Ewaschuk, "Criminal Legislation" (1983-84) 26 Crim. L.Q. 97; Williams, *supra* note 25; D. Stuart, *Canadian Criminal Law: A Treatise,* 3d ed. (Scarborough, ON: Carswell, 1995); D. Stuart & R.J. Delisle, *Learning Canadian Criminal Law,* 4th ed. (Scarborough, ON: Carswell, 1993).

31 Low, Jeffries, & Bonnie, *supra* note 30 at 36.

32 *James Bagg's Case,* (1616) 77 E.R. 1271 at 1277.

33 *Jones v. Randall* (1774), 98 E.R. 706 at 707.

34 *Rex v. Sidley* (1663), 82 E.R. 1036.

35 *Taylor's Case* (1676), 86 E.R. 189.

36 *The King v. Ward* (1727), 92 E.R. 451.

37 *The King v. Lynn* (1788), 100 E.R. 394.

38 This passage from the 1879 commission on the reform of the criminal law is reproduced in Williams, *supra* note 25 at 595-96.

39 During the nineteenth century, two serious attempts were made to codify criminal law in England. Attempts were first made starting in 1833, and led to the introduction of a bill in 1845 by a Royal Commission. The bill was withdrawn to be revised by a second Royal Commission and was reintroduced in 1848, but was not proceeded with. A second series of efforts was made in 1878, based on the works of Sir James Fitzjames Stephen; see L.F. Sturge, ed., *Stephen's Digest of the Criminal Law,* 8th ed. (London: Sweet & Maxwell, 1947). In that work, a draft Criminal Code was introduced and was later withdrawn to be amended by a Royal Commission. It was reintroduced in 1879, too late to be passed into law. It was reintroduced several times in subsequent years, but was never enacted in the House of Commons. See Williams, *supra* note 25 at 582-83.

40 J.F. Stephen, *A History of the Criminal Law of England,* vol. 3 (London: Macmillan, 1883) at 359-60.

41 *R. v. Price* (1884) 12 Q.B.D. 247 (refusing to create the offence of cremation despite the popular feeling at the time, which viewed this conduct as highly offensive).

42 *Rex v. Manley,* [1933] 1 K.B. 529 *[Manley].*

43 See, *e.g.,* W.T.S. Stallybrass, "Public Mischief" (1933) 49 Law Q. Rev. 183; W.C. MacGregor, "Note" (1933) 49 Law Q. Rev. 482. A few years later, see J.A. Coults, "Effecting a Public Mischief" (1957) 21 J. Crim. L. 60.

44 *Shaw v. Director of Public Prosecutions,* [1961] 2 All E.R. 446 *[Shaw].*

45 Although the power to create new crimes is rarely exercised, Viscount Simonds's comments in the *Shaw* case suggest that such power exists in England: "In the sphere of criminal law, I entertain no doubt that there remains in the courts of law a residual power to enforce the supreme and fundamental purpose of the law, to conserve not only the safety and order but also the moral welfare of the state, and that it is their duty to guard it against attacks which may be more insidious because they are novel and unprepared for. That is the broad head (call it public policy if you wish) within which the present indictment falls. It matters little what label is given to the offending act" (at 452).

46 *Knuller v. Director of Public Prosecutions,* [1972] 2 All E.R. 898 *[Knuller].*

47 *Newland,* [1954] 1 Q.B. 167 (Circuit Court of Appeals); *Withers v. Director of Public Prosecutions,* [1975] A.C. 842.

48 *Manley* has been criticized; see *supra* note 43. *Shaw* has been the object of criticism in W. Friedmann, *Law in a Changing Society,* 2d ed. (New York: Columbia University Press, 1972) at 54-62; H.L.A. Hart, *Law, Liberty and Morality* (London: Oxford University Press, 1963) at 7-12; D.S. Davies, "The House of Lords and the Criminal Law" (1961) 6 Journal of the Society of Public Teachers of Law 104. For a criticism of *Knuller,* see J.D. Fine, "Conspiracies Contra Bonos Mores" (1973) 19 McGill L.J. 136.

49 See F.G. Jacobs & R.C.A. White, *The European Convention on Human Rights,* 2d ed. (Oxford: Clarendon Press, 1996) at 164-66.

50 *Ibid.* at 164 [citations omitted].

51 *Ibid.* at 165. See also D. Feldman, *Civil Liberties and Human Rights in England and Wales* (Oxford: Clarendon Press, 1993) at 706-8.

52 See, *e.g.,* the case of *Cantoni v. France,* 15 November 1995, European Court of Human Rights, *Reports of Judgements and Decisions* 1996-V, 1615 at 1627: "As the Court has already held, Article 7 embodies, *inter alia,* the principle that only the law can define a crime and prescribe a penalty *(nullum crimen, nulla poena sine lege)* and the principle that the criminal law must not be extensively construed to an accused's detriment, for instance by analogy. From these principles, it follows that an offence must be clearly defined in the law. This requirement is satisfied where the individual can know from the wording of the relevant provision and, if need be, with the assistance of the courts' interpretation of it, what acts and omissions will make him criminally liable."

53 I will come back later to the similarity between a conviction based on a vague law and an *ex post facto* conviction. See Chapter 4, notes 126-34 and accompanying text.

54 See B. Bailyn, *The Ideological Origins of the American Revolution* (Cambridge, MA: Harvard University Press, 1961).

55 See D.W. Carrithers, ed., *The Spirit of Laws* (Berkeley: University of California Press, 1977) (1st ed. by C. Montesquieu: 1748).
56 See C. Beccaria, *An Essay on Crimes and Punishments* (Brookline, MA: Branden Press, 1983) (1st ed.: 1764).
57 See generally F.W. Hall, "The Common Law: An Account of Its Reception in the United States" (1951) 4 Vand. L. Rev. 791.
58 See G. Beckman, "Three Penal Codes Compared" (1966) 10 Am. J. Legal Hist. 148; M. Bloomfield, "William Sampson and the Codifiers: The Roots of American Legal Reform, 1820-1830" (1967) 11 Am. J. Legal Hist. 234; S.H. Kadish, "Codifiers of the Criminal Law: Wechsler's Predecessors" (1978) 78 Colum. L. Rev. 1098.
59 *Commonwealth v. Taylor*, 5 Binn. 277 at 281 (Pa. 1812).
60 *Pennsylvania v. Gillespie*, 1 Addam's Ecclesiastical Reports 267 (1795) *[Gillespie]*.
61 *State v. Buckman*, 8 New Hampshire Reports 203 (1836) *[Buckman]*.
62 See Jeffries, *supra* note 24 at 191-95, and authorities referred to.
63 See L. Preuss, "Punishment by Analogy in National Socialist Penal Law" (1936) 26 J. Crim. L. & Criminology 847 at 847. A similar provision of the Dantzig Penal Code was condemned by the Permanent Court of International Justice in the *Dantzig Legislative Decrees* case, Advisory Opinion of 4 December 1935, Permanent Court of International Justice, Series A/B, No. 65.
64 Similarly, the American repugnance towards judicial crime creation was perhaps further intensified ideologically by the fact that the principle of punishment by analogy was also resorted to in the Soviet Union. Article 16 of the Soviet Penal Code provided that "if any socially dangerous act is not provided for by the present code, the basis and limits of responsibility for it shall be determined by application of those articles of the Code which provide for crimes most similar to it in nature"; see H. Berman, *Soviet Criminal Law and Procedure*, 2d ed. (Cambridge, MA: Harvard University Press, 1972) at 22.
65 See *Commonwealth v. Donoghue*, 250 Kentucky Reports 343 (1933) (upholding an indictment for usury without support from either statute or precedent); *Commonwealth v. Mochan*, 177 Pa. Super. 454 (1955) (conviction for having made obscene telephone calls, although conduct not prohibited by either statute or precedent).
66 See Jeffries, *supra* note 24 at 190-95 and authorities referred to.
67 See *supra* note 39.
68 Passage quoted in G.H. Crouse, "A Critique of Canadian Criminal Legislation" (1934) 12 Can. Bar Rev. 545 at 566.
69 See Ewaschuk, *supra* note 30 at 104.
70 On the history of the Canadian *Criminal Code* and the influence of the British experience in that regard, see Ewaschuk, *supra* note 30 at 102-7; M.L. Friedland and K. Roach, *Criminal Law and Procedure: Cases and Materials*, 7th ed. (Toronto: E. Montgomery, 1994) at 15-17; G. Parker, "The Origins of the Canadian Criminal Code" in D. Flaherty, ed., *Essays in the History of Canadian Law* (Toronto: University of Toronto Press, 1981) ch. 7; D. Brown, *The Genesis of the Canadian Criminal Code* (Toronto: University of Toronto Press, 1989); A.W. Mewett, "The Criminal Code, 1892-1992" (1993) 72 Can. Bar Rev. 1.
71 Debates of the House of Commons, 1892, vol. 2 at 1313.
72 Ewaschuk, *supra* note 30 at 105.
73 A.W. Mewett, "The Criminal Law, 1867-1967" (1967) 45 Can. Bar Rev. 726 at 729.
74 *R. v. Hastings* (1947) 90 C.C.C. 150 (N.B.S.C. App. Div.) *[Hastings]*.
75 In *Hastings*, the question was the following: In the context of an accusation of bodily harm that a student had inflicted on a police officer, one of the questions was whether the police officer had the right to arrest the accused for indecent exposure considering that he had caught him urinating in a public place at night. The judge concluded that the police officer had acted illegally since there was no definition in the *Criminal Code*, nor in the common law, of indecent exposure.
76 *Frey v. Fedoruk*, [1950] S.C.R. 517 *[Frey]*.
77 *Frey* was in fact a civil action by the "peeping Tom" against the victim's son and a police officer for false imprisonment. His arrest without warrant and his detention would have been legal only if being a "peeping Tom" had been a criminal offence.

78 *Frey, supra* note 76 at 530.
79 On the survival of the common law offence of criminal contempt, see *United Nurses of Alberta v. Alberta (Attorney General)*, [1992] 1 S.C.R. 901 at 931-34 *[United Nurses]*, where the Supreme Court of Canada maintained a conviction for criminal contempt against a labour union that, by going on strike, had violated a court order. As stated by McLachlin J. (as she then was): "It is for Parliament, not the courts, to create new offences ... but this does not mean that the courts should refuse to recognize the common law crime of contempt of court which pre-dated codification and which is expressly preserved by s. 9 of the *Code*" (at 930, citations omitted). From a constitutional standpoint, the offence's lack of codification and alleged vagueness was held not to violate ss. 7, 11(a), or 11(g) of the *Charter*. Another interesting aspect about the *United Nurses* case: it shows that the vagueness doctrine can be applicable not only to legislative enactments but also to common law standards (as long as the *Charter* is applicable), although it is most often applied against statutes.
80 R.S.C. 1985, c. 1 (2d Supp.).
81 R.S.C. 1985, c. F-27.
82 R.S.C. 1985, c. 1 (5th Supp.).
83 R.S.C. 1985, c. C-34.
84 R.S.C. 1985, c. N-1.
85 Ewaschuk, *supra* note 30 at 104.
86 Section 8 of the *Criminal Code* provides that "every rule and principle of the common law that renders any circumstance a justification or excuse for an act or a defence to a charge continues in force and applies in respect of proceedings." However, if a defence is restricted through the common law rather than created, it can arguably equate to judicial crime creation. See the discussion on the *Jobidon* case, *infra* notes 89-91 and accompanying text.
87 See *United Nurses, supra* note 79 at 934.
88 See F. Chevrette and H. Cyr, "La protection en matière de fouilles, perquisitions et saisies, en matière de détention, la non-rétroactivité de l'infraction et la peine la plus douce," in G.A. Beaudoin and E. Mendes, eds., *The Canadian Charter of Rights and Freedoms*, 3d ed. (Scarborough, ON: Carswell, 1996) ch. 10 at 102-3. Note that this has also been recognized in American case law: *Marks v. United States*, 430 U.S. 188 (1977); *Bouie v. City of Columbia*, 378 U.S. 347 (1964).
89 *R. v. Jobidon*, [1991] 2 S.C.R. 714 *[Jobidon]*.
90 *Ibid.* at 774.
91 See *supra* notes 10-29 and accompanying text.
92 *R. v. Cuerrier*, [1998] 2 S.C.R. 371 *[Cuerrier]*.
93 *Ibid.* at 432.
94 *Ibid.* at 400-1.
95 *Ibid.* at 392.
96 *R. v. Clarence* (1888) 22 Q.B.D. 23.
97 *Cuerrier, supra* note 92 at 414.
98 *Ibid.* at 392.
99 Although if the statute on which an interpretation is based is overly vague, the interpretation that is done in an attempt to remedy its vagueness can be problematic, in my view. This issue will be examined later. See Chapter 3, notes 181-94 and accompanying text.
100 Note that before the enactment of the *Charter*, courts developed a principle pursuant to which a statute must be interpreted as having only a prospective effect. This presumption can be put aside only if the statute states expressly or by necessary implication that it will operate in the past. Of course, this rule does not permit the invalidation of expressly retroactive statutes or preclude their application to past situations, as only constitutional provisions can have such a paramount effect on the sovereignty of legislative assemblies. For jurisprudential applications of the presumption against retroactivity, see cases referred to in Côté, *supra* note 14 at 144-46 (footnotes 196-221).
101 In the case law, see *Thorpe v. College of Pharmacists of British Columbia* (1997), 97 D.L.R. (4th) 634 at 638 (B.C.C.A.) *[Thorpe]* – s. 11(g) held not to be applicable to disciplinary

sanctions directed towards professionals; *États-Unis d'Amérique v. Brisson* (1994), 61 Q.A.C. 198 (Qc. C.A.) *[Brisson]* – s. 11(g) held not to be applicable to extradition hearings. In Canadian legal literature, it has thus far been taken for granted that s. 11(g) would be applicable only in penal matters because it refers to "offences": see Chevrette and Cyr, *supra* note 88 at 107; and P.W. Hogg, *Constitutional Law of Canada*, looseleaf, vol. 2 (Scarborough, ON: Carswell, 1997), ch. 48 at 25-27.

102 *Reference re Remuneration of Judges of the Provincial Court of Prince Edward Island; Reference re Independence and Impartiality of Judges of the Provincial Court of Prince Edward Island,* [1997] 3 S.C.R. 3 *[Judges Remuneration Reference]*.

103 See Chapter 2, notes 52-54 and accompanying text.

104 See Chapter 2, notes 81-83.

105 We will come back to this question and explain it in greater detail in Chapter 4; see notes 126-34 and accompanying text.

106 See generally S.R. Munzer, "Retroactive Law" (1977) 6 J. Legal Stud. 373.

107 Fuller, *supra* note 20 at 53-54.

108 *Ibid.* at 53.

109 Hogg, *Constitutional Law of Canada, supra* note 101, ch. 48 at 27.

110 For more on the warning provided by ministerial announcements, see G.Q. Walker, *The Rule of Law* (Melbourne: University of Melbourne Press, 1988) at 320. For more on the legitimacy of certain types of retroactive laws, see also Walker at 319; Edinger, *supra* note 10 at 14-15; Bridge, *supra* note 6 at 138.

111 In the United States, the scope of the *ex post facto* clauses has long been limited to penal statutes; *Calder v. Bull*, 3 U.S. 386 (1798). However, American courts will expand the reach of the prohibition to other laws when they have effects that are similar to penal legislation. See L.H. Tribe, *American Constitutional Law*, 2d ed. (Mineola, NY: Foundation Press, 1988) at 637. In the jurisprudence of the United States Supreme Court, see *Burgess v. Salmon* 97 U.S. 381 at 385 (1878); *Harisiades v. Shaughnessy,* 342 U.S. 580 at 595 (1952). Canadian courts have yet to adopt this reasoning. See, *e.g., Brisson, supra* note 101, where s. 11(g) was held not to be applicable in the context of a statute providing retroactively for grounds for deportation.

112 W. Blackstone, *Commentaries on the Law of England,* vol. 1 (15th ed. by Christian, 1809) at 46.

113 J. Hall, *General Principles of Criminal Law,* 2d ed. (New York: Bobbs, 1960) at 59.

114 Chevrette and Cyr, *supra* note 88.

115 *Ibid.* at 94-95.

116 *Ibid.* at 95-96. But see *Jobidon, supra* note 89 and the accompanying discussion on the *ex post facto* suppression of a defence (or at least of an exculpatory element of the offence) through judicial interpretation.

117 Chevrette and Cyr, *supra* note 88 at 95.

118 *Ibid.* at 96.

119 This calls upon the distinction made by some authors between the retroactive and the retrospective operation of a statute. See E.A. Driedger, "Statutes: Retroactive Retrospective Reflections" (1978) 56 Can. Bar Rev. 264 at 268-69: "A retroactive statute is one that operates as of a time prior to its enactment. A retrospective statute is one that operates for the future only. It is prospective, but it imposes new results in respect of a past event."

120 Chevrette and Cyr, *supra* note 88 at 97.

121 *Ibid.*

122 *Ibid.* at 98.

123 *Ibid.*

124 *Ibid.*

125 *Ibid.* In a rather similar line, Pierre-André Côté goes even further to suggest that retroactive limitations to any of the guarantees of the *Charter* would automatically be unconstitutional. The State would not be given the opportunity to demonstrate that such limitations may be justifiable under s. 1. Professor Côté relies on the requirement in s. 1 that limitations to *Charter* rights be "prescribed by law." Inspired by the jurisprudence

maintaining that a vague law is not a law for the purpose of s. 1, Côté suggests that a retroactive law also fails to satisfy this preliminary requirement. Côté, *supra* note 14 at 148 (footnote 231).

126 See the *Proposed Resolution for Joint Address to Her Majesty the Queen Respecting the Constitution of Canada*, tabled in the House of Commons and the Senate, Catalogue no. YC3-321/5-57, 6 October 1980, s. 11(e), reproduced in A.F. Bayefsky, ed., *Canada's Constitution Act, 1982 & Amendments: A Documented History*, vol. 2 (Toronto: McGraw-Hill, 1989) 743 at 748.

127 *R. v. Finta*, [1994] 1 S.C.R. 701 *[Finta]*.

128 *Ibid.* at 873.

129 *Ibid.*

130 H. Kelsen, "Will the Judgement in the Nuremberg Tribunal Constitute a Precedent in International Law?" (1947), 1 Int'l L. Q. 153 at 165, cited by Cory J. in *Finta, supra* note 127 at 874.

131 *Finta, supra* note 127 at 874. Interestingly, the Court seems to have included an element of justification (which is usually within the ambit of s. 1) in the analysis of s. 11(g) itself. It was decided that even though the law was retroactive, it did not violate s. 11(g) because the alleged acts were so highly reprehensible that they nevertheless deserved to be punished. Usually, this type of justification is made in the framework of the limitation clause, through the *Oakes* method, after the violation to the substantive *Charter* right has been shown. However, it is possible that the requirement that a limitation must be prescribed by law would have prevented the application of s. 1, and perhaps the Court did not want to resort to s. 1 because it intends to rule in the future that a limit imposed by a retroactive law is not "prescribed by law." This theory on the "prescribed by law" element of s. 1 has been touched upon by Pierre-André Côté, as mentioned earlier (*supra* note 125).

132 *C.R. v. United Kingdom*, 22 November 1995, European Court of Human Rights, No. 48/1994/495/577 *[Marital Rape Case]*. See also the companion case of *S.W. v. United Kingdom*, 22 November 1995, European Court of Human Rights, No. 47/1994/494/576.

133 *Ibid., C.R. v. United Kingdom*, at 60-62.

134 *R. v. R.*, [1992] 1 A.C. 599 (House of Lords).

135 R. Higgins, "Time and the Law: International Perspectives on an Old Problem" (1997) 46 I.C.L.Q. 501 at 508.

136 See, *e.g.*, C. Osborne, "Does the Ends Justify the Means? Retrospectivity, Article 7, and the Marital Rape Exemption" (1996) 4 Eur. H.R.L. Rev. 406.

137 *Dobbert v. Florida*, 432 U.S. 282 (1977) *[Dobbert]*.

138 The statute was invalidated by Florida's highest court in *Donaldson v. Sack*, 265 Southern Reporter 2d 499 (Fla. 1972), under the authority of a decision of the Supreme Court in *Furman v. Georgia*, 408 U.S. 238 (1972).

139 *Dobbert, supra* note 137 at 297-98.

140 *Ibid.* at 311.

141 Tribe, *supra* note 111 at 639.

142 See Higgins, *supra* note 135 at 508.

143 *Re B.C. Motor Vehicle Act*, [1985] 2 S.C.R. 486 at 502-3 *[Motor Vehicle Reference]*.

144 *R. v. Gamble*, [1988] 2 S.C.R. 595 *[Gamble]*.

145 This application of s. 7 of the *Charter* to situations that began before 1982 again calls upon the distinction between retroactivity and retrospectivity. See *supra* note 119.

146 *R. v. Nova Scotia Pharmaceutical Society*, [1992] 2 S.C.R. 606 at 634: "The substantive aspect of fair notice is ... a subjective understanding that the law touches upon some conduct, based on the substratum of values underlying the legal enactment."

147 In the Supreme Court of Canada, see, *e.g.*, *Ontario v. Canadian Pacific Ltd.*, [1995] 2 S.C.R. 1031 at 1083ff. *[Canadian Pacific]; Nova Scotia Pharmaceutical, supra* note 146 at 651-58.

148 On the judicial specification of vague laws through interpretation, see criticisms by Jeffries, *supra* note 24 at 207-8; D. Stuart, "The Canadian Void for Vagueness Doctrine Arrives with No Teeth" (1990) 77 C.R. (3d) 101 at 108; G.T. Trotter, "LeBeau: Toward a Canadian Vagueness Doctrine" (1988) 62 C.R. (3d) 183 at 188.

149 See Chapter 3, notes 181-94 and accompanying text.

Chapter 2: The Rule of Law

1 See A. Scalia, "The Rule of Law as a Law of Rules," (1989) 56 U. Chicago L. Rev. 1175 at 1177: "The advantages of the discretion-conferring approach are obvious. All generalizations ... are to some degree invalid, and hence every rule of law has a few corners that do not quite fit. It follows that perfect justice can only be achieved if Courts are unconstrained by such imperfect generalizations."

2 See G.F. Gaus, "Public Reason and the Rule of Law" in I. Shapiro, ed., *The Rule of Law* (New York: New York University Press, 1994) 328 at 345-46.

3 Scalia, *supra* note 1 at 1178.

4 See A.V. Dicey, *Introduction to the Study of the Law of the Constitution,* 10th ed. (London: Macmillan, 1965). The first edition of this treatise was published in 1885.

5 *Ibid.* at 202: "[The rule of law] means, in the first place, the absolute supremacy or predominance of regular law as opposed to the influence of arbitrary power, and excludes the existence of arbitrariness, of prerogative, or even of wide discretionary authority on the part of the government."

6 *Ibid.* at 202-3: "It means, again, equality before the law, or the equal subjection of all classes to the ordinary law of the land administered by the ordinary courts; the 'rule of law' in this sense excludes the idea of any exemption of officials or others from the duty of obedience to the law which governs other citizens or from the jurisdiction of the ordinary tribunals."

7 *Ibid.* at 40.

8 Although it may be considered that the Parliament of Great Britain has lost its total sovereignty to a certain extent because it is now bound by higher norms by virtue of the *European Convention for the Protection of Human Rights and Fundamental Freedoms,* 4 November 1950, 213 U.N.T.S. 222 *[European Convention].*

9 Dicey, *supra* note 4 at 203: "The 'rule of law,' lastly, may be used as a formula for expressing the fact that with us the law of the constitution, the rules which in foreign countries naturally form part of a constitutional code, are not the source but the consequences of the rights of individuals, as defined and enforced by the courts; ... thus the constitution is the result of the ordinary law of the land."

10 See R. Sullivan, *Driedger on the Construction of Statutes,* 3d ed. (Toronto: Butterworths, 1994) at 259-63; P.A. Côté, *The Interpretation of Legislation in Canada,* 3d ed. (Toronto: Carswell, 2000) at 57-60.

11 P.W. Hogg, *Canada Act 1982 Annotated* (Scarborough, ON: Carswell, 1982) at 9. With regard to the rule of law, however, Professor Hogg doubted that it could be very helpful in interpretation merely because the phrase is "notoriously vague" *(ibid.).*

12 See *Gregg v. Georgia,* 428 U.S. 153 at 188 (1976).

13 *R. v. Smith,* [1987] 1 S.C.R. 1045.

14 *Ibid.* at 1074-76.

15 *Ibid.* at 1103-6.

16 *Ibid.* at 1111.

17 *Ibid.* at 1109-10.

18 See P.J. Monahan, "Is the Pearson Airport Legislation Unconstitutional? The Rule of Law as a Limit on Contract Repudiation by Government" (1995) 33 Osgoode Hall L.J. 411.

19 See J. Bakan and S. Schneiderman, "Submissions to the Standing Senate Committee on Legal and Constitutional Affairs Concerning Bill C-22" at 2 [unpublished].

20 In that regard, it is interesting to note that the French version of s. 52 does not refer to constitutional "provisions," but instead to the Constitution in general: "52. (1) La Constitution du Canada est la loi suprême du Canada; elle rend inopérantes les dispositions incompatibles de toute autre règle de droit."

21 Bakan and Schneiderman, *supra* note 19 at 3-4.

22 See Monahan, *supra* note 18 at 420.

23 This leads, for example, to the possibility, as Professor Monahan puts it (*supra* note 18), of challenging the validity of legislation seeking to cancel contracts signed between the government and private parties without compensation. This kind of statute being repugnant to the rule of law, it could be declared unconstitutional despite the fact that no provision of the Constitution protects property rights.

24 *Roncarelli v. Duplessis*, [1959] S.C.R. 121 *[Roncarelli]*.
25 *Ibid.* at 140-42.
26 *Ibid.* at 142.
27 *Reference Re Resolution to Amend the Constitution*, [1981] 1 S.C.R. 753 *[Patriation Reference]*.
28 There were actually two majority opinions in this case. The one being referred to here, which discussed the impact of the unwritten principles of the Constitution, was written by Laskin C.J., as well as Dickson, Beetz, Estey, McIntyre, Chouinard, and Lamer JJ. The other majority opinion, which addressed the degree of provincial support required by constitutional convention for constitutional modifications, was written by Martland, Ritchie, Dickson, Beetz, Chouinard, and Lamer JJ.
29 *Patriation Reference, supra* note 27 at 805.
30 *Ibid.* at 841 and 844-45 [emphasis in original].
31 *Reference Re Manitoba Language Rights*, [1985] 1 S.C.R. 721 *[Manitoba Language Reference]*.
32 R.S.C. 1970, app. 2.
33 *Manitoba Language Reference, supra* note 31 at 747-68.
34 *Ibid.* at 750-51.
35 See passage accompanying note 30. Cited in the *Manitoba Language Reference, supra* note 31 at 752.
36 See passage accompanying note 29.
37 *OPSEU v. Ontario (A.G.)*, [1987] 2 S.C.R. 2 *[OPSEU]*.
38 *Ibid.* at 57.
39 *Switzman v. Elbling*, [1957] S.C.R. 285.
40 *Ibid.* at 328.
41 *OPSEU, supra* note 37 at 57.
42 *Manitoba Language Reference, supra* note 31: "The rule of law [is] a fundamental principle of our Constitution" (at 748); "the constitutional status of the rule of law is beyond question" (at 750); "the Constitution Act, 1982 ... is explicit recognition that the rule of law [is] a fundamental postulate of our constitutional structure" (at 750); "the principle is clearly implicit in the very nature of a Constitution" (at 750); "While it is not set out in a specific provision, the principle of the rule of law is clearly a principle of our Constitution" (at 751).
43 *New Brunswick Broadcasting Co. v. Nova Scotia (Speaker of the House of Assembly)*, [1993] 1 S.C.R. 319 *[New Brunswick Broadcasting]*.
44 *Ibid.* at 375-78.
45 *Reference re Remuneration of Judges of the Provincial Court of Prince Edward Island; Reference re Independence and Impartiality of Judges of the Provincial Court of Prince Edward Island*, [1997] 3 S.C.R. 3 *[Judges Remuneration Reference]*.
46 The text of s. 11(d) states: "Any person charged with an offence has the right ... to be presumed innocent until proven guilty according to law in a fair and public hearing *by an independent and impartial tribunal*" [emphasis added].
47 *Judges Remuneration Reference, supra* note 45 at 63-78.
48 *Ibid.* at 68.
49 *Ibid.* (citing *New Brunswick Broadcasting, supra* note 43 at 355).
50 *Ibid.* at 68.
51 *Ibid.* at 78.
52 *Ibid.* at 69.
53 *Ibid.* at 76-77.
54 *Reference re Secession of Quebec*, [1998] 2 S.C.R. 217 *[Quebec Secession Reference]*.
55 *Ibid.* at 267-68.
56 *Ibid.* at 247-63.
57 *Ibid.* at 249.
58 *OPSEU, supra* note 37 at 57.
59 *Quebec Secession Reference, supra* note 54 at 249.
60 See especially the statements reproduced in *supra* note 42.
61 See passage accompanying note 30.
62 The text of s. 7 states that "everyone has the right to life, liberty and security of the person

and the right not to be deprived thereof except in accordance with the principles of fundamental justice."

63 The text of s. 9 states that "everyone has the right not to be arbitrarily detained or imprisoned."

64 The text of s. 11(g) states that "any person charged with an offence has the right ... not to be found guilty on account of any act or omission unless, at the time of the act or omission, it constituted an offence under Canadian or international law." This provision embodies, at least in part, the protection afforded to the principle of legality studied in Chapter 1. See text accompanying Chapter 1, notes 100-45. In that sense, the principle of legality can be viewed as enjoying a more direct and tangible constitutional protection than the rule of law.

65 *Judges Remuneration Reference, supra* note 45 at 76 [citations omitted].

66 See passage accompanying note 52.

67 See comments following note 23.

68 See Monahan, *supra* note 18 at 428: "The enactment of the *Charter* has placed the Court in the position of second-guessing the legislature on a wide variety of policy matters that previously would have been regarded as off-limits. This, in turn has made the Court much more comfortable with the notion of 'unwritten' or 'implied' constitutional limitations on the authority of Parliament."

69 See *supra* notes 24-26 and accompanying text.

70 *Roncarelli, supra* note 24 at 142.

71 *Patriation Reference, supra* note 27 at 805-6. This was again the first of two majority opinions of the Court in this case (see *supra* note 28).

72 *Manitoba Language Reference, supra* note 31 at 748-49 [citations omitted].

73 See *supra* note 71 and accompanying passage.

74 *R. v. Nova Scotia Pharmaceutical Society,* [1992] 2 S.C.R. 606.

75 *Ibid.* at 640.

76 *Judges Remuneration Reference, supra* note 45 at 34.

77 *Quebec Secession Reference, supra* note 54 at 258.

78 B. McLachlin, "Rules and Discretion in the Governance of Canada" (1992) 56 Sask. L. Rev. 167 at 168.

79 J. Raz, "The Rule of Law and its Virtue" (1977) 93 Law Q. Rev. 195.

80 The related German concept of the Rechtsstaat (law-State) is also divided between a formal view and a more substantive conception. See L.C. Blaau, "The Rechtsstaat Idea Compared with the Rule of Law as a Paradigm for Protecting Rights" (1990) 107 South African Law Journal 76 at 79-88.

81 J. Rawls, *A Theory of Justice* (Cambridge, MA: Harvard University Press, 1971) at 235-39, states that the components of the rule of law are that (1) laws must be capable of being followed; (2) similar cases must be treated similarly; (3) there is no offence without an expressly promulgated, clear, prospective, and general law; and (4) some safeguards must ensure the integrity and impartiality of the judicial process.

82 Raz, *supra* note 79 at 198-202, states that the rule of law includes the following requirements: (1) all laws should be prospective, open, and clear; (2) laws should be relatively stable; (3) the making of particular laws (particular legal orders) should be guided by open, stable, clear, and general rules; (4) the independence of the judiciary should be guaranteed; (5) the principles of natural justice must be observed; (6) the courts should have review powers over the implementation of the other principles; (7) the courts should be easily accessible; and (8) the discretion of the crime-preventing agencies should not be allowed to pervert the law.

83 L. Fuller, *The Morality of Law,* 2d ed. (New Haven, CT: Yale University Press, 1969) at 46-89, states that the following elements are required from laws: (1) generality; (2) promulgation; (3) prospectivity; (4) clarity; (5) absence of contradictions; (6) performability; (7) constancy through time; and (8) congruence between official action and declared rule.

84 See text accompanying notes 1-3.

85 See Raz, *supra* note 79 at 195-96: "If the rule of law is the rule of the good law then to explain its nature is to propound a complete social philosophy. But if so the term lacks any useful function."

86 *Ibid.* at 196.
87 *Ibid.* See also A.C. Hutchinson and P.J. Monahan, "Democracy and the Rule of Law" in A.C. Hutchinson and P.J. Monahan, eds., *The Rule of Law: Ideal or Ideology* (Toronto: Carswell, 1987) 97 at 101.
88 Raz, *supra* note 79 at 196; M.J. Radin, "Reconsidering the Rule of Law" (1989) 69 B.U.L. Rev. 781 at 786.
89 See M.S. Moore, "A Natural Law Theory of Interpretation" (1985) 58 S. Cal. L. Rev. 277.
90 See R. Dworkin, *A Matter of Principle* (Cambridge, MA: Harvard University Press, 1985).
91 See J. Locke, *Two Treatises on Government* (Cambridge: Cambridge University Press, 1967).
92 Clause 1 of the *Report of Committee I of the International Congress of Jurists* (New Delhi: International Congress of Jurists, 1959).
93 Among the contemporary authors referred to thus far, only Moore and Dworkin agree with the inclusion of substantive limits, while all of these authors agree that the rule of law includes at least formal limitations.
94 For example, it has been argued that the rule of law in a "fundamental rights" version is detrimental to democratic philosophy because it favours individual over communal values while achieving an undue judicialization of politics: see Hutchinson and Monahan, *supra* note 87.
95 In most other countries, the rule of law does not enjoy express constitutional recognition, unlike in Canada with the preamble to the *Charter*. The principle is widely recognized in the Western academic literature, however. The expression "rule of law" is mainly used in the Anglo-Saxon world: see, for example, Raz, *supra* note 79, and F.A. Hayek, *The Constitution of Liberty* (Chicago: University of Chicago Press, 1960) (United States); Dicey, *supra* note 4, and I. Jennings, *The Law and the Constitution,* 5th ed. (London: University of London Press, 1959) (Great Britain); G.Q. Walker, *The Rule of Law* (Melbourne: University of Melbourne Press, 1988) (Australia). Outside the Anglo-Saxon world, the principle is recognized under different names, such as "stato di diritto," see B. Leoni, "Diritto e politica" (1961) Rivista Internazionale di Filosofia del Diritto 89 (Italy); or "Rechtsstaat," see works cited and extensive description in Blaau, *supra* note 80 (Germany); or "L'État de droit," see R.C. de Malberg, *Contribution à la théorie générale du droit,* t.1 (Paris: Sirey, 1920) (France).
96 However, note that a minority of commentators have criticized the legitimacy of the ideal. See, *e.g.,* D. Kennedy, "Form and Substance in Private Law Adjudication" (1976) 89 Harv. L. Rev. 1685; R. Unger, "The Critical Legal Studies Movement" (1983) 96 Harv. L. Rev. 563; D. Kairis, "The Politics of Law" (1984) 36 Stan. L. Rev. 1. It is outside the scope of this study to explore these criticisms. Rather, this study examines the rule of law's internal perspective and develops the concepts related to the vagueness doctrine within that framework.
97 Scalia, *supra* note 1 at 1175-76 [citations omitted].
98 Walker, *supra* note 95 at 266. Note that the importance of limiting discretion is particularly important in relation to laws that have a coercive aspect. See *infra* notes 124-33 and accompanying text.
99 See *supra* notes 24-67 and accompanying text.
100 *Nova Scotia Pharmaceutical, supra* note 74.
101 *Ibid.* at 639-40.
102 The Court does mention that "a delicate balance must be maintained between social interests and individual rights" (*ibid.* at 642), but this concern is not included in the general test of legal debate. Instead, the Court seems to consider only the interests of State by stating a very low standard and declaring it applicable to all laws. The Court seems to disregard the fact that some legislative subject matters may allow more precision in drafting than mere basis for legal debate. A "delicate balance" would require the Court to take this reality into consideration in framing the test of the vagueness doctrine. (This "balancing" approach will be further explained below.)
103 Hayek, *supra* note 95 at 213.
104 *Ibid.* at 217.
105 The text of s. 1 states that "the *Canadian Charter of Right and Freedoms* guarantees the rights and freedoms set out in it subject only to such reasonable limits prescribed by law as can be demonstrably justified in a free and democratic society."

106 *R. v. Oakes*, [1986] 1 S.C.R. 103 *[Oakes]*.
107 See the evolution of s. 1 jurisprudence described by E.P. Mendes, "The Crucible of the *Charter:* Judicial Deference in the Context of Section 1" in G.A. Beaudoin and E. Mendes, eds., *The Canadian Charter of Rights and Freedoms*, 3d ed. (Scarborough, ON: Carswell, 1996) ch. 3 at 12 and ff.
108 *Oakes, supra* note 106 at 138-39.
109 For an conservative inventory of some 14,885 discretionary powers within the 1970 *Revised Statutes of Canada* alone, see P. Anisman, *A Catalogue of Discretionary Powers in the Revised Statutes of Canada 1970* (Ottawa: Law Reform Commission of Canada, 1975) at 23.
110 See *supra* notes 78-95 and accompanying text.
111 *First Report of the Royal Commission Inquiry into Civil Rights* (Toronto; Queen's Printer, 1968) *[McRuer Report]*.
112 *Ibid.* at 95. See similarly Scalia, *supra* note 1 at 1182.
113 E. Baker, ed., *The Politics of Aristotle* (Oxford: Clarendon Press, 1946) at 127.
114 *McRuer Report, supra* note 111 at 96.
115 R.S.O. 1960, c. 312.
116 *McRuer Report, supra* note 111 at 97.
117 *Ibid.*
118 *Ibid.*
119 R.S.O. 1960, c. 338.
120 *McRuer Report, supra* note 111 at 98.
121 *Nova Scotia Pharmaceutical, supra* note 74 at 641.
122 The criterion for constitutional evaluation is whether the law is an "adequate basis for legal debate" (*Nova Scotia Pharmaceutical, supra* note 74 at 639). This criterion is very permissive. As Peter Hogg has noted, "almost any provision, no matter how vague could provide a basis for legal debate"; Hogg, *Constitutional Law of Canada*, 4th ed. (Scarborough, ON: Carswell, 1996) at 867. In fact, only one piece of legislation has thus far been found defective by the Supreme Court of Canada on grounds of vagueness: see *R. v. Morales,* [1992] 3 S.C.R. 711 *[Morales]; R. v. Hall*, 2002 S.C.C. 64, file no. 28223 *[Hall]*. See discussion in Chapter 3, notes 196-97 and accompanying text.
123 In that framework, jurisprudence on s. 1 of the *Charter* can shed light on considerations related to judicial deference towards legislative choice. See generally Mendes, *supra* note 107. For example, it is recognized under s. 1 that greater deference is especially appropriate in cases involving the delivery of social programs; *Irwin Toy Ltd. v. Quebec (A.G.),* [1989] 1 S.C.R. 927 *[Irwin Toy]*. In that regard, it is interesting to note that Dicey himself was more inclined to tolerate the influence of arbitrary power in the context of social legislation: see A.V. Dicey, "The Development of Administrative Law in England" (1915) 31 Law Q. Rev. 148.
124 Hayek, *supra* note 95 at 206.
125 *Ibid.* at 133-47.
126 *Ibid.* at 213: "So long as the government administers its own resources, there are strong arguments for giving it as much discretion as any business management would require in similar circumstances. As Dicey has pointed out, 'in the management of his own business, properly so called, the government will be found to need that freedom of action, necessarily possessed by every private person in the management of his own personal concerns'" [citations omitted].
127 On the rule of law's "gap-filling" potential, see previous discussion in *supra* notes 52-57 and accompanying text.
128 *Ontario Public School Boards' Assn. v. Ontario (A.G.)* (1997), 151 D.L.R. (4th) 346 (Ont. G.D.) *[Ontario School Boards]*. This decision was affirmed on appeal: *Ontario Public School Boards' Assn. v. Ontario (A.G.)* (1999), 175 D.L.R. (4th) 609 (Ont. C.A.). Note that the appeal rested on other grounds, and therefore the rule of law issue was not discussed in the Court of Appeal's decision.
129 S.O. 1997, c. 3.
130 *Ontario School Boards, supra* note 128 at 360.
131 *Ibid.*

132 For other examples of this tendency, see, *e.g., East York (Borough) v. Ontario (Attorney General)* (1997), 34 O.R. (3d) 789 (Ont. G.D.) *[Megacity Case]* (upholding the validity of broad delegations to the executive to restructure municipalities in the Toronto area); *Ontario English Catholic Teachers' Assn. v. Ontario (Attorney General)* (1999), 172 D.L.R. (4th) 193 (Ont. C.A.) *[Ontario Teachers]* (upholding the validity of broad delegations to the executive to restructure the education funding system in Ontario).

133 *Ontario School Boards, supra* note 128 at 363.

Chapter 3: The Content of the Vagueness Doctrine

1 *R. v. Nova Scotia Pharmaceutical Society,* [1992] 2 S.C.R. 606.

2 *R. v. Morales,* [1992] 3 S.C.R. 711.

3 *Canadian Bar Assn. v. British Columbia (Attorney-General); Law Society of British Columbia v. British Columbia (Attorney-General)* (1996), 101 D.L.R. (4th) 410 (B.C.S.C.) *[Canadian Bar Assn. No. 1].*

4 *Canadian Bar Assn. v. British Columbia (Attorney-General)* (1994), 91 B.C.L.R. 207 (B.C.S.C.) *[Canadian Bar Assn. No. 2].*

5 See L.H. Tribe, *American Constitutional Law,* 2d ed. (Mineola, NY: Foundation Press, 1988) at 684 (where the void-for-vagueness doctrine is presented among *procedural* due process guarantees). See also G. Gunther and K.M. Sullivan, *Constitutional Law,* 13th ed. (Westbury, NY: Foundation Press, 1997) at 1337; R.A. Collings, "Unconstitutional Uncertainty: An Appraisal" (1955) 40 Cornell L.Q. 195 at 196. On the distinction between procedural and substantive due process review, see J.E. Nowak, R.D. Rotunda, & J.N. Young, *Constitutional Law,* 3d ed. (St. Paul, MN: West Publishing, 1986) at 322.

6 See, *e.g., Stromberg v. California,* 283 U.S. 359 (1931); *Herndon v. Lowry,* 301 U.S. 242 (1937); *Thornhill v. Alabama,* 310 U.S. 88 (1940); *Winters v. New York,* 333 U.S. 507 at 524 (1948) (dissenting opinion) *[Winters]; Baggett v. Bullitt,* 377 U.S. 360 (1964) *[Baggett]; Coates v. Cincinnati,* 402 U.S. 611 (1971) *[Coates]; Smith v. Goguen,* 415 U.S. 566 (1974); *Colautti v. Franklin,* 439 U.S. 379 (1979) *[Colautti]; Kolender v. Lawson,* 461 U.S. 360 (1983) *[Kolender].* See also cases referred to *infra* note 13.

7 *The Slaughter-House Cases,* 83 U.S. 36 at 81 (1873).

8 *Allgeyer v. Louisiana,* 165 U.S. 578 at 591-92 (1897).

9 *Lochner v. New York,* 198 U.S. 45 (1905).

10 *West Coast Hotel v. Parrish,* 300 U.S. 379 at 399 (1937).

11 *United States v. Carolene Products Co.,* 304 U.S. 144 at 152-53 (1938).

12 See A.G. Amsterdam, "The Void-for-Vagueness Doctrine in the Supreme Court" (1960) 109 U. Pa. L. Rev. 67 at n. 38: "The Void-for-Vagueness doctrine was born in the reign of substantive due process."

13 See *International Harvester Co. v. Kentucky,* 234 U.S. 216 (1914) (striking down legislation prohibiting price-fixing combinations "for the purpose or with the effect of fixing a price that was greater or less than the real value of the article"); *United States v. Cohen Grocery Co.,* 255 U.S. 81 (1921) *[Cohen Grocery]* (invalidating law that made it illegal to willfully "make any unjust or unreasonable rate or charge in handling or dealing in or with any necessaries"); *Connally v. General Construction Company,* 269 U.S. 385 (1926) *[Connally]* (invalidating a law that made it a crime for a contractor to pay his employees "less than the current rate of per diem wages in the locality where the work is performed"); *Cline v. Frink Dairy Co.,* 274 U.S. 445 (1927) (invalidating legislation that outlawed conspiracies and combinations of restraint of trade except when the purposes were "to conduct operations at a reasonable profit"); *Smith v. Cahoon,* 283 U.S. 553 (1931) (striking down legislation that left it unclear, after state court interpretations, whether certain requirements of a regulatory scheme on motor transport were "legally applicable" to contract carriers as opposed to common carriers); *Champlin Refining Co. v. Commission,* 286 U.S. 210 (1932) (invalidating a statute that outlawed the production of "crude oil or petroleum in the State of Oklahoma, in such a manner and under such conditions as to constitute a waste").

14 *Cohen Grocery, supra* note 13.

15 *United States v. National Dairy Products Corp.,* 372 U.S. 29 (1963).

16 Amsterdam, "The Void-for-Vagueness Doctrine in the Supreme Court," *supra* note 12 at 85.

17 See Collings, *supra* note 5 at 212: "It is hard to read the procedural due process uncertainty cases without a feeling that their value as precedents at least on the merits, may be subject to a considerable doubt. They are generally cases involving economic regulation, decided before the mid-thirties"; Amsterdam, "The Void-for-Vagueness Doctrine in the Supreme Court," *supra* note 12 at n. 39: "Had each of the claims carried sufficient conviction to determine the outcome independently, the vagueness syntax need never – and probably would never – have been used. It becomes necessary insomuch as the individual claimant fails to establish that his economic ... interests have been unconstitutionally curtailed," and at 77: "Most of them date from an era when economic laissez-faire was for the Court the sanctum sanctorum that free speech has become today, and decisions like Cohen and International Harvester display unmistakable signs of ... extraneous constitutional compulsion."
18 Tribe, *supra* note 5 at 769-70; Gunther and Sullivan, *supra* note 5 at 1030.
19 See especially *N.A.A.C.P. v. Button,* 371 U.S. 415 at 432-33 (1963) *[Button]; Winters, supra* note 6 at 509-10 (1948); *Smith v. California,* 361 U.S. 147 at 150-51 (1959); *Smith v. Goguen, supra* note 6 at 573. Note that the Court has occasionally treated other civil liberties of the Bill of Rights as having a preferred status similar to speech in vagueness cases. See, for example, *Colautti, supra* note 6 (right to abortion); *Kolender, supra* note 6 (freedom of movement); *Coates, supra* note 6 (freedom of association).
20 Gunther and Sullivan, *supra* note 5 at 1326, and ff.; on the overbreadth doctrine, see generally "The First Amendment Overbreadth Doctrine" (1970) 83 Harv. L. Rev. 844; R.H. Fallon, "Making Sense of Overbreadth" (1991) 100 Yale L.J. 853.
21 Gunther and Sullivan, *supra* note 5 at 1337; Tribe, *supra* note 5 at 1033.
22 J.C. Jeffries Jr., "Legality, Vagueness, and the Construction of Penal Statutes" (1985) 71 Va. L. Rev. 189 at 217; R.D. Rotunda and J.E. Nowak, *Treatise on Constitutional Law,* 2d ed. (St. Paul, MN: West Publishing, 1992) at 37.
23 Tribe, *supra* note 5 at 1034; Rotunda and Nowak, *supra* note 22 at 36.
24 *Speiser v. Randall,* 357 U.S. 513 at 526 (1958).
25 On the question of "chilling effect" in Canada, see Chapter 4, notes 21-47 and accompanying text.
26 See Collings, *supra* note 5 at 218-20. However, traditional elements related to vagueness (legality and the rule of law) can still be concerns, although of lesser analytical importance, in cases involving overbreadth. See Amsterdam, "The Void-for-Vagueness Doctrine in the Supreme Court," *supra* note 12 at 76-77.
27 *United States v. Raines,* 362 U.S. 17 at 21 (1960) *[Raines].*
28 *Parker v. Levy,* 417 U.S. 733 at 756 (1974) *[Parker]; Hoffman Estates v. Flipside, Hoffman Estates, Inc.,* 455 U.S. 489 at 495 (1982) *[Hoffman Estates].*
29 *Gooding v. Wilson,* 405 U.S. 518 at 521 (1972).
30 See Tribe, *supra* note 5 at 1030-32.
31 *Ibid.* at 1035-37.
32 *Kolender, supra* note 6 at 358 (footnote 8).
33 See Amsterdam, "The Void-for-Vagueness Doctrine in the Supreme Court," *supra* note 12 at 96-102.
34 *Fox v. Washington,* 236 U.S. 273 (1915).
35 *Ibid.* at 277.
36 *Connally, supra* note 13.
37 Collings, *supra* note 5 at 201.
38 *Connally, supra* note 13 at 391.
39 Amsterdam, "The Void-for-Vagueness Doctrine in the Supreme Court," *supra* note 12 at 75.
40 I may occasionally refer to cases involving other constitutionally protected guarantees, such as freedom of speech, but mainly in situations where the vagueness argument failed. We know that cases of invalidation of vague laws involving speech are not reliable in the way they reflect the protection given to legality and the rule of law, but we can at least consider the cases in which the argument failed to show *a fortiori* how legality and the rule of law were of insufficient strength.

41 *Papachristou v. City of Jacksonville,* 405 U.S. 156 (1972) *[Papachristou].*
42 *Jacksonville Ordinance Code,* 1965, para. 26-57.
43 P.W. Low, J.C. Jeffries Jr., & R.J. Bonnie, *Criminal Law: Cases and Materials* (Mineola, NY: Foundation Press, 1982) at 147; A.G. Amsterdam, "Federal Constitutional Restrictions on the Punishment of Crimes of General Obnoxiousness, Crimes of Displeasing Police Officers, and the Like" (1967) 3 Crim. L. Bull. 205 at 209 ["Vagrancy Note"].
44 See *Winters, supra* note 6 at 540 (Frankfurter J., dissenting opinion).
45 Amsterdam, "Vagrancy Note," *supra* note 43 at 223.
46 *Lanzetta v. New Jersey,* 306 U.S. 451 (1939) *[Lanzetta].*
47 *Ibid.* at 456.
48 Collings, *supra* note 5 at 213.
49 The *Lanzetta* case is generally perceived as being of the same essence as cases dealing with traditional vagrancy and other "street-cleaning" statutes. See Collings, *supra* note 5 at 212-13; Amsterdam, "Vagrancy Note," *supra* note 43 at 219. See also *Winters, supra* note 6 at 540 (Frankfurter J., dissenting opinion).
50 *Roth v. United States,* 354 U.S. 476 (1957) *[Roth].*
51 *Ibid.* at 489.
52 *Ibid.* at 492.
53 *Memoirs v. Massachusetts,* 383 U.S. 413 (1966).
54 *Miller v. California,* 413 U.S. 15 (1973).
55 *Rose v. Locke,* 423 U.S. 48 (1975) *[Rose].*
56 *Ibid.* at 52, where the majority shows how other states' decisions and their apparent approval by the Tennessee court was sufficient to provide fair warning to the accused. See, however, the dissenting opinion by Justice Brennan, who argues (at 55-57) that state court cases were too unclear and inconsistent to provide fair warning as to the proscribed conduct.
57 *Roth, supra* note 50 at 491, quoting from *United States v. Petrillo,* 332 U.S. 1 at 7-8 (1947): "The Constitution does not require impossible standards."
58 See Amsterdam, "Vagrancy Note," *supra* note 43 at 219-20: "The *[Lanzetta]* case is broadly significant because it implicitly rejects the notion that 'crime-control' concerns, a legitimate legislative purpose to nip future criminality in the bud ... justif[ies] dragnet, open-ended penal liability ... In declining to accept this notion, *Lanzetta* at the least withdraws from those who would support the constitutionality of vagrancy legislation the argument of *necessity* recognized in some areas as justifying relatively indefinite criminal laws" [emphasis in original]. See also on this issue P.E. Johnson, *Criminal Law,* 2d ed. (St. Paul, MN: West Publishing, 1980) at 286-87.
59 See *Grayned v. City of Rockford,* 408 U.S. 104 at 108 (1972), and cases cited therein.
60 See *Connally, supra* note 13 at 391; *Cramp v. Board of Public Instruction of Orange County, Fla.,* 368 U.S. 278 at 283 (1961).
61 *Connally, supra* note 13 at 391.
62 Jeffries, *supra* note 22 at 211.
63 *Ibid.*
64 *Lambert v. California,* 355 U.S. 225 (1957) *[Lambert].*
65 *Ibid.* at 220-30 [references omitted].
66 See *supra* note 42 and accompanying text.
67 *Papachristou, supra* note 41.
68 *Ibid.* at 163-64.
69 *Lanzetta, supra* note 46.
70 *Ibid.* at 458.
71 *Roth, supra* note 50.
72 *Rose, supra* note 55.
73 See *Grayned v. City of Rockford, supra* note 59 at 108-09, and cases cited.
74 See *Papachristou, supra* note 41 at 171; Jeffries, *supra* note 22 at 212.
75 See Johnson, *supra* note 58 at 280-81; H.L. Packer, *The Limits of the Criminal Sanction* (Stanford, CA: Stanford University Press, 1968) at 79-80; Jeffries, *supra* note 22 at 214-15.
76 Jeffries, *supra* note 22 at 213.

77 See *supra* notes 41-49 and accompanying text.

78 *Papachristou, supra* note 41.

79 *Lanzetta, supra* note 46 at 357.

80 See Collings, *supra* note 5 at 213.

81 See Amsterdam, "Vagrancy Note," *supra* note 43 at 218, 223, 232.

82 *Ibid.* at 230.

83 Although "the arresting officers denied that the racial mixture in the car played any part in the decision to make the arrest" (*Papachristou, supra* note 41 at 159).

84 *Roth, supra* note 50.

85 *Rose, supra* note 55.

86 *Giacco v. State of Pennsylvania*, 382 U.S. 399 (1966) *[Giacco]*.

87 *Ibid.* at 404.

88 *Ibid.* at 403.

89 *Jordan v. De George*, 341 U.S. 223 (1951) *[Jordan]*.

90 *Ibid.* at 227.

91 *Ibid.* at 231-32.

92 *Ibid.* at 239-40.

93 Other decisions of the Supreme Court of Canada had addressed the question of vagueness prior to *Nova Scotia Pharmaceutical* (*supra* note 1). However, these cases did not purport to explain to a significant extent the meaning of the two rationales, nor did they indicate a threshold of constitutional validity. See, *e.g., R. v. Morgentaler*, [1988] 1 S.C.R. 30 at 64-70 (Dickson C.J.); *Irwin Toy Ltd. v. Quebec (A.G.)*, [1989] 1 S.C.R. 927 at 980-83 *[Irwin Toy]*; *Reference re ss. 193 and 195.1(1)(c) of the Criminal Code (Man.)*, [1990] 1 S.C.R. 1123 at 1150-61 (Lamer J., concurring) *[Prostitution Reference]*.

94 See *supra* notes 59-61 and accompanying text.

95 *Nova Scotia Pharmaceutical, supra* note 1 at 633.

96 *Ibid.*

97 *Ibid.* at 633-34.

98 *Ibid.* at 634-35, Gonthier J. writes: "I do not mean to suggest that the State can only intervene through law when some non-legal basis for intervention exists. Many enactments are relatively narrow in scope and echo little of society at large; this is the case with many regulatory enactments. The weakness or the absence of substantive notice before the enactment can be compensated by bringing to the attention of the public the actual terms of the law, so that substantive notice is achieved."

99 *Ibid.* at 635. For another example of how publicity and advertisement can compensate for a lack of "substratum of values," see *R. v. Yorke* (1998), 122 C.C.C. (3d) 298 at 316-18 (N.S.C.A.).

100 See *supra* notes 62-72 and accompanying text.

101 *Jeffries, supra* note 22.

102 *Lambert, supra* note 64.

103 *Jeffries, supra* note 22 at 211-12, 231.

104 *Lambert, supra* note 64 at 229, citing O.W. Holmes, *The Common Law,* 42d printing (Boston: Little, Brown and Company, 1948) at 50.

105 *Nova Scotia Pharmaceutical, supra* note 1 at 635 [emphasis added].

106 *Ibid.* at 634, citing *Jeffries, supra* note 22 at 211.

107 See ss. 253 to 260 of the *Criminal Code*, R.S.C., 1985, c. C-46.

108 *Nova Scotia Pharmaceutical, supra* note 1 at 639.

109 *Ibid.*

110 See, in the same sense, L. Huppé, "La fonction des lois et la théorie de l'imprécision" (1992) 52 R. du B. 831 at 833-36.

111 R.S.O. 1980, c. 141, s. 13(1)(a).

112 *Ontario v. Canadian Pacific Ltd.*, [1995] 2 S.C.R. 1031 at 1076 *[Canadian Pacific]*.

113 *Ibid.* at 1078.

114 Similarly, see *R. v. Finta*, [1994] 1 S.C.R. 701 at 869 *[Finta]* (by Cory J.): "War crimes or crimes against humanity are so repulsive, so reprehensible, and so well understood that it simply cannot be argued that the definition of crimes against humanity and war crimes

are vague or uncertain ... The standards which guide the determination and definition of crimes against humanity are the values that are known to all people and shared by all."

115 *Canadian Pacific, supra* note 112 at 1078.

116 For another example of a criminal provision that, although not vague, seems remote from the values of society (and might therefore be constitutionally vulnerable), see s. 143(a) of the *Criminal Code*. This provision states that "every one who ... publicly advertises a reward for the return of anything that has been stolen or lost, and in the advertisement uses words to indicate that no questions will be asked if it is returned ... is guilty of an offence punishable on summary conviction."

117 *Finta, supra* note 114.

118 *Dobbert v. Florida*, 432 U.S. 282 (1977) *[Dobbert]*.

119 *C.R. v. United Kingdom*, 22 November 1995, European Court of Human Rights, No. 48/1994/495/577 *[Marital Rape Case]*.

120 See Chapter 1, notes 126-42 and accompanying text.

121 H. Kelsen, "Will the Judgement in the Nuremberg Tribunal Constitute a Precedent in International Law?" (1947), 1 Int'l L. Q. 153 at 165, cited in *Finta, supra* note 114 at 874.

122 See, in Chapter 1, text accompanying notes 141-42.

123 *Morales, supra* note 2.

124 In the Supreme Court of Canada, for instance, the presence of broad discretion was held valid on some occasions in the context of the administration of criminal justice; see *R. v. Lyons*, [1987] 2 S.C.R. 309 at 348; *R. v. Beare*, [1988] 2 S.C.R. 386 at 410-11 *[Beare]*.

125 *Nova Scotia Pharmaceutical, supra* note 1 at 636.

126 Huppé, *supra* note 110 at 836. In that respect, see also the cases of *Liyanage v. The Queen*, [1967] 1 A.C. 259 (Privy Council); and *Gagnon and Vallières v. The Queen*, [1971] C.A. 454 (Qc. C.A.). These cases provide examples of laws that were challenged on the basis that they would arguably lead to automatic convictions, thus offending the separation of powers between the legislative assembly and the judiciary.

127 See *supra* notes 41-49; 73-92 and accompanying text.

128 *Papachristou, supra* note 41.

129 *Lanzetta, supra* note 46.

130 *Nova Scotia Pharmaceutical, supra* note 1 at 630.

131 *Morales, supra* note 2.

132 The same provision was re-enacted by Parliament and was again found partly defective on grounds of vagueness in the case of *R. v. Hall*, 2002 S.C.C. 64, file no. 28223 *[Hall]*. See discussion *infra* notes 196-97 and accompanying text. In other cases, vagueness has contributed to the invalidation of statutory provisions by the Supreme Court of Canada, but was not the only cause. See *Morgentaler, supra* note 93 at 68-69 (per Dickson C.J. and Lamer J.), where vagueness as a "principle of fundamental justice" under s. 7 contributed, *inter alia*, to the invalidity of s. 251 of the *Criminal Code* (which prohibited abortions unless "the continuation of the pregnancy of the female person ... would be likely to endanger her ... health"). See also *R. v. Zundel*, [1992] 2 S.C.R. 731 at 769-70 *[Zundel]*, where s. 181 of the *Criminal Code*, prohibiting the publication of false news likely to "cause injury or mischief to a public interest," was held contrary to s. 2(b) of the *Charter* and could not be saved under s. 1 because of its vagueness and overbreadth. In addition, see *Committee for the Commonwealth of Canada v. Canada*, [1991] 1 S.C.R. 139 at 213-14 *[Commonwealth of Canada]* (concurring opinion per L'Heureux-Dubé J; see also Cory J., concurring, at 227), holding a restriction on s. 2(b) not to be "prescribed by law" within the meaning of s. 1 because of its vagueness. (The regulation under scrutiny prohibited the "conduct [of] any business or undertaking, commercial or otherwise, at an airport").

133 Lamer C.J. wrote the majority opinion with the concurrence of La Forest, Sopinka, McLachlin, and Iacobucci JJ., holding that the public interest criterion in s. 515(10)(b) did not meet the legal debate test set out in *Nova Scotia Pharmaceutical*. Gonthier J. dissented (with the concurrence of L'Heureux-Dubé J.), holding that the standard in s. 515(10)(b) was sufficiently precise, mainly on the basis that "public interest" was informed by the notion of "just cause" in s. 11(e) of the *Charter*.

134 *Giacco, supra* note 86. See discussion in text accompanying notes 86-89.

135 *Zundel, supra* note 132 at 805-6 (dissenting opinion).
136 *R. v. Farinacci* (1993), 86 C.C.C. (3d) 32 (Ont. C.A.) *[Farinacci]*.
137 *Ibid*. at 46.
138 *Ibid*. at 47-48.
139 *Protection de la Jeunesse – 618*, [1993] R.J.Q. 1603 (C.Q.).
140 *Ibid*. at 1610.
141 In that regard, compare the decision of the Court in *R. v. Butler, infra* note 145, with the minority decision by Iacobucci J. in *Little Sisters Book and Art Emporium v. Canada (Minister of Justice)*, [2000] 2 S.C.R. 1120.
142 This reaches again the importance of the interpretative context of the provision at stake. See *Canadian Pacific, supra* note 112 at 1081; *R. v. Keegstra*, [1990] 3 S.C.R. 697 at 779 *[Keegstra]; Nova Scotia Pharmaceutical, supra* note 1 at 651.
143 *Canadian Pacific, supra* note 112 at 1081.
144 *Ibid*. at 1085-86; *Suresh v. Canada (Minister of Citizenship and Immigration)*, [2002] 1 S.C.R. 3 at 55 *[Suresh]*.
145 *Ibid*. at 1083; *R. v. Butler*, [1992] 1 S.C.R. 419 at 491 *[Butler]; Prostitution Reference, supra* note 93 at 1141 (Dickson C.J.) and 1157 (Lamer J.); *Nova Scotia Pharmaceutical, supra* note 1 at 651.
146 *Butler, supra* note 145.
147 See authorities referred to in Chapter 1, note 148.
148 See *infra* notes 181-94 and accompanying text.
149 *Nova Scotia Pharmaceutical, supra* note 1 at 632.
150 *Ibid*. at 639-40.
151 P.W. Hogg, *Constitutional Law of Canada*, 4th ed. (Scarborough, ON: Carswell, 1996) at 867. Other authors have expressed skepticism towards the Court's deferential approach. See, *e.g.*, D. Stuart, *Canadian Criminal Law: A Treatise*, 3d ed. (Scarborough, ON: Carswell, 1995) at 26; A. Jodouin, "La Charte canadienne et la nouvelle légalité" in G.A. Beaudoin and E. Mendes, eds., *The Canadian Charter of Rights and Freedoms*, 3d ed. (Scarborough, ON: Carswell, 1996) ch. 13; Huppé, *supra* note 110. In contrast, it is interesting to note the absence of any substantial doctrinal analysis published thus far supporting the Court's approach.
152 *Nova Scotia Pharmaceutical, supra* note 1 at 640.
153 *Ibid*. at 638: "An unintelligible provision gives insufficient guidance for legal debate and is therefore unconstitutionally vague"; at 642: "Once more, an unpermissibly vague law will not provide a sufficient basis for legal debate"; at 643: "The doctrine of vagueness can therefore be summed up in this proposition: a law will be found unconstitutionally vague if it so lacks in precision as not to give sufficient guidance for legal debate."
154 See, *e.g., Canadian Pacific, supra* note 112 at 1042, 1044 (Lamer C.J.), 1069-70 (Gonthier J.); *Zundel, supra* note 132 at 804 (per Cory and Iacobucci JJ., dissenting); *Morales, supra* note 2 at 727; *Ruffo v. Conseil de la Magistrature*, [1995] 4 S.C.R. 267 at 330 *[Ruffo]; P.(D.) v. S.(C.)*, [1993] 4 S.C.R. 141 at 181; *Young v. Young*, [1993] 4 S.C.R. 3 at 73-74 *[Young]; Suresh, supra* note 144 at 47; *Hall, supra* note 132, para. 34.
155 *Canadian Pacific, supra* note 112.
156 *Ibid*. at 1047.
157 *Ibid*. at 1090-91.
158 *Luscher v. Deputy Minister, Revenue Canada, Customs and Excise*, [1985] 1 C.F. 85 at 94 *[Luscher]*.
159 See *supra* notes 94-122 and accompanying text.
160 See also *supra* notes 125-34 and accompanying text.
161 The issue of reasonable necessity was discussed in relation to the rule of law in Chapter 2 (see notes 111-23 and accompanying text). More will be said on it below (see *infra* notes 176-80 and accompanying text).
162 On the impact of this issue (type of law involved), see Chapter 1, notes 101-11; Chapter 2, notes 124-33 and accompanying text. See also *infra* notes 167-75 and accompanying text.
163 For example, the issues of chilling effect and overbreadth on fundamental freedoms can have an impact on the constitutional assessment of vague legislation, depending on the

constitutional basis invoked to support the vagueness challenge. These issues will be discussed in Chapter 4 (see notes 15-47; 135-48 and accompanying text).

164 On the first factor, see *supra* notes 94-122 and accompanying text. On the second factor, see *supra* notes 125-34 and accompanying text.

165 The question of necessity was used to support a deferential attitude in the following cases: *Canadian Pacific, supra* note 112 at 1070; *Butler, supra* note 145 at 506; *Young, supra* note 154 at 76; *Ruffo, supra* note 154 at 332; *P.(D.) v. S.(C.), supra* note 154 at 179; *Suresh, supra* note 144 at 55. The relevance of the type of law involved was invoked to lower the threshold of constitutional validity in the following cases: *Canadian Pacific, supra* note 112 at 1069-76; and *Young, supra* note 154 at 76. We can also note the use of the "substratum of values" issue to relax the requirement of precision in a number of cases: *Nova Scotia Pharmaceutical, supra* note 1 at 649; *Canadian Pacific, supra* note 112 at 1075-77; *Ruffo, supra* note 154 at 331; *Young, supra* note 154 at 75; *Finta, supra* note 114 at 868-69; *P.(D.) v. S.(C.), supra* note 154 at 180.

166 See cases referred to in the previous note.

167 The provision challenged for vagueness was s. 13(1)(a) of the Ontario *Environmental Protection Act,* R.S.O. 1980, c. 141, which contains a general interdiction of the pollution "of the natural environment for any use that can be made of it."

168 *Canadian Pacific, supra* note 112 at 1072.

169 *Ibid.* at 1075.

170 *Ibid.* at 1071-72, 1077-78.

171 Although the result in that case was in my view appropriate because the subject matter involved was so indefinite that it could hardly lend itself to more precise legislative drafting, it would nevertheless have been useful in order to provide guidance for further cases to acknowledge the need for careful drafting when penal laws are involved.

172 *Nova Scotia Pharmaceutical, supra* note 1 at 642-43.

173 See, *e.g., Ontario Public School Boards' Assn. v. Ontario (A.G.)* (1997), 151 D.L.R. (4th) 346 at 359 (Ont. G.D.) *[Ontario School Boards]* (see discussion of the case in Chapter 2, in text accompanying notes 128-33).

174 *Prostitution Reference, supra* note 93 at 1152 (concurring opinion) [emphasis added].

175 In the context of the principle of legality, see Chapter 1, notes 105-11 and accompanying text. In the context of the rule of law, see Chapter 2, notes 124-33 and accompanying text.

176 See cases referred to *supra* note 165.

177 *Butler, supra* note 145 at 506

178 This phenomenon has also been noticed in the American context by Professor Laurence Tribe: "In practice, the Court rarely rests a finding of overbreadth or vagueness upon its discovery of a genuinely 'less restrictive alternative,' although an affirmation showing that any alternative to the statute would be seriously ineffectual might negate the overbreadth of vagueness conclusion." L.H. Tribe, *American Constitutional Law,* 2d ed. (Mineola, NY: Foundation Press, 1988) at 1037.

179 *Nova Scotia Pharmaceutical, supra* note 1 at 639.

180 *Canadian Pacific, supra* note 112 at 1070.

181 *Ibid.* at 1074.

182 Jeffries, *supra* note 22 at 208. The preferability of legislative as opposed to judicial specification of the law is acknowledged by the Supreme Court of Canada in *Hall, supra* note 132, para. 37.

183 R.S.C. 1970, c. C-23.

184 K.C. Davis, *Discretionary Justice: A Preliminary Inquiry* (Chicago: University of Illinois Press, 1971) at 47.

185 *Nova Scotia Pharmaceutical, supra* note 1 at 647.

186 A series of factors, some of which are derived from prior interpretations by lower courts, are presented by Gonthier J. to circumscribe the meaning of the provision. These factors are divided into two categories: (1) the structure of the market, and (2) the behaviour of the parties to the agreement. See *Nova Scotia Pharmaceutical, supra* note 1 at 651-57.

187 The notice is still not optimal because it is contained in case law rather than legislation.

As noted earlier, it would be preferable that the standard be directly expressed in the legislation because it would make it more easily accessible to individuals. Of course, the gravity of this reality is attenuated considering that the judicial specification of the law is contained in a single decision of the Supreme Court of Canada. Problems of accessibility are thus less important than if the standards were dispersed in several lower courts' decisions, in addition to the fact that their analysis is simplified. Also, Supreme Court of Canada decisions receive greater media and academic attention, which improves the notice associated with them.

188   *Zundel, supra* note 132 at 807.

189   *Ibid.* at 771.

190   *Prostitution Reference, supra* note 93 at 1156.

191   *Ibid.*

192   In Canada, see, *e.g.,* P.A. Côté, *The Interpretation of Legislation in Canada,* 3d ed. (Toronto: Carswell, 2000); R. Sullivan, *Driedger on the Construction of Statutes,* 3d ed. (Toronto: Butterworths, 1994).

193   As Beetz J. observed in the first case before the Supreme Court of Canada dealing with vagueness as a constitutional vice, "flexibility and vagueness are not synonymous" (*Morgentaler, supra* note 93 at 107). See also *Suresh, supra* note 144 at 55. It has even been held that the presence of discretion in certain legislative schemes can actually be *required* to ensure compliance with the *Charter.* Thus, in *Baron v. Canada,* [1993] 1 S.C.R. 416, a provision of the *Income Tax Act* was held to be invalid when compared to s. 8 of the *Charter* because it had taken away the discretionary power of courts to refuse to grant search warrants.

194   *Nova Scotia Pharmaceutical, supra* note 1 at 641.

195   On the operation of this principle, see Côté, *supra* note 192 at 315-21; *Driedger on the Construction of Statutes, supra* note 192 at 203-13.

196   *Morales, supra* note 2.

197   *Hall, supra* note 144, para. 22ff. For another illustration of how this technique can be useful in solving problems of vagueness, see text accompanying and following note 215 below.

198   Davis, *supra* note 184.

199   *Ibid.* at 55ff.

200   *Ibid.* at 56.

201   See M.R. MacGuigan, *Third Report of the Special Committee on Statutory Instruments* (Ottawa: Queen's Printer for Canada, 1969).

202   *Ibid.* at 4.

203   See *Nova Scotia Pharmaceutical, supra* note 1 at 642: "A very detailed enactment would not provide the required flexibility, *and it might furthermore obscure its purposes behind a veil of detailed provisions*" [emphasis added]. See also *Canadian Pacific, supra* note 112 at 1073-74. For a doctrinal account of this question, see L.P. Pigeon, *Drafting and Interpreting Legislation* (Toronto: Carswell, 1988) at 3-11.

204   Davis, *supra* note 184 at 65 [references omitted]. For a more detailed account of the operation of § 553 of the *Administrative Procedure Act* (5 U.S.C.), see K.C. Davis, *Administrative Law Treatise,* 2d ed. (San Diego: University of San Diego, 1978) at 447ff.

205   The province of Quebec is an exception, as the *Regulations Act,* S.Q. 1986, c. 22, requires any proposed regulation to be published in the *Gazette officielle du Québec* (s. 8) and to be accompanied by a notice inviting the public to submit comments (s. 10). For a discussion of the operation of the Quebec scheme, see J.M. Evans, H.N. Janish, & D.J. Mullan, *Administrative Law,* 4th ed. (Toronto: Emond Montgomery Publications, 1995) at 365-66.

206   For a recent account of this evolution, see Evans, Janish, & Mullan, *supra* note 205 at 359ff. For a jurisdiction-by-jurisdiction description of public consultation practices or requirements for the adoption of regulations, see *How Regulators Regulate: A Guide to Regulatory Process in Canada* (Ottawa: Treasury Board Secretariat, 1992).

207   The first case, decided by Lysyk J., is *Canadian Bar Assn. No. 1, supra* note 3. The second case, decided by Humphries J., is *Canadian Bar Assn. No. 2, supra* note 4.

208   *Social Service Tax Amendment Act, 1992,* S.B.C. 1992, c. 22.

209   *Ibid.,* s. 2.01(1).

210   *Ibid.,* s. 2.01(2) [emphasis added].

211 *Canadian Bar Assn. No. 1, supra* note 3 at 441.
212 *Canadian Pacific, supra* note 112 at 1047. See discussion in text accompanying notes 155-58.
213 *Social Service Tax Amendment Act, 1993,* S.B.C. 1993, c. 24.
214 *Ibid.,* s. 2.012(3) [emphasis added].
215 *Canadian Bar Assn. No. 2, supra* note 4 at 225.

Chapter 4: The Place of the Vagueness Doctrine in the Charter

1 Since the case of *R. v. Morgentaler,* [1988] 1 S.C.R. 30 *[Morgentaler],* and especially since the *Reference re ss. 193 and 195.1(1)(c) of the Criminal Code (Man.),* [1990] 1 S.C.R. 1123 *[Prostitution Reference],* vagueness is recognized as a constitutional vice under the *Charter.*
2 *R. v. Nova Scotia Pharmaceutical Society,* [1992] 2 S.C.R. 606 at 631: "Vagueness may be raised under the substantive sections of the *Charter* whenever these sections comprise some *internal limitation*" [emphasis added].
3 See *Operation Dismantle v. The Queen,* [1985] 1 S.C.R. 441; *R. v. Therens,* [1985] 1 S.C.R. 613; *Reference Re Manitoba Language Rights,* [1985] 1 S.C.R. 721 *[Manitoba Language Reference].*
4 *Irwin Toy Ltd. v. Quebec (A.G.),* [1989] 1 S.C.R. 927 at 983 *[Irwin Toy].*
5 *European Convention for the Protection of Human Rights and Fundamental Freedoms,* 4 November 1950, 213 U.N.T.S. 222 *[European Convention].*
6 *Sunday Times,* 26 April 1979, European Court of Human Rights, Series A, No. 30.
7 *Malone,* 2 August 1984, European Court of Human Rights, Series A, No. 82.
8 *Irwin Toy, supra* note 4.
9 *Ibid.* at 983 [emphasis added].
10 *Ontario Film and Video Appreciation Society v. Ontario Board of Censors* (1984), 5 D.L.R. (4th) 766 (Ont. C.A.) *[Board of Censors].*
11 *Committee for the Commonwealth of Canada v. Canada,* [1991] 1 S.C.R. 139 at 215 *[Commonwealth of Canada]* (concurring opinion). It may be noted, however, that L'Heureux-Dubé J. did not stop the analysis at this stage; she went on to apply the *Oakes* test subsidiarily to conclude that it was not satisfied.
12 Section 7(b) of the *Government Airport Concession Regulations,* S.O.R./1979-373, was to the effect that "except as authorized in writing by the minister, no person shall ... advertise or solicit at an airport on his own behalf or on behalf of any person."
13 Other cases where the "prescribed by law" requirement was not satisfied include the following: *International Fund for Animal Welfare Inc. v. Canada (Minister of Fisheries and Oceans)* (1983), 83 N.R. 303 (F.C.A.); *Reference re Minority Language Educational Rights* (1988), 49 D.L.R. (4th) 499 (P.E.I.S.C. App. Div.); *Henry v. Canada* (1987), 10 F.T.R. 176 (Fed. T.D.).
14 For example, if a statute states that "the film commission will not grant licences to movies that *shock public morals*," it can be considered vague because the meaning of the expression "shock public morals" is highly uncertain. We therefore cannot determine what the legislature meant by this phrase. In contrast, if another statute states that "the film commission will have *complete discretion* to deny licences," it is not, strictly speaking, vague because its meaning is clear: the commission is given "complete discretion." There is no controversy as to the meaning of the statute. However, it is obvious how both statutes involve the same types of problems related to the rule of law, and are therefore sometimes analyzed together under the vagueness doctrine.
15 *R. v. Oakes,* [1986] 1 S.C.R. 103 *[Oakes].*
16 *Ibid.* at 246.
17 *Nova Scotia Pharmaceutical, supra* note 2 at 629.
18 *R. v. Heywood,* [1994] 3 S.C.R. 761 at 792 *[Heywood].*
19 *Nova Scotia Pharmaceutical, supra* note 2 at 627. See also *Commonwealth of Canada, supra* note 11 at 208 (per L'Heureux-Dubé J., concurring); and *Osborne v. Canada (Treasury Board),* [1991] 2 S.C.R. 69 at 95 *[Osborne].*
20 In an attempt to emphasize this distinction, Gonthier J. stated in the *Nova Scotia Pharmaceutical* case that under the "minimal impairment" branch, problems of legislative precision shall not be qualified as "vagueness" but rather "overbreadth" (*Nova Scotia Pharmaceutical, supra* note 2 at 630-31). Therefore, as already mentioned in the Introduction

of this book, the vagueness doctrine *per se* is concerned only with the rationales of fair notice and law enforcement discretion, but not with overbreadth. I have attempted to respect this distinction as much as possible when I explored the content of the vagueness doctrine in the first three chapters. However, I will in the context of this chapter address vagueness and overbreadth together when applicable in order to assess the impact of their interaction in the context of the different provisions of the *Charter*.

21 *Commonwealth of Canada, supra* note 11 at 214 (concurring opinion).

22 See J. Ross, "Applying the Charter to Discretionary Authority" (1991) 29 Alta. L. Rev. 382 at 411-13.

23 In the Supreme Court of Canada, see *R. v. Keegstra*, [1990] 3 S.C.R. 697 at 859-61 *[Keegstra]*, per McLachlin J., dissenting (*Criminal Code* prohibiting willful promotion of hatred against identifiable groups); *Canada (Human Rights Commission) v. Taylor*, [1990] 3 S.C.R. 892 at 959-60, per McLachlin J., dissenting (*Federal Human Rights Act* prohibiting telephone messages likely to expose a person or a group to hatred or contempt) [hereinafter *Taylor*]; *Commonwealth of Canada, supra* note 11 at 213-15, per L'Heureux-Dubé J., concurring (prohibition of expressive activities in airports); *Rocket v. Royal College of Dental Surgeons of Ontario*, [1990] 2 S.C.R. 232 at 251-52 (profession restricting member's advertising) *[Rocket]; R. v. Zundel* (1987), 58 O.R. (2d) 129 (Ont. C.A.) at 772 *[Zundel]* (*Criminal Code* prohibiting willful publication of false news likely to cause injury or mischief to a public interest).

24 See *Baggett v. Bullitt*, 377 U.S. 360 at 372 (1964) *[Baggett]* (loyalty oath for teachers which required them "by precept and example [to] promote respect for the flag"); *Grayned v. City of Rockford*, 408 U.S. 104 at 108-9 (1972) (statute prohibiting noises which tend to "disturb the peace" near schools); *N.A.A.C.P. v. Button*, 371 U.S. 415 at 433 (1963) *[Button]* (statutory ban against "the improper solicitation of any legal or professional business").

25 See *Schachter v. Canada*, [1992] 2 S.C.R. 679 at 700.

26 L.H. Tribe, *American Constitutional Law*, 2d ed. (Mineola, NY: Foundation Press, 1988) at 1031.

27 *Osborne, supra* note 19.

28 R.S.C., 1985, c. P-33.

29 *P.S.C. v. Osborne*, [1986] 3 C.F. 206.

30 See *United States v. Raines*, 362 U.S. 17 at 21 (1960) *[Raines]*. For illustrations of this rule in the context of the vagueness doctrine, see G. Parker, "The Origins of the Canadian Criminal Code" in D. Flaherty, ed., *Essays in the History of Canadian Law* (Toronto: University of Toronto Press, 1981) at 756; *Hoffman Estates v. Flipside, Hoffman Estates, Inc.*, 455 U.S. 489 at 495 (1982) *[Hoffman Estates]*.

31 See *Gooding v. Wilson*, 405 U.S. 518 at 521 (1972); Tribe, *supra* note 26 at 1030-32.

32 C. Rogerson, "The Judicial Search for Appropriate Remedies under the *Charter*: The Examples of Overbreadth and Vagueness" in R.J. Sharpe, dir., *Charter Litigation* (Toronto: Butterworths, 1987) 233 at 262-63.

33 *Rocket, supra* note 23.

34 *Ibid.* at 252.

35 *Ibid.* at 252-53.

36 See *Hoffman Estates, supra* note 30 at 498. See also discussion in *Kolender v. Lawson*, 461 U.S. 360 at 358, footnote 8 (1983) *[Kolender]*.

37 *Rocket, supra* note 23 at 251-52.

38 *Ruffo v. Conseil de la Magistrature*, [1995] 4 S.C.R. 267 at 330 *[Ruffo]*.

39 *Judicial Code of Ethics*, O.C. 643-82, 1982, G.O.Q. 1982.II.1253 *[Code]*.

40 Y. Ouellette, "L'imprécision des codes de déontologie professionnelle" (1977) 37 R. du B. 669 at 671, as quoted and translated in *Ruffo, supra* note 38 at 333-34.

41 See *Ruffo, supra* note 38 at 355: "The duty to act in a reserved manner is not found to be *unconstitutional* for vagueness" [emphasis added].

42 *Ibid.* at 334.

43 See *Ville de Montréal v. Arcade Amusements Ltd.*, [1985] 1 S.C.R. 368 at 401; *913719 Ontario Ltd. v. Mississauga (City)* (1998), 40 O.R. (3d) 413 at 415 (Ont. C.A.), leave to appeal to Supreme Court of Canada denied: S.C.C. Bulletin, 1999, at 257; *Martin c. Granby (Ville)*

(1999), R.J.Q. 674 at 678-79 (Qc. C.A.). Although the constitutional vagueness doctrine has sometimes been applied to delegated legislation interchangeably with the administrative law doctrine – see, *e.g., Brown v. Alberta Dental Assn.*, [2002] 5 W.W.R. 221 at 231-32 (Alta C.A.); *2550-9613 Quebec Inc. c. Val d'Or*, [1997] R.J.Q. 2090 at 2098-99 (Qc. C.A.) – one must be careful not to confuse the two notions, as they may not always both be applicable in the same manner to every situation. On the distinction between administrative and constitutional vagueness doctrines, see generally G. Pepin, "La nullité des lois et règlements pour cause d'imprécision: une norme unique ou deux normes distinctes de contrôle?" (1996) 56 R. du B. 643; P. Garant, "L'imprécision en droit administratif et en droit constitutionnel: un défi à l'intelligence moyenne" (1994) 4 National Journal of Constitutional Law 75.

44 *Ruffo, supra* note 38 at 329, 335.

45 The Supreme Court of Canada has taken a very broad approach towards s. 2(b) of the *Charter*. Any activity designed to convey a message is *prima facie* protected under s. 2(b), and is to be subjected to s. 1 scrutiny. See P.W. Hogg, *Constitutional Law of Canada*, 4th ed. (Scarborough, ON: Carswell, 1996) at 785-86. Only expression that takes the form of violence is not protected by s. 2(b): *Zundel, supra* note 23 at 1185; *Irwin Toy, supra* note 4 at 970; *Keegstra, supra* note 23 at 731.

46 Vagueness does not, to this day, have an autonomous status in Canadian constitutional law. This means that it must always be invoked in conjunction with another *Charter* interest in order to become relevant (see *infra* notes 90-114 and accompanying text). It is possible that the vagueness doctrine may be given a broader scope in the future, which might even go as far as rendering it autonomous (see *infra* notes 115-34 and accompanying text), but without an explicit statement to this effect by the Court, we must consider that the doctrine was analyzed in the context of s. 1 in the *Ruffo* case. (Since no violation of a substantive *Charter* guarantee had actually been proven, the vagueness analysis in *Ruffo* may be seen as a *dictum*.)

47 *Ruffo, supra* note 38 at 332-33.

48 *Osborne, supra* note 19 at 95; *Nova Scotia Pharmaceutical, supra* note 2 at 627.

49 *Ibid.*, Osborne at 95.

50 *Slaight Communications v. Davidson*, [1989] 1 S.C.R. 1038 *[Slaight]*.

51 R.S.C. 1970, c. L.1.

52 By "formal sense," I refer to the very *existence* of a law under s. 1, and not to the question of whether a law is sufficiently precise.

53 *Irwin Toy, supra* note 4 at 983.

54 See *Board of Censors, supra* note 10.

55 See *Commonwealth of Canada, supra* note 11.

56 *Nova Scotia Pharmaceutical, supra* note 2 at 631.

57 *Prostitution Reference, supra* note 1 at 1155.

58 *R. v. Morales*, [1992] 3 S.C.R. 711 *[Morales]*.

59 Note that s. 7 would in any event have been applicable in *Morales* under the banner of "liberty," but Lamer C.J. chose to analyze the question in the framework of s. 11(e), which offered a more specific protection in the circumstances (at 725-26).

60 In the Supreme Court of Canada, see *Morgentaler, supra* note 1 (*Criminal Code* prohibiting abortions except if the health of the mother is in danger); *Prostitution Reference, supra* note 1 (*Criminal Code* prohibiting communications in public for the purpose of prostitution and the keeping of common bawdy-houses); *Nova Scotia Pharmaceutical, supra* note 2 (offence of conspiracy to prevent or lessen competition unduly); *United Nurses of Alberta v. Alberta (Attorney General)*, [1992] 1 S.C.R. 901 *[United Nurses]* (common law offence of criminal contempt); *R. v. Finta*, [1994] 1 S.C.R. 701 *[Finta]* (*Criminal Code* punishment of war crimes and crimes against humanity); *Ontario v. Canadian Pacific Ltd.*, [1995] 2 S.C.R. 1031 *[Canadian Pacific]* (act prohibiting the pollution "of the natural environment for any use that can be made of it").

61 *Heywood, supra* note 18 at 792-93 (invalidating as overbroad under s. 7 a provision of the *Criminal Code* prohibiting convicted sexual offenders from loitering in schoolyards, playgrounds, and public parks); see also *Nova Scotia Pharmaceutical, supra* note 2 at 629.

However, note reservations as to the appropriateness of the overbreadth doctrine under s. 7 in *Canadian Pacific, supra* note 60 at 1093.

62 *Heywood, supra* note 18 at 793-94.

63 *Taylor, supra* note 23.

64 S.C. 1976-77, c. 33.

65 It may be noted that in *Taylor,* a majority of the Court saw s. 13(1) as sufficiently precise to meet the test under s. 1 (at 929). Let us, however, ignore this reality for the purposes of the analysis to ascertain whether it would have been possible to raise the vagueness argument in the framework of s. 7.

66 *Re B.C. Motor Vehicle Act,* [1985] 2 S.C.R. 486 at 502-3 *[Motor Vehicle Reference].*

67 *Ibid.* at 515.

68 See *supra* notes 61-62 and accompanying text.

69 See, *e.g., Prostitution Reference, supra* note 1 at 1155: "Clearly, it seems to me that if a person is placed at risk of being deprived of his liberty when he has not been given fair notice that his conduct falls within the scope of the offence as defined by Parliament, then surely this would offend the principles of fundamental justice" (per Lamer J.).

70 *Morgentaler, supra* note 1.

71 On the possibilities of invoking the benefit of other people's constitutional rights, see *R. v. Big M. Drug Mart Ltd.,* [1985] 1 S.C.R. 295 *[Big M. Drug Mart]; R. v. Wholesale Travel Group Inc.,* [1991] 3 S.C.R. 154.

72 *R. v. Morgentaler* (1985), 52 O.R. (2d) 353 at 387-88 (Ont. C.A.), cited and approved by McIntyre J. (dissenting) in *Morgentaler, supra* note 1 at 153-54 (I have reduced the length of the citation, not McIntyre J.).

73 It is even probable that according to the current standards of legislative precision as stated in *Nova Scotia Pharmaceutical,* the "danger for health" criterion would not even be considered imprecise in the strict sense (rule of law), contrary to what Dickson C.J. seemed to suggest in *Morgentaler (supra* note 1 at 68-69) when he took into consideration the lack of statutory definiteness, *inter alia,* to conclude that the "principles of fundamental justice" had been breached.

74 *Taylor, supra* note 23 at 929.

75 *Nova Scotia Pharmaceutical, supra* note 2 at 631.

76 Section 6 provides the following:

> (1) Every citizen of Canada has the right to enter, remain in, and leave Canada.
> (2) Every citizen of Canada and every person who has the status of a permanent resident of Canada has the right
>   (a) to move to and take up residence in any province; and
>   (b) to pursue the gaining of a livelihood in any province.
> (3) The rights specified in subsection (2) are subject to
>   (a) any laws or practices of general application in force in a province other than those that discriminate among persons primarily on the basis of province of present or previous residence; and
>   (b) any laws providing for reasonable residency requirements as a qualification for the receipt of publicly provided social services.
> (4) Subsections (2) and (3), do not preclude any law, program or activity that has as its object the amelioration in a province of conditions of individuals in that province who are socially or economically disadvantaged if the rate of employment in that province is below the rate of employment in Canada.

77 F. Chevrette and H. Cyr, "La protection en matière de fouilles, perquisitions et saisies, en matière de détention, la non-rétroactivité de l'infraction et la peine la plus douce," in G.A. Beaudoin and E. Mendes, eds., *The Canadian Charter of Rights and Freedoms,* 3d ed. (Scarborough, ON: Carswell, 1996) at 23.

78 *Ibid.*

79 *R. v. Hufsky,* [1988] 1 S.C.R. 621; *R. v. Ladouceur,* [1990] 1 S.C.R. 1257; *R. v. Wilson,* [1990] 1 S.C.R. 1291.

80 Chevrette and Cyr, *supra* note 77 at 63-68.

81 See, in the same sense, Hogg, *Constitutional Law of Canada, supra* note 45 at 868.

82 The following comments by United States District Judge Marvin E. Frankel concerning the overwhelming presence of discretion in the American sentencing process can apply equally to the Canadian situation: "The sentencing power is so far unregulated that even matters of a relatively technical, seemingly 'legal' nature are left for the individual judge, and thus for whimsical handling, at least in the sense that no two judges need be the same. Should a defendant be deemed to deserve some leniency if he has pled guilty rather than going to trial? Many judges say yes; many, perhaps a minority, say no; all do as they please. Should a prior criminal record enhance punishment? Most judges seem to think so. Some take the view that having 'paid the price' for prior offences, the defendant should not pay again now. Again, dealer's choice. Many judges believe it a mitigating factor if defendant yields to the pressure, moral or other, to pay back what he has taken. Others condemn this view as an illicit use of criminal sanctions for private redress. Once more, no rule of law enforces either of these contradictory judgements. There are other illustrations – relating, for example, to family conditions, defendant's behavior at trial, the consideration, if any for turning State's evidence – all subject to the varying and unregulated views of judges"; M.E. Frankel, *Criminal Sentences: Law without Order* (New York: Hill and Wang, 1972) at 24-25.

83 *R. v. Smith*, [1987] 1 S.C.R. 1045 at 1074-76.

84 *Ibid.* at 1109-10.

85 *Ibid.* at 1103-6.

86 *Ibid.* at 1111.

87 See *Gregg v. Georgia*, 428 U.S. 153 at 188 (1976).

88 *Furman v. Georgia*, 408 U.S. 238 (1972).

89 See especially Chapter 2, notes 13-17 and accompanying text, which considered specifically the possible impact of the rule of law on the interpretation of s. 12, to render relevant the question of whether a punishment is imposed in an arbitrary manner.

90 *Motor Vehicle Reference, supra* note 66 at 501. See also *R. v. Beare*, [1988] 2 S.C.R. 386 at 401 *[Beare]*.

91 *Nova Scotia Pharmaceutical, supra* note 2 at 642.

92 *Canadian Bar Assn. v. British Columbia (Attorney-General); Law Society of British Columbia v. British Columbia (Attorney-General)* (1996), 101 D.L.R. (4th) 410 (B.C.S.C.) *[Canadian Bar Assn. No. 1]*.

93 R.S.B.C. 1979, c. 388, s. 2.01.

94 *Canadian Bar Assn. No. 1, supra* note 92 at 433-38. Let us note that, subsidiarily, Lysyk J. also relied on a second explanation for rendering s. 7 applicable. He considered a broad interpretation of the concept of liberty in s. 7 to include all penal laws, therefore rendering the vagueness doctrine applicable to laws providing for the imposition of fines. This reasoning is based in large part on a separate opinion by Lamer J. in the *Prostitution Reference, supra* note 1 at 1177-78. This issue will be discussed further below (see *infra* notes 115-25 and accompanying text).

95 *Nova Scotia Pharmaceutical, supra* note 2 at 627-33.

96 *Ibid.* at 632.

97 *Morales, supra* note 58.

98 *Ibid.* at 727-28.

99 *Ibid.* at 726-32. Section 7 could have been applicable in the same manner, but Lamer J. chose to analyze the question under s. 11(e), which offered a more specific protection in the circumstances (at 725-26).

100 *Ibid.* at 729.

101 *Levy Leasing Co. v. Siegel*, 258 U.S. 242 (1922).

102 *Ibid.* at 250. The Court thus distinguished the statute at stake in the case at bar from a similarly worded statute invalidated one year before in *United States v. Cohen Grocery Co.*, 255 U.S. 81 (1921) *[Cohen Grocery]*, which made it criminal to willfully "make any unjust or unreasonable rate or charge in handling or dealing in or with any necessaries."

103 *Young v. Young*, [1993] 4 S.C.R. 3 *[Young]*.

104 R.S.C. (1985), c. 3 (2d Supp.).

105 *Young, supra* note 103 at 71-77.

106 *P.(D.) v. S.(C.),* [1993] 4 S.C.R. 141.

107 *Civil Code of Lower Canada,* 1980, c. 39 *[C.C.L.C.].*

108 *P.(D.) v. S.(C.), supra* note 106 at 178-81.

109 *Ibid.* at 180.

110 *Ibid.*

111 *Ruffo, supra* note 38.

112 *Code, supra* note 39.

113 *Ruffo, supra* note 38 at 329-34.

114 Similarly, these cases could hardly be read under s. 7 of the *Charter* since there was no apparent breach to either life, liberty, or security of the person. A broad conception of liberty in these cases could have been imagined to trigger the applicability of the "principles of fundamental justice." For example, in *Young,* the father could have tried to include the right to give religious education to his children as a fundamental parental right protected by liberty in s. 7; for a discussion of this issue, see *B.(R.) v. Children's Aid Society of Metropolitan Toronto,* [1995] 1 S.C.R. 315 at 362-74. The same could have been tried in *Ruffo* in relation to the right to exercise a profession: see *Wilson v. B.C. (Medical Services Com'n)* (1988), 53 D.L.R. (4th) 171 at 184-87 (B.C.C.A); *Re Khaliq-Kareemi* (1989), 57 D.L.R. (4th) 505 at 515 (N.S.S.C.). However, this path would have required an express acknowledgment by the Court, which is totally absent from these cases.

115 See Hogg, *Constitutional Law of Canada, supra* note 45 at 830-31.

116 For applications of the concept of liberty outside of the scope of imprisonment in the Supreme Court of Canada, see: *Beare, supra* note 90 (submission to fingerprinting); *Thomson Newspapers v. Canada,* [1990] 1 S.C.R. 425 (production of documents); *Stelco v. Canada,* [1990] 1 S.C.R. 617 (statutory duty to give oral testimony); *Heywood, supra* note 18 (access to public places).

117 See P. Garant, "Fundamental Right, Fundamental Justice" in G.A. Beaudoin and E. Mendes, eds., *The Canadian Charter of Rights and Freedoms,* 3d ed. (Scarborough, ON: Carswell, 1996) ch. 9 at 12-16.

118 Hogg, *Constitutional Law of Canada, supra* note 45 at 832 (see, however, cases referred to *supra* note 114).

119 *Prostitution Reference, supra* note 1 at 1177.

120 See, *e.g.,* G. Gunther and K.M. Sullivan, *Constitutional Law,* 13th ed. (Westbury, NY: Foundation Press, 1997) at 453-627.

121 Most major commentators on the rule of law view the principle as implying a preference for rules over discretion and arbitrary powers in general (see Chapter 2, notes 78-88 and accompanying text), and as including a requirement of legislative precision: see J. Raz, "The Rule of Law and its Virtue" (1977) 93 Law Q. Rev. 195 at 198-99; G.Q. Walker, *The Rule of Law* (Melbourne: University of Melbourne Press, 1988) at 25; F.A. Hayek, *The Constitution of Liberty* (Chicago: University of Chicago Press, 1960) at 208-9; L. Fuller, *The Morality of Law,* 2d ed. (New Haven, CT: Yale University Press, 1969) at 63-65. In Supreme Court of Canada jurisprudence, see *Commonwealth of Canada, supra* note 11 at 209-15 (per L'Heureux-Dubé J., concurring); *Nova Scotia Pharmaceutical, supra* note 2 at 632. See also Chapter 2, notes 74-75 and accompanying text.

122 See Chapter 2, notes 24-67 and accompanying text.

123 See *Reference re Remuneration of Judges of the Provincial Court of Prince Edward Island; Reference re Independence and Impartiality of Judges of the Provincial Court of Prince Edward Island,* [1997] 3 S.C.R. 3 at 69 *[Judges Remuneration Reference].* See, in Chapter 2, text accompanying notes 52-54.

124 See Chapter 2, notes 124-33 and accompanying text.

125 *Ontario Public School Boards' Assn. v. Ontario (A.G.)* (1997), 151 D.L.R. (4th) 346 (Ont. G.D.) *[Ontario School Boards].* Recall that this case involved a challenge in the Ontario Court General Division to the *Fewer School Boards Act,* S.O. 1997, c. 3, which purported to restructure the school boards system in the province and gave wide discretionary powers to the administration to operate the transition. See Chapter 2, notes 128-33 and accompanying text.

126 See, in the same sense, Chevrette and Cyr, *supra* note 77 at 102-3; A. Jodouin, "La Charte canadienne et la nouvelle légalité" in G.A. Beaudoin and E. Mendes, eds., *The Canadian Charter of Rights and Freedoms*, 3d ed. (Scarborough, ON: Carswell, 1996) at 11-12.
127 *Irwin Toy*, *supra* note 4 at 983. See *supra* notes 3-14 and accompanying text.
128 *Nova Scotia Pharmaceutical*, *supra* note 2 at 631.
129 *European Convention*, *supra* note 5.
130 F.G. Jacobs & R.C.A. White, *The European Convention on Human Rights*, 2d ed. (Oxford: Clarendon Press, 1996) at 164-65.
131 *Reference re Public Service Employee Relations Act (Alta.)*, [1987] 1 S.C.R. 313 at 348 (per Dickson C.J., dissenting on other issues).
132 *Big M. Drug Mart*, *supra* note 71 at 344.
133 *Judges Remuneration Reference*, *supra* note 123. See comments accompanying notes 45-67 in Chapter 2.
134 Of course, the degree of precision required would have to vary depending on the type of law involved. Nonpenal laws generally call for a greater tolerance of vagueness. See, in Chapter 3, text accompanying notes 162 and 167-75. See also, on the impact of the type of law involved, Chapter 1, notes 101-11 and accompanying text (in the context of the principle of legality), and Chapter 2, notes 124-33 and accompanying text (in the context of the principle of the rule of law).
135 *Nova Scotia Pharmaceutical*, *supra* note 2 at 631.
136 See *supra* notes 90-114 and accompanying text.
137 *Nova Scotia Pharmaceutical*, *supra* note 2 at 630-31: "For the sake of clarity, I would prefer to reserve the term 'vagueness' for the most serious degree of vagueness, where a law is so vague as not to constitute a 'limit prescribed by law' under s. 1 *in limine*. The other aspect of vagueness, being an instance of overbreadth, should be considered as such." Note that this conception is subject to variations in the jurisprudence of the Supreme Court itself. See, for example, the following comments by LaForest J. in *Canadian Broadcasting Corp. v. New-Brunswick (Attorney General)*, [1996] 3 S.C.R. 480 at 510: "I note that Gonthier J. writing in *Nova Scotia Pharmaceutical Society*, *supra* preferred to reserve the term 'vagueness' for the most serious degree of vagueness where the law could not be said to constitute a 'limit prescribed by law' and to use overbreadth for the other aspect of vagueness. My use of 'vagueness' in this case should be construed as meaning 'overbreadth.'"
138 *Morales*, *supra* note 58.
139 *Ibid.* at 726-32.
140 *Ibid.* at 733.
141 *Ibid.* at 734.
142 S. Beaulac, "Les bases constitutionnelles de la théorie de l'imprécision: partie d'une précaire dynamique globale de la Charte" (1995) 55 R. du B. 257 at 287.
143 *Nova Scotia Pharmaceutical*, *supra* note 2 at 631.
144 Such provisions include ss. 1 *in limine* ("prescribed by law"), s. 6(3) and (4), as well as the possible future basis of s. 11(g) of the *Charter*.
145 This would be the case of the "minimal impairment" branch under s. 1 of the *Charter*.
146 These provisions are ss. 7, 8, 9, and 11(e) of the *Charter*.
147 See *Heywood*, *supra* note 18, and accompanying text.
148 See, in the same sense, Garant, "L'imprécision en droit administratif et en droit constitutionnel," *supra* note 43 at 95. Since the analysis under minimal impairment implies a proven breach to a substantive *Charter* right (which, unlike vagueness and the rule of law, is expressly guaranteed), it is legitimate to require greater precision to avoid restricting this right more than necessary in the context of s. 1. See Chapter 2, notes 105-9 and accompanying text, where I explain in greater detail how breaches to the rule of law, although highly repugnant to our Constitution, call for a greater deference than breaches to substantive *Charter* rights.
149 A.G. Amsterdam, "The Void-for-Vagueness Doctrine in the Supreme Court" (1960) 109 U. Pa. L. Rev. 67 at 75. Note that in this leading article on the American vagueness doctrine, the author uses the expression "buffer zone" to designate an idea that is quite similar, although different in some regards, to the one I am expressing in relation to the Canadian

situation. The applicability of the vagueness doctrine rarely poses any problems in the United States because the due process clauses of the Fifth and Fourteenth Amendments protect "property" rights, which is not the case for s. 7 of the *Charter*. As a result, in contemporary American jurisprudence, there are hardly any formal obstacles to the applicability of the vagueness doctrine in most situations. However, an analysis of vagueness cases in the Supreme Court of the United States since the beginning of the twentieth century shows that in practice, the doctrine is invoked successfully on the merits mostly in cases where the Court is attempting to protect some other pressing substantive interest. (We have already discussed this issue; see Chapter 3, notes 5-39 and accompanying text.) In Canada, *Charter* jurisprudence is still too embryonic for us to tell whether vagueness will be used in practice to protect indirectly some constitutional guarantees more than others. However, the formal conditions of applicability of the doctrine reveal, to this day, the accessory character of vagueness in the sense that it must always be invoked in conjunction with another *Charter* interest in order to be applicable.

Conclusion

1 *Fraser v. Public Service Staff Relations Board*, [1985] 2 S.C.R. 455 at 469-70.
2 For more on the creative role of courts, see L. Reid, "Judge as Law Maker" (1972) 12 Journal of the Society of Public Teachers of Law (N.S.) 22; J. Deschesnes, "Le rôle législatif du pouvoir judiciaire" (1974) 5 R.D.U.S. 1; D. Gibson, "Judges as Legislators: Not Whether but How" (1986-87) 25 Alta. L. Rev. 249.
3 See *R. v. Power*, [1994] 1 S.C.R. 601 at 620: "In contrast to the U.S. Constitution, no general 'separation of powers' doctrine is spelled out in the *Constitution Act, 1867*. However ... such a separation of powers does in fact exist" (referring to an intrusion of the judiciary on executive powers); *Cooper v. Canada (H.R.C.)*, [1996] 3 S.C.R. 854 at 871: "One of the defining features of the Canadian Constitution, in my opinion, is the separation of powers" (per Lamer C.J., concurring, referring to an intrusion of the executive on judicial powers); *Judges Remuneration Reference, supra* note 123 at 90: "[The separation of powers is] a fundamental principle of the Canadian Constitution" (referring to encroachments of the executive and legislative bodies on the judiciary).

Bibliography

Legislation

Constitutional Documents
Canadian Charter of Rights and Freedoms, Part I of the *Constitution Act, 1982*, being Schedule B to the *Canada Act 1982* (U.K.), 1982, c. 11.
Constitution Act, 1867 (U.K.) 30 & 31 Vict., c. 3, reprinted in R.S.C. 1985, App. II, No. 5.
Manitoba Act, 1870, R.S.C. 1970, App. II.

Statutes
Canadian Human Rights Act, S.C. 1976-77, c. 33.
Canadian Labour Code, R.S.C. 1970, c. L.1.
Civil Code of Lower Canada, 1980, c. 39.
Combines Investigation Act, R.S.C. 1970, c. C-23.
Competition Act, R.S.C. 1985, c. C-34.
Criminal Code, R.S.C. 1985, c. C-46.
Customs Act, R.S.C. 1985 (2d Supp.), c. 1.
Divorce Act, R.S.C. 1985 (2d Supp.), c. 3.
Environmental Protection Act, R.S.O. 1980, c. 141.
Fewer School Boards Act, S.O. 1997, c. 3.
Food and Drugs Act, R.S.C. 1985, c. F-27.
Income Tax Act, R.S.C. 1985 (5th Supp.), c. 1.
Narcotics Control Act, R.S.C. 1985, c. N-1.
Provincial Auctioneers Act, R.S.O. 1960, c. 312.
(Federal) Public Service Employment Act, R.S.C. 1985, c. P-33.
Regulations Act, S.Q. 1986, c. 22.
Social Service Tax Act, R.S.B.C. 1979, c. 388.
Social Service Tax Amendment Act, 1992, S.B.C. 1992, c. 22.
Social Service Tax Amendment Act, 1993, S.B.C. 1993, c. 24.
Young Offenders Act, R.S.C. 1985, c. Y-1.

Regulations
Government Airport Concession Regulations, S.O.R./1979-373.
Judicial Code of Ethics, O.C. 643-82, 1982, G.O.Q. 1982.II.1253.

Foreign and International Documents
Administrative Procedure Act, 5 U.S.C. (United States)
European Convention for the Protection of Human Rights and Fundamental Freedoms, 4 November 1950, 213 U.N.T.S. 222.
International Covenant on Civil and Political Rights, 19 December 1966, 999 U.N.T.S. 171.

Jacksonville Ordinance Code, 1965. (United States)
Universal Declaration of Human Rights, GA Res. 217(III), UN GAOR, 3d Sess., Supp. No. 13, UN Doc. A/810 (1948).

Preliminary Documents
Bakan, J., and S. Schneiderman, "Submissions to the Standing Senate Committee on Legal and Constitutional Affairs Concerning Bill C-22" [unpublished].
Debates of the House of Commons, 1892, vol. 2.
Proposed Resolution for Joint Address to Her Majesty the Queen Respecting the Constitution of Canada, tabled in the House of Commons and the Senate, Catalogue no. YC3-321/5-57, 6 October 1980.

Jurisprudence

Canada
2550-9613 Québec Inc. c. Val d'Or, [1997] R.J.Q. 2090 (Qc. C.A.).
913719 Ontario Ltd. v. Mississauga (City) (1998) 40 O.R. (3d) 413 (Ont. C.A.) (Leave to appeal to Supreme Court of Canada denied: S.C.C. Bulletin, 1999, at 257).
B.(R.) v. Children's Aid Society of Metropolitan Toronto, [1995] 1 S.C.R. 315.
Baron v. Canada, [1993] 1 S.C.R. 416.
Brown v. Alberta Dental Assn., [2002] W.W.R. 221 (Alta C.A.).
Canada (Human Rights Commission) v. Taylor, [1990] 3 S.C.R. 892.
Canadian Bar Assn. v. British Columbia (Attorney-General) (1994), 91 B.C.L.R. 207 (B.C.S.C.).
Canadian Bar Assn. v. British Columbia (Attorney-General); Law Society of British Columbia v. British Columbia (Attorney-General) (1996), 101 D.L.R. (4th) 410 (B.C.S.C.).
Canadian Broadcasting Corp. v. New-Brunswick (Attorney General), [1996] 3 S.C.R. 480.
Committee for the Commonwealth of Canada v. Canada, [1991] 1 S.C.R. 139.
Cooper v. Canada (H.R.C.), [1996] 3 S.C.R. 854.
East York (Borough) v. Ontario (Attorney General) (1997), 34 O.R. (3d) 789 (Ont. G.D.).
États-Unis d'Amérique v. Brisson (1994), 61 Q.A.C. 198 (Qc. C.A.).
Fraser v. Public Service Staff Relations Board, [1985] 2 S.C.R. 455.
Frey v. Fedoruk, [1950] S.C.R. 517.
Gagnon and Vallières v. The Queen, [1971] C.A. 454 (Qc. C.A.).
Henry v. Canada (1987), 10 F.T.R. 176 (Fed. T.D.).
International Fund for Animal Welfare Inc. v. Canada (Minister of Fisheries and Oceans) (1983), 83 N.R. 303 (F.C.A.).
Irwin Toy Ltd. v. Quebec (A.G.), [1989] 1 S.C.R. 927.
Little Sisters Book and Art Emporium v. Canada (Minister of Justice), [2000] 2 S.C.R. 1120.
Luscher v. Deputy Minister, Revenue Canada, Customs and Excise, [1985] 1 C.F. 85 (Fed. C.A.).
Martin c. Granby (Ville) (1999) R.J.Q. 674 (Qc. C.A.).
New Brunswick Broadcasting Co. v. Nova Scotia (Speaker of the House of Assembly), [1993] 1 S.C.R. 319.
Ontario v. Canadian Pacific Ltd., [1995] 2 S.C.R. 1031.
Ontario English Catholic Teachers' Assn. v. Ontario (Attorney General) (1999), 172 D.L.R. (4th) 193 (Ont. C.A.).
Ontario Film and Video Appreciation Society v. Ontario Board of Censors (1984), 5 D.L.R. (4th) 766 (Ont. C.A.).
Ontario Public School Boards' Assn. v. Ontario (A.G.) (1997), 151 D.L.R. (4th) 346 (Ont. G.D.).
Ontario Public School Boards' Assn. v. Ontario (A.G.) (1999), 175 D.L.R. (4th) 609 (Ont. C.A.).
Operation Dismantle v. The Queen, [1985] 1 S.C.R. 441.
OPSEU v. Ontario (A.G.), [1987] 2 S.C.R. 2.
Osborne v. Canada (Treasury Board), [1991] 2 S.C.R. 69.
P.(D.) v. S.(C.), [1993] 4 S.C.R. 141.
Protection de la Jeunesse – 618, [1993] R.J.Q. 1603 (C.Q.).

P.S.C. v. Osborne, [1986] 3 C.F. 206 (Fed. T.D.).
R. v. Beare, [1988] 2 S.C.R. 386.
R. v. Big M. Drug Mart Ltd., [1985] 1 S.C.R. 295.
R. v. Butler, [1992] 1 S.C.R. 419.
R. v. Cuerrier, [1998] 2 S.C.R. 371.
R. v. Edwards, [1996] 1 S.C.R. 128.
R. v. Farinacci (1993), 86 C.C.C. (3d) 32 (Ont. C.A.).
R. v. Finta, [1994] 1 S.C.R. 701.
R. v. Gamble, [1988] 2 S.C.R. 595.
R. v. Hall, 2002 S.C.C. 64, file no. 28223 (not yet reported in S.C.R. series).
R. v. Hastings (1947), 90 C.C.C. 150 (N.B.S.C. App. Div.).
R. v. Heywood, [1994] 3 S.C.R. 761.
R. v. Hufsky, [1988] 1 S.C.R. 621.
R. v. Jacobson (1988), 46 C.C.C. (3d) 50 (Sask. C.A.).
R. v. Jobidon, [1991] 2 S.C.R. 714.
R. v. Keegstra, [1990] 3 S.C.R. 697.
R. v. Ladouceur, [1990] 1 S.C.R. 1257.
R. v. Lyons, [1987] 2 S.C.R. 309.
R. v. Morales, [1992] 3 S.C.R. 711.
R. v. Morgentaler (1985), 52 O.R. (2d) 353 (Ont. C.A.).
R. v. Morgentaler, [1988] 1 S.C.R. 30.
R. v. Nova Scotia Pharmaceutical Society, [1992] 2 S.C.R. 606.
R. v. Oakes, [1986] 1 S.C.R. 103.
R. v. Power, [1994] 1 S.C.R. 601.
R. v. Silveira, [1995] 2 S.C.R. 297.
R. v. Smith, [1987] 1 S.C.R. 1045.
R. v. Therens, [1985] 1 S.C.R. 613.
R. v. Wholesale Travel Group Inc., [1991] 3 S.C.R. 154.
R. v. Wilson, [1990] 1 S.C.R. 1291.
R. v. Yorke (1998), 122 C.C.C. (3d) 298 (N.S.C.A.).
R. v. Zundel (1987), 58 O.R. (2d) 129 (Ont. C.A.).
R. v. Zundel, [1992] 2 S.C.R. 731.
Re Khaliq-Kareemi (1989), 57 D.L.R. (4th) 505 (N.S.S.C.).
Reference re B.C. Motor Vehicle Act, [1985] 2 S.C.R. 486.
Reference re Manitoba Language Rights, [1985] 1 S.C.R. 721.
Reference re Minority Language Educational Rights (1988), 49 D.L.R. (4th) 499 (P.E.I.S.C. App. Div.).
Reference re Public Service Employee Relations Act (Alta.), [1987] 1 S.C.R. 313.
Reference re Remuneration of Judges of the Provincial Court of Edward Island; Reference re Independence and Impartiality of Judges of the Provincial Court of Prince Edward Island, [1997] 3 S.C.R. 3.
Reference re Resolution to Amend the Constitution, [1981] 1 S.C.R. 753.
Reference re Secession of Quebec, [1998] 2 S.C.R. 217.
Reference re ss. 193 and 195.1(1)(c) of the Criminal Code (Man.), [1990] 1 S.C.R. 1123.
Rocket v. Royal College of Dental Surgeons of Ontario, [1990] 2 S.C.R. 232.
Roncarelli v. Duplessis, [1959] S.C.R. 121.
Ruffo v. Conseil de la Magistrature, [1995] 4 S.C.R. 267.
Schachter v. Canada, [1992] 2 S.C.R. 679.
Slaight Communications v. Davidson, [1989] 1 S.C.R. 1038.
Stelco v. Canada, [1990] 1 S.C.R. 617.
Suresh v. Canada (Minister of Citizenship and Immigration), [2002] 1 S.C.R. 3.
Switzman v. Elbling, [1957] S.C.R. 285.
Taylor v. The Queen, [1877] 1 S.C.R. 65.
Thomson Newspapers v. Canada, [1990] 1 S.C.R. 425
Thorpe v. College of Pharmacists of British Columbia (1997), 97 D.L.R. (4th) 634 (B.C.C.A.).
United Nurses of Alberta v. Alberta (Attorney General), [1992] 1 S.C.R. 901.

Ville de Montréal v. Arcade Amusements Ltd., [1985] 1 S.C.R. 368.
Wilson v. B.C. (Medical Services Com'n) (1988), 53 D.L.R. (4th) 171 (B.C.C.A).
Young v. Young, [1993] 4 S.C.R. 3.

United States
Allgeyer v. Louisiana, 165 U.S. 578 (1897).
Baggett v. Bullitt, 377 U.S. 360 (1964).
Burgess v. Salmon, 97 U.S. 381 (1878).
Calder v. Bull, 3 U.S. 386 (1798).
Champlin Refining Co. v. Commission, 286 U.S. 210 (1932).
Cline v. Frink Dairy Co., 274 U.S. 445 (1927).
Coates v. Cincinnati, 402 U.S. 611 (1971).
Colautti v. Franklin, 439 U.S. 379 (1979).
Commonwealth v. Donoghue, 250 Kentucky Reports (1933).
Commonwealth v. Mochan, 177 Pa. Super. 454 (1955).
Commonwealth v. Taylor, 5 Binn. 277 (Pa. 1812).
Connally v. General Construction Company, 269 U.S. 385 (1926).
Cramp v. Board of Public Instruction of Orange County, Fla., 368 U.S. 278 (1961).
Dobbert v. Florida, 432 U.S. 282 (1977).
Donaldson v. Sack, 265 Southern Reporter 2d 499 (Fla. 1972).
Fox v. Washington, 236 U.S. 273 (1915).
Furman v. Georgia, 408 U.S. 238 (1972).
Giacco v. State of Pennsylvania, 382 U.S. 399 (1966).
Gooding v. Wilson, 405 U.S. 518 (1972).
Grayned v. City of Rockford, 408 U.S. 104 (1972).
Gregg v. Georgia, 428 U.S. 153 (1976).
Harisiades v. Shaughnessy, 342 U.S. 580 (1952).
Herndon v. Lowry, 301 U.S. 242 (1937).
Hoffman Estates v. Flipside, Hoffman Estates, Inc., 455 U.S. 489 (1982).
International Harvester Co. v. Kentucky, 234 U.S. 216 (1914).
Jordan v. De George, 341 U.S. 223 (1951).
Kolender v. Lawson, 461 U.S. 360 (1983).
Lambert v. California, 355 U.S. 225 (1957).
Lanzetta v. New Jersey, 306 U.S. 451 (1939).
Levy Leasing Co. v. Siegel, 258 U.S. 242 (1922).
Lochner v. New York, 198 U.S. 45 (1905).
Memoirs v. Massachusetts, 383 U.S. 413 (1966).
Miller v. California, 413 U.S. 15 (1973).
N.A.A.C.P. v. Button, 371 U.S. 415 (1963).
Papachristou v. City of Jacksonville, 405 U.S. 156 (1972).
Parker v. Levy, 417 U.S. 733 (1974).
Pennsylvania v. Gillespie, 1 Addam's Ecclesiastical Reports 267 (1795).
Rose v. Locke, 423 U.S. 48 (1975).
Roth v. United States, 354 U.S. 476 (1957).
The Slaughter-House Cases, 83 U.S. 36 (1873).
Smith v. Cahoon, 283 U.S. 553 (1931).
Smith v. California, 361 U.S. 147 (1959).
Smith v. Goguen, 415 U.S. 566 (1974).
Speiser v. Randall, 357 U.S. 513 (1958).
State v. Buckman, 8 New Hampshire Reports 203 (1836).
Stromberg v. California, 283 U.S. 359 (1931).
Thornhill v. Alabama, 310 U.S. 88 (1940).
United States v. Carolene Products Co., 304 U.S. 144 (1938).
United States v. Cohen Grocery Co., 255 U.S. 81 (1921).
United States v. National Dairy Products Corp., 372 U.S. 29 (1963).
United States v. Petrillo, 332 U.S. 1 (1947).

United States v. Raines, 362 U.S. 17 (1960).
West Coast Hotel v. Parrish, 300 U.S. 379 (1937).
Winters v. New York, 333 U.S. 507 (1948).

Europe
Cantoni v. France, 15 November 1995, European Court of Human Rights, *Reports of Judgements and Decisions* 1996-V, 1615.
C.R. v. United Kingdom, 22 November 1995, European Court of Human Rights, No. 48/1994/495/577.
Dantzig Legislative Decrees case, Advisory Opinion of 4 December 1935, Permanent Court of International Justice, Series A/B, No. 65.
James Bagg's Case (1616), 77 E.R. 1271.
Jones v. Randall (1774), 98 E.R. 706.
The King v. Lynn (1788), 100 E.R. 394.
The King v. Ward (1727), 92 E.R. 451.
Knuller v. Director of Public Prosecutions, [1972] 2 All E.R. 898.
Liyanage v. The Queen, [1967] 1 A.C. 259 (Privy Council).
Malone, 2 August 1984, European Court of Human Rights, Series A, No. 82.
Newland, [1954] 1 Q.B. 167 (C.C.A.).
R. v. Clarence (1888), 22 Q.B.D. 23.
R. v. Price (1884), 12 Q.B.D. 247.
R. v. R., [1992] 1 A.C. 599 (House of Lords).
Rex v. Manley, [1933] 1 K.B. 529.
Rex v. Sidley (1663), 82 E.R. 1036.
Shaw v. Director of Public Prosecutions, [1961] 2 All E.R. 446.
Sunday Times, 26 April 1979, European Court of Human Rights, Series A, No. 30.
S.W. v. United Kingdom, 22 November 1995, European Court of Human Rights, No. 47/1994/494/576.
Taylor's Case (1676), 86 E.R. 189.
Withers v. Director of Public Prosecutions, [1975] A.C. 842.

Secondary Materials

Monographs
Anisman, P. *A Catalogue of Discretionary Powers in the Revised Statutes of Canada 1970* (Ottawa: Law Reform Commission of Canada, 1975).
Bailyn, B. *The Ideological Origins of the American Revolution* (Cambridge, MA: Harvard University Press, 1961).
Baker, F., ed. *The Politics of Aristotle* (Oxford: Clarendon Press, 1946).
Bayefsky, A.F., ed. *Canada's Constitution Act, 1982 & Amendments: A Documented History,* vol. 2 (Toronto: McGraw-Hill, 1989).
Beccaria, C. *An Essay on Crimes and Punishments* (Brookline, MA: Branden Press, 1983) (1st ed.: 1764).
Bennion, F.A.R. *Statutory Interpretation* (London: Butterworths, 1984).
Berman, H. *Soviet Criminal Law and Procedure,* 2d ed. (Cambridge, MA: Harvard University Press, 1972).
Blackstone, W. *Commentaries on the Law of England,* vol. 1 (London: Strahan, 1809) (15th ed. by Christian, 1809).
Broom, H. *A Selection of Legal Maxims,* 10th ed. (London: Sweet & Maxwell, 1939).
Brown, D. *The Genesis of the Canadian Criminal Code* (Toronto: University of Toronto Press, 1989).
Carrithers, D.W., ed. *The Spirit of Laws* (Berkeley: University of California Press, 1977) (1st ed. by C. Montesquieu: 1748).
Conac, G., M. Debene, and G. Teboul, eds. *La déclaration des droits de l'homme et du citoyen de 1789* (Paris: Economica, 1993).
Cooke, J.E., ed. *The Federalist,* No. 44 (Cleveland: World Publishing, 1961).

Côté, P.A. *The Interpretation of Legislation in Canada*, 3d ed. (Toronto: Carswell, 2000).

Davis, K.C. *Administrative Law Treatise*, 2d ed. (San Diego: University of San Diego, 1978).

–. *Discretionary Justice: A Preliminary Inquiry* (Chicago: University of Illinois Press, 1971).

Debbasch, C., and J.-M. Pointier. *Les Constitutions de la France* (Paris: Dalloz, 1989).

Dicey, A.V. *Introduction to the Study of the Law of the Constitution*, 10th ed. (London: Macmillan, 1965) (1st ed.: 1885).

Dworkin, R. *A Matter of Principle* (Cambridge, MA: Harvard University Press, 1985).

Edgar, S.G.G., ed. *Craies on Statute Law*, 7th ed. (London: Sweet & Maxwell, 1971).

Evans, J.M., H.N. Janish, and D.J. Mullan. *Administrative Law*, 4th ed. (Toronto: Emond Montgomery Publications, 1995).

Feldman, D. *Civil Liberties and Human Rights in England and Wales* (Oxford: Clarendon Press, 1993).

Feuerbach, P. *Lehrbuch des peinlichen Rechts* (Goldbach: Keip Verlag, 1997) (1st ed. by P. Feuerbach: 1801).

First Report of the Royal Commission Inquiry into Civil Rights (Toronto: Queen's Printer, 1968).

Frankel, M.E. *Criminal Sentences: Law without Order* (New York: Hill and Wang, 1972).

Friedland, M.L., and Roach, K. *Criminal Law and Procedure: Cases and Materials*, 7th ed. (Toronto: E. Montgomery, 1994).

Friedmann, W. *Law in a Changing Society*, 2d ed. (New York: Columbia University Press, 1972).

Fuller, L. *The Morality of Law*, 2d ed. (New Haven, CT: Yale University Press, 1969).

Goerner, E.A., ed. *The Constitutions of Europe* (Chicago: H. Regnery, 1967).

Gunther, G., and K.M. Sullivan. *Constitutional Law*, 13th ed. (Westbury, NY: Foundation Press, 1997).

Hall, J. *General Principles of Criminal Law*, 2d ed. (New York: Bobbs, 1960).

Hart, H.L.A. *Law, Liberty and Morality* (London: Oxford University Press, 1963).

Hayek, F.A. *The Constitution of Liberty* (Chicago: University of Chicago Press, 1960).

Hogg, P.W. *Canada Act 1982 Annotated* (Scarborough, ON: Carswell, 1982).

–. *Constitutional Law of Canada*, 4th ed. (Scarborough, ON: Carswell, 1996).

–. *Constitutional Law of Canada*, looseleaf, vol. 2 (Scarborough, ON: Carswell, 1997).

Holmes, O.W. *The Common Law*, 42d printing (Boston: Little, Brown and Company, 1948).

How Regulators Regulate: A Guide to Regulatory Process in Canada (Ottawa: Treasury Board Secretariat, 1992).

Jacobs, F.G., and R.C.A. White. *The European Convention on Human Rights*, 2d ed. (Oxford: Clarendon Press, 1996).

Jennings, I. *The Law and the Constitution*, 5th ed. (London: University of London Press, 1959).

Johnson, P.E. *Criminal Law*, 2d ed. (St. Paul, MN: West Publishing, 1980).

Locke, J. *Two Treatises on Government* (Cambridge: Cambridge University Press, 1967).

Low, P.W., J.C. Jeffries Jr., and R.J. Bonnie. *Criminal Law: Cases and Materials* (Mineola, NY: Foundation Press, 1982).

MacGuigan, M.R. *Third Report of the Special Committee on Statutory Instruments* (Ottawa: Queen's Printer for Canada, 1969).

Malberg, R.C. de. *Contribution à la théorie générale du droit*, t.1 (Paris: Sirey, 1920).

Maslowski, T. *De Domo Sua* (Leipzig: B.G. Teubner, 1981).

Molesworth, W., ed. *The English Works of Thomas Hobbes*, vol. 6 (London: J. Bohn, 1840).

Nowak, J.E., R.D. Rotunda, and J.N. Young. *Constitutional Law*, 3d ed. (St. Paul, MN: West Publishing, 1986).

Packer, H.L. *The Limits of the Criminal Sanction* (Stanford, CA: Stanford University Press, 1968).

Pigeon, L.P. *Drafting and Interpreting Legislation* (Toronto: Carswell, 1988).

Rawls, J. *A Theory of Justice* (Cambridge, MA: Harvard University Press, 1971).

Report of Committee I of the International Congress of Jurists (New Delhi: International Congress of Jurists, 1959).

Rotunda, R.D., and J.E. Nowak. *Treatise on Constitutional Law*, 2d ed. (St. Paul, MN: West Publishing, 1992).

Stuart, D. *Canadian Criminal Law: A Treatise*, 3d ed. (Scarborough, ON: Carswell, 1995).

Stuart, D., and R.J. Delisle. *Learning Canadian Criminal Law*, 4th ed. (Scarborough, ON: Carswell, 1993).

Stephen, J.F. *A History of the Criminal Law of England*, vol. 3 (London: Macmillan, 1883).

Sturge, L.F., ed. *Stephen's Digest of the Criminal Law*, 8th ed. (London: Sweet & Maxwell, 1947).

Sullivan, R., ed. *Driedger on the Construction of Statutes*, 3d ed. (Toronto: Butterworths, 1994).

Thompson, E.P. *Whigs and Hunters: The Origin of the Black Act* (New York: Pantheon Books, 1975).

Troy, D.E. *Retroactive Legislation* (Washington, DC: A.E.I. Press, 1998).

Walker, G.Q. *The Rule of Law* (Melbourne: University of Melbourne Press, 1988).

Williams, G. *Criminal Law: The General Part*, 2d ed. (London: Stevens & Sons, 1961).

Articles

Amsterdam, A.G. "Federal Constitutional Restrictions on the Punishment of Crimes of General Obnoxiousness, Crimes of Displeasing Police Officers, and the Like" (1967) 3 Crim. L. Bull. 205.

–. "The Void-for-Vagueness Doctrine in the Supreme Court" (1960) 109 U. Pa. L. Rev. 67.

Beaulac, S. "Les bases constitutionnelles de la théorie de l'imprécision: partie d'une précaire dynamique globale de la Charte" (1995) 55 R. du B. 257.

Beckman, G. "Three Penal Codes Compared" (1966) 10 Am. J. Legal Hist. 148.

Blaau, L.C. "The Rechtsstaat Idea Compared with the Rule of Law as a Paradigm for Protecting Rights" (1990) 107 South African Law Journal 76.

Bloomfield, M. "William Sampson and the Codifiers: The Roots of American Legal Reform, 1820-1830" (1967) 11 Am. J. Legal Hist. 234.

Bridge, J.W. "Retrospective Legislation and the Rule of Law in Britain" (1967) 35 UMKC L. Rev. 132.

Chevrette, F., and H. Cyr. "La protection en matière de fouilles, perquisitions et saisies, en matière de détention, la non-rétroactivité de l'infraction et la peine la plus douce" in G.A. Beaudoin and E. Mendes, eds., *The Canadian Charter of Rights and Freedoms*, 3d ed. (Scarborough, ON: Carswell, 1996) ch. 10.

Collings, R.A. "Unconstitutional Uncertainty: An Appraisal" (1955) 40 Cornell L.Q. 195.

Colvin, E. "Criminal Law and the Rule of Law" in P. Fitzgerald, ed., *Crime, Justice and Codification* (Toronto: Carswell, 1986) ch. 9.

Coults, J.A. "Effecting a Public Mischief" (1957) 21 J. Crim. L. 60.

Crouse, G.H. "A Critique of Canadian Criminal Legislation" (1934) 12 Can. Bar Rev. 545.

Davies, D.S. "The House of Lords and the Criminal Law" (1961) 6 Journal of the Society of Public Teachers of Law 104.

Deschesnes, J. "Le rôle législatif du pouvoir judiciaire" (1974) 5 R.D.U.S. 1.

Dicey, A.V. "The Development of Administrative Law in England" (1915) 31 Law Q. Rev. 148.

Driedger, E.A. "Statutes: Retroactive Retrospective Reflections" (1978) 56 Can. Bar Rev. 264.

Edinger, E. "Retrospectivity in Law" (1995) 29 U.B.C. L. Rev. 5.

Ewaschuk, E.G. "Criminal Legislation" (1983-84) 26 Crim. L.Q. 97.

Fallon, R.H. "Making Sense of Overbreadth" (1991) 100 Yale L.J. 853.

Fine, J.D. "Conspiracies Contra Bonos Mores" (1973) 19 McGill L.J. 136.

"The First Amendment Overbreadth Doctrine" (1970) 83 Harv. L. Rev. 844.

Garant, P. "Fundamental Right, Fundamental Justice" in G.A. Beaudoin and E. Mendes, eds., *The Canadian Charter of Rights and Freedoms*, 3d ed. (Scarborough, ON: Carswell, 1996) ch. 9.

–. "L'imprécision en droit administratif et en droit constitutionnel: un défi à l'intelligence moyenne" (1994) 4 National Journal of Constitutional Law 75.

Gaus, G.F. "Public Reason and the Rule of Law" in I. Shapiro, ed., *The Rule of Law* (New York: New York University Press, 1994) ch. 14.

Gibson, D. "Judges as Legislators: Not Whether but How"·(1986-87) 25 Alta. L. Rev. 249.

Hall, F.W. "The Common Law: An Account of Its Reception in the United States" (1951) 4 Vand. L. Rev. 791.

Higgins, R. "Time and the Law: International Perspectives on an Old Problem" (1997) 46 I.C.L.Q. 501.

Huppé, L. "La fonction des lois et la théorie de l'imprécision" (1992) 52 R. du B. 831.

Hutchinson, A.C., and P.J. Monahan. "Democracy and the Rule of Law" in A.C. Hutchinson and P.J. Monahan, eds., *The Rule of Law: Ideal or Ideology* (Toronto: Carswell, 1987) 97.

Jeffries, J.C. Jr. "Legality, Vagueness, and the Construction of Penal Statutes" (1985) 71 Va. L. Rev. 189.

Jodouin, A. "La Charte canadienne et la nouvelle légalité" in G.A. Beaudoin and E. Mendes, eds., *The Canadian Charter of Rights and Freedoms,* 3d ed. (Scarborough, ON: Carswell, 1996) ch. 13.

Kadish, S.H. "Codifiers of the Criminal Law: Wechsler's Predecessors" (1978) 78 Colum. L. Rev. 1098.

Kairis, D. "The Politics of Law" (1984) 36 Stan. L. Rev. 1.

Kelsen, H. "Will the Judgement in the Nuremberg Tribunal Constitute a Precedent in International Law?" (1947) 1 Int'l L. Q. 153.

Kennedy, D. "Form and Substance in Private Law Adjudication" (1976) 89 Harv. L. Rev. 1685.

Leoni, B. "Diritto e politica" (1961) Rivista Internazionale di Filosofia del Diritto 89.

MacGregor, W.C. "Note" (1933) 49 Law Q. Rev. 482.

McLachlin, B. "Rules and Discretion in the Governance of Canada" (1992) 56 Sask. L. Rev. 167.

Mendes, E.P. "The Crucible of the *Charter:* Judicial Deference in the Context of Section 1" in G.A. Beaudoin and E. Mendes, eds., *The Canadian Charter of Rights and Freedoms,* 3d ed. (Scarborough, ON: Carswell, 1996) ch. 3.

Mewett, A.W. "The Criminal Code, 1892-1992" (1993) 72 Can. Bar Rev. 1.

–. "The Criminal Law, 1867-1967" (1967) 45 Can. Bar Rev. 726.

Monahan, P.J. "Is the Pearson Airport Legislation Unconstitutional? The Rule of Law as a Limit on Contract Repudiation by Government" (1995) 33 Osgoode Hall L.J. 411.

Moore, M.S. "A Natural Law Theory of Interpretation" (1985) 58 S. Cal. L. Rev. 277.

Munzer, S.R. "Retroactive Law" (1977) 6 J. Legal Stud. 373.

Osborne, C. "Does the Ends Justify the Means? Retrospectivity, Article 7, and the Marital Rape Exemption" (1996) 4 Eur. H.R.L. Rev. 406.

Ouellette, Y. "L'imprécision des codes de déontologie professionnelle" (1977) 37 R. du B. 669.

Parker, G. "The Origins of the Canadian Criminal Code" in D. Flaherty, ed., *Essays in the History of Canadian Law* (Toronto: University of Toronto Press, 1981) ch. 7.

Pepin, G. "La nullité des lois et règlements pour cause d'imprécision: une norme unique ou deux normes distinctes de contrôle?" (1996) 56 R. du B. 643.

Preuss, L. "Punishment by Analogy in National Socialist Penal Law" (1936) 26 J. Crim. L. & Criminology 847.

Radin, M.J. "Reconsidering the Rule of Law" (1989) 69 B.U.L. Rev. 781.

Raz, J. "The Rule of Law and Its Virtue" (1977) 93 Law Q. Rev. 195.

Reid, L. "Judge as Law Maker" (1972) 12 Journal of the Society of Public Teachers of Law (N.S.) 22.

Rogerson, C. "The Judicial Search for Appropriate Remedies under the *Charter:* The Examples of Overbreadth and Vagueness" in R.J. Sharpe, dir., *Charter Litigation* (Toronto: Butterworths, 1987) ch. 10.

Ross, J. "Applying the Charter to Discretionary Authority" (1991) 29 Alta. L. Rev. 382.

Scalia, A. "The Rule of Law as a Law of Rules" (1989) 56 U. Chicago L. Rev. 1175.

Smead, E.E. "The Rule against Retroactive Legislation: A Basic Principle of Jurisdiction" (1936) 20 Minn. L. Rev. 775.

Stallybrass, W.T.S. "Public Mischief" (1933) 49 Law Q. Rev. 183.

Stuart, D. "The Canadian Void for Vagueness Doctrine Arrives with No Teeth" (1990) 77 C.R. (3d) 101.

Trotter, G.T. "LeBeau: Toward a Canadian Vagueness Doctrine" (1988) 62 C.R. (3d) 183.

Unger, R. "The Critical Legal Studies Movement" (1983) 96 Harv. L. Rev. 563.

Index